IARIA

AA004020

eKNOW 2020

The Twelfth International Conference on Information, Process, and Knowledge Management

November 21 – 25, 2020

Valencia, Spain

eKNOW 2020 Editors

Samia Aitouche, University Batna 2, Algeria
Aksa Karima, University Batna 2, Algeria
Susan Gauch, University of Arkansas, USA
Roy Oberhauser, Aalen University, Germany
Nitin Agarwal, University of Arkansas at Little Rock, USA

Printed from e-media with permission by:

Curran Associates, Inc.
57 Morehouse Lane
Red Hook, NY 12571

CURRAN ASSOCIATES INC.
proceedings
.com

Some format issues inherent in the e-media version may also appear in this print version.

Printed with permission by Curran Associates, Inc. (2020)

International Academy, Research, and Industry Association (IARIA)
412 Derby Way
Wilmington, DE 19810

Phone: (408) 893-6407
Fax: (408) 527-6351

petre@iaria.org

Additional copies of this publication are available from:

Curran Associates, Inc.
57 Morehouse Lane
Red Hook, NY 12571 USA
Phone: 845-758-0400
Fax: 845-758-2633
Email: curran@proceedings.com
Web: www.proceedings.com

Table of Contents

eKNOW 2020

Forward

The Twelfth International Conference on Information, Process, and Knowledge Management (eKNOW 2020) was driven by the complexity of the current systems, the diversity of the data, and the challenges for mental representation and understanding of environmental structure and behavior.

Capturing, representing, and manipulating knowledge was and still is a fascinating and extremely useful challenge from both theoretical and practical perspective. Using validated knowledge for information and process management and for decision support mechanisms raised a series of questions the eKNOW 2020 conference was aimed at.

eKNOW 2020 provided a forum where researchers were able to present recent research results and new research problems and directions related to them. The topics covered aspects from knowledge fundamentals to more specialized topics such as process analysis and modeling, management systems, semantics processing and ontology.

We take this opportunity to thank all the members of the eKNOW 2020 Technical Program Committee as well as the numerous reviewers. The creation of such a broad and high-quality conference program would not have been possible without their involvement. We also kindly thank all the authors who dedicated much of their time and efforts to contribute to the eKNOW 2020. We truly believe that, thanks to all these efforts, the final conference program consists of top quality contributions.

This event could also not have been a reality without the support of many individuals, organizations, and sponsors. We are grateful to the members of the eKNOW 2020 organizing committee for their help in handling the logistics and for their work to make this professional meeting a success.

We hope that eKNOW 2020 was a successful international forum for the exchange of ideas and results between academia and industry and for the promotion of progress in knowledge management research.

eKNOW 2020 Chairs

eKNOW 2020 Steering Committee
Susan Gauch, University of Arkansas, USA

eKNOW 2020 Publicity Chair
Javier Rocher, Universitat Politecnica de Valencia, Spain

eKNOW 2020 Advisory Committee
Roy Oberhauser, Aalen University, Germany
Nitin Agarwal, University of Arkansas at Little Rock, USA

eKNOW 2020
Committee

eKNOW 2020 Steering Committee
Susan Gauch, University of Arkansas, USA

eKNOW 2020 Publicity Chair
Javier Rocher, Universitat Politecnica de Valencia, Spain

eKNOW 2020 Advisory Committee
Roy Oberhauser, Aalen University, Germany
Nitin Agarwal, University of Arkansas at Little Rock, USA

eKNOW 2020 Technical Program Committee
Giuseppe A. Di Lucca, University of Sannio | RCOST (Research Center on Software Technology), Italy
Rocío Abascal Mena, Universidad Autónoma Metropolitana - Cuajimalpa, Mexico City, Mexico
Raoua Abdelkhalek, LARODEC | Institut Supérieur de Gestion de Tunis | Université de Tunis, Tunisia
Marie-Hélène Abel, Sorbonne universités - Université de technologie de Compiègne, France
Awais Adnan, Center of Excellence in Information Technology (CEIT) | Institute of Management Sciences, Peshawar, Pakistan
Nitin Agarwal, University of Arkansas at Little Rock, USA
Maroi Agrebi, Université Polytechnique Hauts-de-France, France
Joyce Aguiar, Center for Psychology at University of Porto (CPUP), Portugal
Samia Aitouche, University Batna 2, Algeria
Mohammad T. Alshammari, University of Hail, Saudi Arabia
Gil Ad Ariely, Lauder School of Government, Diplomacy and Strategy - Interdisciplinary Center Herzliya (IDC), Israel
Adham Atyabi, University of Colorado Colorado springs / Seattle Children's Research Institute, USA
Mohamed Anis Bach Tobji, ESEN – University of Manouba | LARODEC Laboratory – ISG of Tunis, Tunisia
Michal Baczynski, University of Silesia in Katowice, Poland
Zbigniew Banaszak, Koszalin University of Technology, Poland
Basel Bani-Ismail, Oman College of Management and Technology, Oman
Peter Bellström, Karlstad University, Sweden
Asmaa Benghabrit, Moulay Ismaïl University, Meknès, Morocco
José Alberto Benítez Andrades, University of León, Spain
Julita Bermejo-Alonso, Universidad Isabel I, Spain
Carlos Bobed Lisbona, everis / NTT Data & University of Zaragoza, Spain
Zorica Bogdanovic, University of Belgrade, Serbia
Gregory Bourguin, LISIC | Université Littoral Côte d'Opale(ULCO), France

Loris Bozzato, FBK-Irst | Fondazione Bruno Kessler, Trento, Italy
Ricardo Campos, Polytechnic Institute of Tomar / LIAAD INESC TEC, Portugal
Massimiliano Caramia, University of Rome "Tor Vergata", Italy
Dickson K.W. Chiu, The University of Hong Kong, Hong Kong
Ritesh Chugh, Central Queensland University, Australia
Miguel Couceiro, University of Lorraine | CNRS | Inria Nancy G.E. | Loria, France
Juan Pablo D'Amato, Universidad Nacional del Centro de la PRov (UNCPBA) / CONICET, Argentina
Anca Daniela Ionita, University Politehnica of Bucharest, Romania
Gustavo de Assis Costa, Federal Institute of Education, Science and Technology of Goiás, Brazil / LIAAD - INESC TEC, Portugal
Andrea De Salve, University of Palermo, Italy
Cláudio de Souza Baptista, University of Campina Grande, Brazil
Chiara Di Francescomarino, Fondazione Bruno Kessler (FBK), Trento, Italy
Vasiliki Diamantopoulou, University of the Aegean, Greece
Mihaela Dinsoreanu, Technical University of Cluj-Napoca, Romania
Tome Eftimov, Jožef Stefan Institute, Ljubljana, Slovenia / Stanford University, Palo Alto, USA
Amélia Ferreira da Silva, Centre for Organizational and Social Studies of Porto Polytechnic, Portugal
Joan Francesc Fondevila, Universitat de Girona / Universitat Pompeu Fabra, Spain
Susan Gauch, University of Arkansas, USA
Dipesh Gautam, Institute for Intelligent Systems (IIS) | The University of Memphis, USA
James Geller, New Jersey Institute of Technology, USA
Markus Grube, VOQUZ IT Solutions GmbH, Germany
Teresa Guarda, Universidad Estatal Peninsula Santa Elena - UPSE / Universidad de las Fuerzas Armadas – ESPE / ALGORITMI Research Centre | ESPE | UPSE, Ecuador
Michael Guckert, Technische Hochschule Mittelhessen, Germany
Carolina Guerini, Cattaneo University Castellanza (Varese) / Sda Bocconi, Milan, Italy
Barbara Guidi, University of Pisa, Italy
Juncal Gutiérrez-Artacho, Universidad de Granada, Spain
Stijn Hoppenbrouwers, HAN University of Applied Sciences, Arnhem / Radboud University, Nijmegen, Netherlands
Marjan Hosseinia, University of Houston, USA
Richard Jiang, Lancaster University, UK
Maria José Sousa, ISCTE-Instituto Universitário de Lisboa, Portugal
Maria José Angélico Gonçalves, P.Porto/ ISCAP / CEOS.PP, Portugal
Katerina Kabassi, Ionian University, Greece
Yasushi Kambayashi, Nippon Institute of Technology, Japan
Jean Robert Kala Kamdjoug, Catholic University of Central Africa, Cameroon
Dimitris Kanellopoulos, University of Patras, Greece
Michael Kaufmann, Hochschule Luzern, Switzerland
Ron Kenett, Samuel Neaman Institute for National Policy Research - Technion, Israel
Sandi Kirkham, Staffordshire University, UK
Wilfried Kirschenmann, Aldwin by ANEO, France

Olivera Kotevska, Oak Ridge National Laboratory (ORNL), Tennessee, USA
Chaya Liebeskind, Jerusalem College of Technology - Lev Academic Center, Israel
Erick López Ornelas, Universidad Autónoma Metropolitana, Mexico
Paulo Maio, ISEP - School of Engineering of Polytechnic of Porto, Portugal
Carlos Alberto Malcher Bastos, Universidade Federal Fluminense, Brazil
Federica Mandreoli, Universita' di Modena e ReggioEmilia, Italy
Andrea Marrella, SAPIENZA - Università di Roma, Italy
Claudia Martínez Araneda, Universidad Católica de la Santísima Concepción (UCSC), Chile
Yobani Martínez Ramírez, Universidad Autónoma de Sinaloa, Mexico
Michele Melchiori, Università degli Studi di Brescia, Italy
Vincenzo Moscato, University of Naples "Federico II", Italy
Tathagata Mukherjee, The University of Alabama in Huntsville, USA
Mirna Muñoz, CIMAT, Mexico
Phivos Mylonas, Ionian University, Greece
Vilem Novak, University of Ostrava - Institute for Research and Applications of Fuzzy Modeling, Czech Republic
Roy Oberhauser, Aalen University, Germany
Daniel O'Leary, University of Southern California, USA
Eva Oliveira, 2Ai Polytechnic Institute of Cávado and Ave, Barcelos, Portugal
João Paulo Costa, University of Coimbra, Portugal
Adriano Peron, University of Napoli "Federico II", Italy
Lukas Pichl, International Christian University, Japan
Rodica Potolea, Technical University of Cluj-Napoca, Romania
Saqib Qamar, Huazhong University of Science and Technology (HUST), China
Paulo Quaresma, University of Évora, Portugal
Lukasz Radlinski, West Pomeranian University of Technology in Szczecin, Poland
Simona Riurean, University of Petrosani, Romania
Polina Rozenshtein, Aalto University, Helsinki, Finland
Inès Saad, Amiens Business School & University Picardie Jules Verne, France
Tanik Saikh, Indian Institute of Technology Patna, India
Virginie Sans, INRISA/IRISA Université of Rennes 1, France
Domenico Fabio Savo, Università degli Studi di Bergamo, Italy
Erwin Schaumlechner, DS Development GmbH (part of the HRS group), Astria
Hartmut Schweizer, Institute for Applied Computer Science - TU Dresden, Germany
Filippo Sciarrone, ROMA TRE University, Italy
Christian Seel, University of Applied Sciences Landshut, Germany
Houcine Senoussi, Quartz laboratory - EISTI, Cergy, France
Luciano Serafini, FBK - Fondazione Bruno Kessler, Italy
Nuno Silva, ISEP - IPP (School of Engineering - Polytechnic of Porto), Portugal
Andrzej M.J. Skulimowski, AGH University of Science and Technology, Krakow, Poland
Christophe Soares, Universidade Fernando Pessoa, Portugal
Darielson Souza, Federal University of Ceará (UFC), Brazil
Deborah Stacey, University of Guelph, Canada
Efstathios Stamatatos, University of the Aegean, Greece

Gernot Steindl, TU Wien - Institute of Computer Engineering, Austria
Takao Terano, Chiba University of Commerce / Tokyo Institute of Technology / University of Tsukuba, Japan
Giorgio Terracina, University of Calabria, Italy
Michele Tomaiuolo, Università di Parma, Italy
Christos Troussas, Department of Informatics - University of Piraeus, Greece
Marco Viviani, University of Milano-Bicocca, Italy
Hans Weigand, Tilburg University, Netherlands
Rihito Yaegashi, Kagawa University, Japan
Elmoukhtar Zemmouri, Moulay Ismail University, Meknes, Morocco
Yu-Dong Zhang (Eugene), University of Leicester, UK
Qiang Zhu, University of Michigan - Dearborn, USA
Mounir Zrigui, Faculté des Sciences de Monastir, Tunisia

Copyright Information

For your reference, this is the text governing the copyright release for material published by IARIA.

The copyright release is a transfer of publication rights, which allows IARIA and its partners to drive the dissemination of the published material. This allows IARIA to give articles increased visibility via distribution, inclusion in libraries, and arrangements for submission to indexes.

I, the undersigned, declare that the article is original, and that I represent the authors of this article in the copyright release matters. If this work has been done as work-for-hire, I have obtained all necessary clearances to execute a copyright release. I hereby irrevocably transfer exclusive copyright for this material to IARIA. I give IARIA permission or reproduce the work in any media format such as, but not limited to, print, digital, or electronic. I give IARIA permission to distribute the materials without restriction to any institutions or individuals. I give IARIA permission to submit the work for inclusion in article repositories as IARIA sees fit.

I, the undersigned, declare that to the best of my knowledge, the article is does not contain libelous or otherwise unlawful contents or invading the right of privacy or infringing on a proprietary right.

Following the copyright release, any circulated version of the article must bear the copyright notice and any header and footer information that IARIA applies to the published article.

IARIA grants royalty-free permission to the authors to disseminate the work, under the above provisions, for any academic, commercial, or industrial use. IARIA grants royalty-free permission to any individuals or institutions to make the article available electronically, online, or in print.

IARIA acknowledges that rights to any algorithm, process, procedure, apparatus, or articles of manufacture remain with the authors and their employers.

I, the undersigned, understand that IARIA will not be liable, in contract, tort (including, without limitation, negligence), pre-contract or other representations (other than fraudulent misrepresentations) or otherwise in connection with the publication of my work.

Exception to the above is made for work-for-hire performed while employed by the government. In that case, copyright to the material remains with the said government. The rightful owners (authors and government entity) grant unlimited and unrestricted permission to IARIA, IARIA's contractors, and IARIA's partners to further distribute the work.

A Scientometric Framework: Application for Knowledge Management (KM) in Industry Between 2014 and 2019

Samia Aitouche, Khaoula Sahraoui, Karima Aksa, Fadhila Djouggane, Walid Cherrid, Souleyman Belayati
Laboratory of Automatics and manufacturing, Industrial engineering department, University Batna 2, Batna, Algeria
e-mail: s.aitouche@univ-batna2.dz, sahraouikhaoula12@gmail.com, k.aksa@univ-batna2.dz, djougganefadila@yahoo.com, cheridwalid@gmail.com, belayati.souleyman@hotmail.com

Abstract— **It is always difficult to identify the most recent works that have been published, especially those published in recent years, due to delays in putting publications online, citations indexe, etc. Scientometry offers to researchers various concepts, models and techniques that can be applied to knowledge management (KM) in order to explore its foundations, its state, its intellectual core, and its potential future development. To this end, we have developed a scientometric KM framework to calculate the scientometric indexes related to a query introduced in the Scopus database, to facilitate research and monitoring of productivity and collaboration between the authors of KM in particular and also the dissemination of knowledge. The works between 2014 and 2019 are taken, the industry of services was omitted. It might help the decision makers and researchers to optimize their time and efforts. We used Unified Modeling Language (UML) to translate the development ideas of the scientometric framework structure into diagrams, and Delphi 7 to calculate the indexes and ensure other operations of research (about: articles, their authors, conferences, etc). This framework is only valid for Excel files extracted from Scopus or similar format. Finally, the relation between KM and industry 4.0 was established on found articles in Scopus.**

Keywords-Scientometric indexes; Knowledge management; Industry; industry 4.0, Scopus; UML; Delphi.

I. INTRODUCTION

KM is a concept having more attention in the last years; it was applied to the industry field as a process of creating, acquiring, transferring and using knowledge in order to improve the companies' performance. It is related to two types of activities: a) activities by which one attempts to document and appropriate individual knowledge within the organization and b) activities that facilitate human exchanges, in which uncodified knowledge is shared [1]. However, because of its novelty and for the reasons of delays in posting, indexes of citations, it is always difficult to identify the most recent and impacting published works. The sociology of sciences has exploited certain possibilities that mathematics and computer tools offer today to provide new analytical tools (library analysis, method of co-citations, method of associated words, etc.), around which a new discipline has been formed: the scientometry [2]. This discipline seeks to characterize science by the constitution of the objective laws of its development and finds its practicalities on the one hand in the quality of the tools it manipulates and on the other hand in the model of science on which it relies. It is based on the use of mathematical tools, and in particular on the statistical analysis of long series of clues deemed objectives, gradually extends.

In this context, a scientometric framework for KM was developed, able to calculate the scientometric indexes relating to a query in the Scopus database, to facilitate research and follow-up, productivity and collaboration between KM authors in particular, and the dissemination of knowledge.

Section 2 gathers some scientometric works. The followed methodology is presented in Section 3. Section 4 was devoted to realization and implementation of the scientometric framework. In Section 5, the relation between KM and Industry 4.0 is established and followed by a conclusion.

II. RELATED WORK

There are several precedent works related to KM. A relative scientometric analysis of KM [3] was presented, as a comparison between KM and Intellectual Capital (IC) journals, by the implantation of scientometric indexes using the programming language R. The results highlighted the best journals in KM and IC. Aitouche et al. [4] found that IC is an emerging field and scientific researchers are more productive and have immediate impact in it than those of KM field even though it is novelty. This comparison was observed through a bibliometric analysis of the evolution of KM and IC fields. Aitouche et al. [5] have done a keywords analysis in KM and IC. They observed that KM and IC have many common concepts such as management, performance, model, value. The keywords analysis allowed the identification of existing levels of meaning in scientific articles as well as the unexpected trends in each area. This work could be useful to prepare glossaries, ontologies and all semantic researches. In industry, Caviggioli and Ughetto [6] proposed a bibliometric analysis of the literature dealing with the impact of additive manufacturing on industry. It has gained momentum since 2012, in terms of the number of articles, received citations and number of involved authors. Empirical studies represent more than 50% of the sample, but they have mostly employed a case study approach. The result suggests that future empirical research could contribute further with the analysis of larger datasets and through the adoption of methods relying on surveys or action research.

Gonçales Filho and Campos [7] analyzed the lean manufacturing as a viable operations strategy; thereby identifying the lean production strategy adopted by companies in the various segments.

III. Methodology

In this section, we will present the used scientometric indexes, UML for design of the framework and used data.

A. *Scientometric indexes*

Table 1 describes the relative indexes used in this work; each index has an interpretation according to its definition.

TABLE I. Most Used Indexes.

Indexes	Description and/or formula
I-index	Number of citations of articles published in year N/ number of articles published in the journal in year N.
I10 index	Number of articles with at least 10 citations.
H index	Number of articles N, cited at least N times.
N index	It is calculated by dividing the H index by the number of years since first publication.
G index	Is the rank g of the article accumulating at least g^2 of citations?
Π-index	The introduction of a new impact index (π-index) aimed to privilege articles from highly influential journal, i.e. those that obtained a relatively high number of citations in all the analyzed articles. Π-index = 0.01 C(Pπ) / C(Pπ); hundredth of the number of citations.
Citescore	Citescore = Number of citations of a journal / Number of articles in a journal
SCImago Journal Rank (SJR)	SCImago Journal Rank measures weighted citations received by the serial. Citation weighting depends on subject field and prestige (SJR) of the citing serial.
Source Normalized Impact per Paper (SNIP)	Source Normalized Impact per Paper measures actual citations received relative to citations expected for the serial's subject field.

B. *Design with UML*

«Unified Modeling Language» is a visual language consisting of a set of diagrams, each diagram gives a different vision of the project to be dealt with. Thereby, StarUml is used to form the essential diagrams (use case diagram and class diagram).

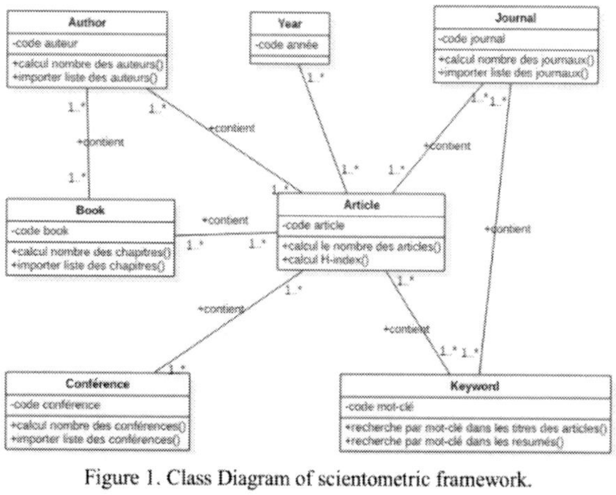

Figure 1. Class Diagram of scientometric framework.

In Fig. 1, we presented the class diagram. It contains 7 classes: author, who is the principal actor of research, then the article containing the majority of information. This latter is related to its keywords. The classes book, conference and journal represent the container of article. We need the class year to separate articles in time.

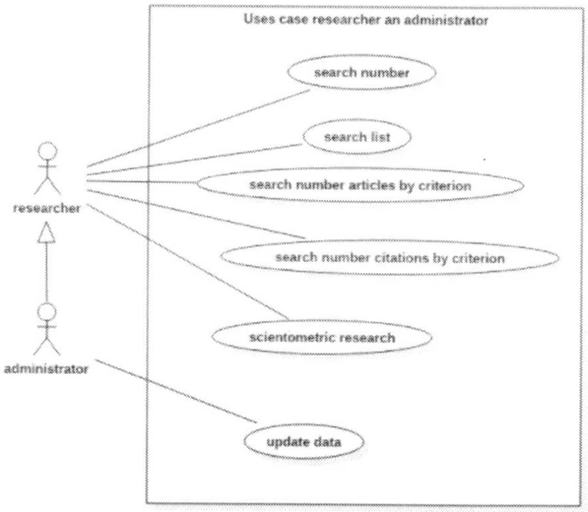

Figure 2. Uses cases of scientometric framework.

The uses cases diagram (Fig. 2) represents the functionalities of the proposed computing framework. It contains calculation of numbers, displaying lists, number articles by criterion, number citations by criterion, scientometric indexes and updating used data. The details are given in Section 4.

C. *Collected data*

The collected data for this framework is a set of articles concerning KM extracted, as an "excel" file, from Scopus (Fig. 3). The search in Scopus is accomplished with a query that finding articles, witch their titles contained the expression (KM AND (industry OR industrial OR manufacturing OR factory OR production OR product OR company OR firm OR enterprise OR organization)).

IV. Realization and Interpretation

The framework offers several functionalities to calculate some scientometric indexes using an Excel database exported from Scopus containing the items of articles requested.

A. *Calculation of numbers*

This functionality (Fig. 3) allows calculating the number of articles, authors, journals, chapters, laboratory, and conferences. We found 198 articles, 542 authors, 9 chapters, and 50 conferences in our integrated database. These numbers reflect the huge practices of KM in industries.

Figure 3. Menu calculation of numbers.

B. *Lists*

This functionality (Fig. 4) allows importing the lists of authors, journals, chapters, laboratory, conferences, and country. It imports the list of the indicated criterion.

Figure 4. Interface of lists.

The lists allow the researcher to have a primary idea on who are the authors, what are the journals, conferences, books and countries, laboratories, participating to the KM in industry.

C. *Number of articles by criterion*

In this functionality (Fig. 5), we search the number of articles by criterion (author, journal, chapter, laboratory, conference, country) or even further, the number of articles for author, journal, chapter, laboratory, conference, country, using names everyone needed.

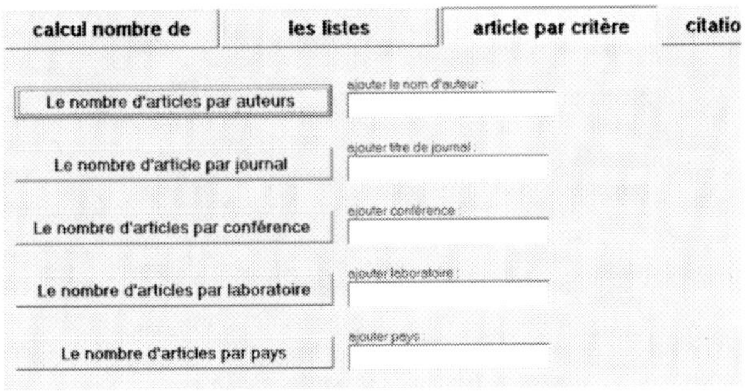

Figure 5. Number articles by criterion.

For countries, as it is observed from Table 2, the most producing countries are Germany, India, China, UK, Iran, USA and Malaysia. The more productive authors in KM applied to industry are Kifor C.V. with 4 articles, and, Tan L.P., Wong K.Y. and Paszek A., with 3 articles.

TABLE II. NUMBER ARTICLES PER AUTHOR AND PER COUNTRY

Author	Number articles	Country	Number articles
Kifor C.V.	**4**	**Germany**	**21**
Tan L.P.	**3**	**India**	**18**
Wong K.Y.	**3**	**China**	**14**
Paszek A.	**3**	**United Kingdom**	**13**
Samsir	2	**Iran**	**13**
Gao J.	2	**United States**	**13**
Twongyirwe T.M.	2	**Malaysia**	**12**
Lubega J.	2	Brazil	9

Table 3 shows that the biggest number of articles belongs to the ECKM (European Conference on KM Management) conference with 5 articles, then the journals "Advances in Transdisciplinary Engineering", "journal of KM management", "Lecture Notes in Computer Science", "Advanced Science Letters" and "KM Research and Practice" with 4 articles.

TABLE III. ARTICLES BY JOURNAL OR CONFERENCE OR BOOK.

Journal or conference or book	Number articles
Proceedings of the European Conference on KM, ECKM	5
Advances in Transdisciplinary Engineering	4
Journal of KM	4
Lecture Notes in Computer Science	4
Advanced Science Letters	4
KM Research and Practice	3
Quality - Access to Success	3
Advances in Intelligent Systems and Computing	3
Procedia CIRP	3
International Journal of Applied Business and Economic Research	3

D. *Number of citations by criterion*

As the previous functionality, our search would be by criterion too for searching the number of citations (Fig. 6). The criteria are the same used in Section C.

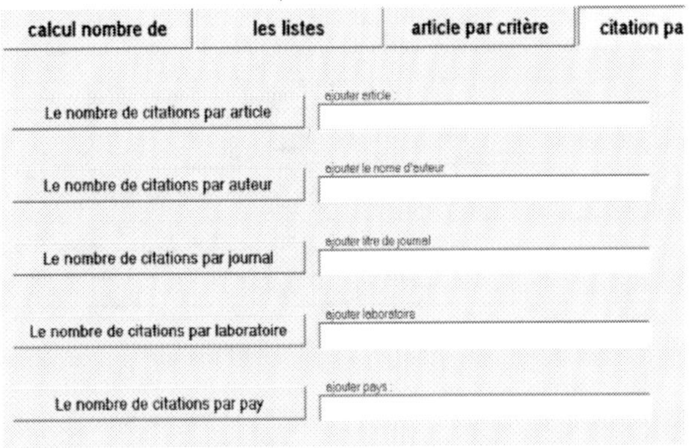

Figure 6. Number citations by criterion.

Table 4 represents an ascendant classification of articles by number of citations. The most cited article is entitled "The effects of industry cluster KM on innovation performance" with 71 citations. The second cited one is entitled "KM and innovation in knowledge-based and high-tech industrial markets: The role of openness and absorptive capacity". The precedent articles highlight the relation between KM and innovation.

Table 5 shows the most cited authors: Lai Y.-L., Hsu M.-S., Lin F.-J., Chen Y.-M., with 71 citations and Martín-de Castro G. with 23 citations. They are the pioneers of KM in industry, even if they are less productive than the authors mentioned in section B. They are not really evaluated by their productivity, but by their impact on the scientific society.

TABLE IV. CITATIONS OF ARTICLES

Article	Number citations
Lai Y.-L., Hsu M.-S., Lin F.-J., Chen Y.-M., Lin Y.-H., "The effects of industry cluster KM on innovation performance", 2014,"Journal of Business Research"	71
Martín-de Castro G., "KM and innovation in knowledge-based and high-tech industrial markets: The role of openness and absorptive capacity", 2015, "Industrial Marketing Management"	47
Hussain M., Ajmal M.M., Khan M., Saber H., "Competitive priorities and KM: An empirical investigation of manufacturing companies in UAE", 2015,"Journal of Manufacturing Technology Management"	23
Tan L.P., Wong K.Y., "Linkage between KM and manufacturing performance: a structural equation modeling approach", 2015,"Journal of KM"	22
Gonzalez R.V.D., Martins M.F., "Mapping the organizational factors that support KM in the Brazilian automotive industry", 2014,"Journal of KM"	22
Assouroko I., Ducellier G., Boutinaud P., Eynard B., "KM and reuse in collaborative product development - A semantic relationship management-based approach", 2014,"International Journal of Product Lifecycle Management"	17

The most countries having impact on the scientific society (Table 5) are Taiwan (98), Germany (51), Spain (47), Malaysia (41), UK (40), USA (38), India (38), Brazil (37) and China (36).

TABLE V. NUMBER CITATIONS BY AUTHOR AND COUNTRY

Author	Number citations	Country	Number citations
Lai Y.-L.	71	Taiwan	98
Hsu M.-S.	71	Germany	51
Lin F.-J.	71	Spain	47
Chen Y.-M.	71	Malaysia	41
Lin Y.-H.	71	United Kingdom	40
Martín-de Castro G.	47	United States	38
Saber H.	23	India	38
Eynard B.	23	Brazil	37
Tan L.P.	23	China	36
Wong K.Y.	23	France	27
Hussain M.	23	Austria	24

Table 6 indicates that the most cited institutions are Feng Chia University in Taiwan, University of Kaohsiung, Kaohsiung in Taiwan, University of Madrid in Spain, Cunef Business School in Spain and Abu Dhabi University in United Arab Emirates.

TABLE VI. NUMBER CITATIONS BY LABORATORY

Laboratory	Citations
Feng Chia University, Taichung, Taiwan	71
Department of Business Administration, Feng Chia University, Taichung, Taiwan	71
Department of Asia-Pacific Industrial and Business Management, University of Kaohsiung, Kaohsiung, Taiwan	71
Department of Leisure and Recreation Management, Asia University, Taichung, Taiwan	71
Business Administration Department, Complutense University of Madrid, Spain	47
Nonaka Centre for Knowledge and Innovation, CUNEF Business School, Spain	47
College of Business Administration, Abu Dhabi University, Abu Dhabi, United Arab Emirates	23
Department of Manufacturing and Industrial Engineering, University of Technology Malaysia, Skudai, Malaysia	22

Table 7 represents the most cited journals. It is found that the first cited journal is "Journal of business research" with 71 citations and the second one is "journal of KM" with 52 citations, followed by "Industrial Marketing Management" with 47 citations.

TABLE VII. CITATIONS BY JOURNAL

Journal	citations
Journal of Business Research	71
Journal of KM	52
Industrial Marketing Management	47
Journal of Manufacturing Technology Management	26
International Journal of Product Lifecycle Management	17
Total Quality Management and Business Excellence	16
International Journal of Computer Integrated Manufacturing	15
Journal of International Marketing	14
Business Process Management Journal	13
Journal of the Knowledge Economy	12
DFX 2014: 25th Symposium Design for X	12
Procedia CIRP	12

"European Conference on KM" (Table 8) is the most cited conference with 5 citations. The second and the third ones are "Advances in Transdisciplinary Engineering" and "Lecture notes in computer science" with 4 citations.

TABLE VIII. CITATIONS BY CONFERENCE

Conference	Citations
Proceedings of the European Conference on KM, ECKM	5
Advances in Transdisciplinary Engineering	4
Lecture Notes in Computer Science (including subseries Lecture Notes in Artificial Intelligence and Lecture Notes in Bioinformatics)	4
Proceedings of the ASME Design Engineering Technical Conference	3
Advances in Intelligent Systems and Computing	3
Procedia CIRP	3
Proceedings of the International Conference on Engineering Design, ICED	3
Procedia Engineering	3
Applied Mechanics and Materials	3

E. Scientometric indexes

This is where we could calculate the scientometric indexes (H-index, G-index, etc.). As it is exposed in Fig. 7, there is a group of authors where the i-10 index equals to 1; the highest value of H index is 2, and the highest value of G index is 3.

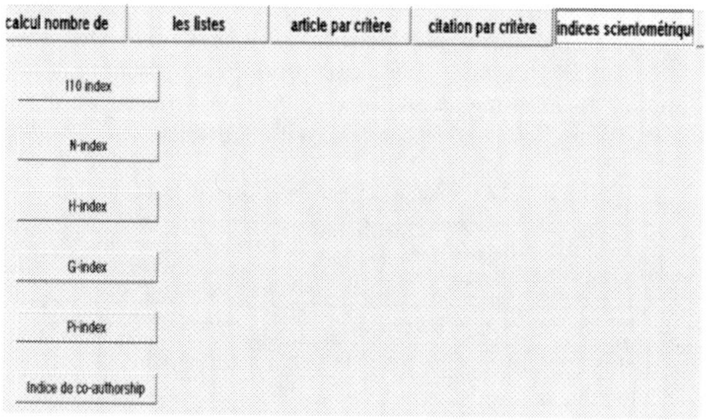

Figure 7. Menu scientometric indexes.

Table 9 indicates that all authors have an i-10 equal to 1 or 0. This means that the best author has 1 article cited with 10 citations: this is true only for the selected data.

The author could have an i10 index superior to 1 but using all his articles which are not present in our data.

The highest h index is 2. This means that these authors have 2 articles cited with 2 citations.

The highest G index is 3. This means these authors are the most cited, relatively; the exponential 2 of citations represents an improved h-index.

TABLE IX. SCIENTOMETRIC INDEXES OF AUTHORS

Author	I10-index	Author	H-index	Author	G-index
Eynard B.	1	Eynard B.	2	Paszek A.	3
Gonzalez R.V.D.	1	Richter A.	2	Tan L.P.	3
Tan L.P.	1	Kifor C.V.	2	Wong K.Y.	3
Wong K.Y.	1	Sivri S.D.	2	Krishnamurty S.	2
Al-Sa'di A.F.	1	Krallmann H.	2	Zhang C.	2
Abdallah A.B.	1	Shirouyehzad H.	2	Wang Y.	2
Dahiyat S.E.	1	Popescu D.I.	1	Eynard B.	2
Marques C.S.	1	Yildirmaz H.	1	Gonzalez R.V.D.	2
Leal C.	1	Atilla Öner M.	1	Gao J.	2
Marques C.P.	1	Herrmann N.	1	Eddy D.	2
Cardoso A.R.	1	Sarina T.	1	Richter A.	2

Table 10 represents the Π-index of journals (138), conferences (50) and books (9). It means that the journals are more cited and productive than conferences and books, because Π-index is an index reflecting the productivity and the impact in the same time.

TABLE X. Π-INDEX OF JOURNALS, CONFERENCES AND BOOKS

Π-index type	Value
Π-index for journals	138
Π-index for conferences	50
Π-index for books	9

It can be justified by the nature of journal articles containing more exhaustive insights, their experimentation and interpretation of results.

F. Update the data

Modifying or changing the file of the database, updating and integrating it, would be possible (Fig. 8). Data should have the same Excel format of the Scopus Excel exportation.

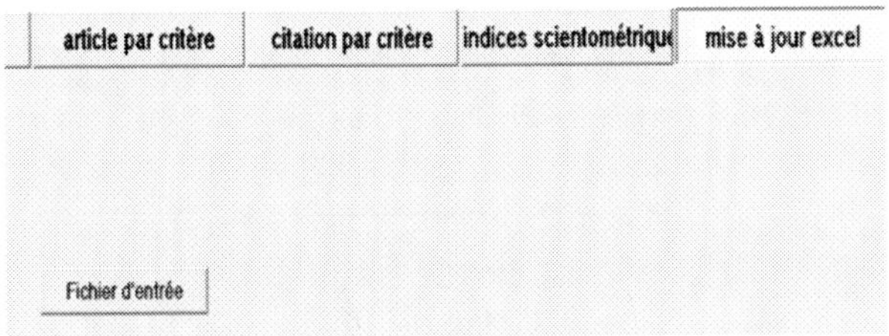

Figure 8. Update input data.

One can use this data or another database and introduce them in the Excel file, having the same items, and introduce it to the framework to have results.

V. SCIENTOMETRIC ANALYSIS OF KNOWLEDGE MANAGEMENT IN INDUSTRY 4.0

For this analysis, the expression (*"industry 4.0"* OR *iiot* OR *"industrial internet of things"* OR *"fourth industrial revolution"*) AND *"knowledge management"* in titles is used in Scopus to find 7 articles.

Table 11 shows that the number of articles on knowledge management and Industry 4.0 has been increasing over time. Germany is the most productive country. All authors have one article.

TABLE XI. PRODUCTION BY YEAR, COUNTRY AND AUTHOR

Year	Nb	Country	Nb	Authors and co-authors	Nb
2019	3	Germany	2	Arifiani, L., Budiastuti, I.D., Erika, W.K.	1
2018	2	Australia	1	Jermsittiparsert, K., Boonratanakittiphumi,	1
2017	1	Austria	1	Neumann, G., Evangelista, P.	1
2016	0	Colombia	1	Sarina, T.	1
2015	1	Finland	1	Cárdenas, L.J.A., Ramírez, W.F.T.,	1
2014	0	Indonesia	1	Möllenstädt, O.	1
		Italy	1	Brandl, P., Aschbacher, H., Hösch, S.	1

Table 12 presents the source of an article, even if it is a journal, conference or a book. Nb, N, CS, SJR and SNIP represent number of articles by source, notoriety, citescore, scimago journal rank, and source normalized impact per paper, respectively. Scopus does not find indexes for certain items. The Lecture Notes in Computer Science is the most cited (highest indexes) and it is the oldest source. It is followed by the CEUR conference.

TABLE XII. SOURCES BY INDEXES N, CS, SJR AND SNIP

Source title	Nb	N	CS	SJR	SNIP
International Journal of Engineering and Advanced Technology	1	2011	0.10	-	-
International Journal of Innovation, Creativity and Change	1	2013	0.20	0.187	0.306
Proceedings of the European Conference on Knowledge Management, ECKM	1	1999	-	-	-
The Palgrave Handbook of Knowledge Management	1	2018	-	-	-
Lecture Notes in Computer Science (including subseries Lecture Notes in Artificial Intelligence and Lecture Notes in Bioinformatics)	1	1937	1.06	0.283	0.713
CEUR Workshop Proceedings	1	1989	0.32	0.166	0.301
Mensch und Computer 2015 - Workshop	1	2015	-	-	-

Table 13 presents the affiliations of the authors of the articles; this is useful for a researcher to eventually collaborate with them.

Two German laboratories appear to make Germany one of the most productive countries in Industry 4.0 (third and fourth article). The collaboration between countries (Table 13) exists in the fourth article (Germany, Italy and Finland).

TABLE XIII. AFFILIATIONS OF THE AUTHORS OF KM AND INDUSTRY 4.0

Affiliation	Nb
Social Research Institute, Chulalongkorn University, Bangkok, Thailand; King Mongkul's Institute of Technology Ladkrabang, Prince of Chumphon Campus, Chumphon, Thailand.	1
Smart Production Solutions, Evolaris Next Level GmbH, Hugo-Wolf-Gasse 8-8A, Graz, A-8010, Austria; R and D Projects and Service Management, XiTrust Secure Technologies GmbH, Grazbachgasse 67, Graz, A-8010, Austria; Consulting and Project Management, XiTrust Secure Technologies GmbH, Grazbachgasse 67, Graz, A-8010, Austria.	1
Hauptgeschäftsführer Gesamtverband Kunststoffverarbeitende Industrie e. V. (GKV), Germany.	1
Technical University of Applied Sciences, Wildau, Germany; CNR-IRISS, Naples, Italy; School of Business and Management, Lappeenranta University of Technology, Finland.	1
Bina Nusantara University, Jakarta, Indonesia.	1
Universidad Distrital Francisco José de Caldas, Bogotá, Colombia.	1
Department of Marketing and Management, Macquarie University, Sydney, NSW, Australia.	1

Table 14 contains the frequencies of keywords proposed by authors in their articles. The keywords "knowledge management" (4) and "industry 4.0" (3) appear more than the others because they are contained in the titles of articles.

TABLE XIV. KEYWORDS FREQUENCIES IN ARTICLES

Keyword	Nb	Keyword	Nb	Keyword	Nb
Knowledge management	4	Data mining	1	Logistics	1
Industry 4.0	3	Degree of flexibility	1	Logistics and supply chain management	1
Supply chain	2	Digital technologies	1	Market situation	1
Academic literature	1	Disruption technology	1	Productivity improvements	1
Big data	1	Effective management	1	Service innovation	1
Big data analytics	1	Fundamental tools	1	Supply chain management	1
Business innovation	1	Information flows	1	Supply chains	1
Comparative advantage	1	Internet of things	1	Technological solution	1
Competitive advantage	1	Literature-based analysis	1	Thailand	1

"Logistics" and "supply chain" gathered appear 6 times; we understand primarily that industry 4.0 and KM are applied almost in logistics. "Technology" appears 7 times and "advantage" appears 2 times. Keywords give insights on trends of the researches on industry 4.0 and KM.

VI. CONCLUSION

In this work, we put to the researcher's hands a framework to facilitate finding what they are looking for, related to KM in the field of industry; KM is considered as a new discipline, so it is hard to find documentation related to it. Scopus is the biggest database containing abstracts, citations, conferences, books, subjects of research in various sciences. The data contains articles talking about KM and industry, extracted from Scopus, omitted the service industries and were introduced to the framework. Moreover, we chose Delphi to be the workspace of programming the scientometric framework. The value of the framework consists in the relative indexes calculated for a specific request; they do not exist in research databases.

The type of the updating file has to be "Excel" or a similar type, so, in this framework, we suggest that a computer scientist concentrates on developing this point, or even better searching for a way to integrate Scopus or other important database directly with the programming application.

A scientometric analysis is applied manually on 7 articles, making the relation between KM and Industry 4.0. The productivity and the impact of these researches is increasing over time and domains.

An interesting future development could be updating more than one database, and comparing them according to the calculation of the scientometric indexes using the framework. Furthermore, the databases could be related to different sciences.

REFERENCES

[1] H. Ben Amor, "The role of trust in knowledge management: case of community of practice at Schneider Electric", Ph.D thesis, 2007, Paris 13.

[2] J. M. Trouve, "Models of growth and evolution of scientific and technological knowledge", Second days of study on developed information systems, Paris, 1989.

[3] S. Aitouche et al, "Relative scientometric analysis of KM journals in Scopus", proc. The 3rd International Conference on Pattern Analysis and Intelligent Systems (PAIS), Oct. 2018, Tebessa, Algeria, ISBN: 978-153864238-2.

[4] S. Aitouche et al, "Relative bibliometrics of intellectual capital and KM in Scopus", Proc. Industrial Engineering and Operations Management (IOEM), Jul. 2018, Paris, France, pp. 3166-3177, ISSN: 2169-8767, ISBN: 978-1-5323-5945-3

[5] S. Aitouche, A. Laggoune, M. D. Mouss, A. Kanit and N. Zerari, "Keyword analysis of intellectual capital and KM in Scopus", proc. International Conference on Information, Process, and KM (EKNOW), Mar. 2017, Nice, France, pp 26-32, ISSN: 2308-4375 ISBN: 978-1-61208-542-5.

[6] F. Caviggioli and E. Ughetto, "A bibliometric analysis of the research dealing with the impact of additive manufacturing on industry, business and society", (2019) International Journal of Production Economics, vol. 208, pp. 254-268.

[7] M. Gonçales Filho, F.C. De Campos and M.R.P. Assumpção, "Systematic literature review with bibliometric analysis on Lean Strategy and manufacturing in industry segments", (2016) Gestao e Producao, vol. 23 (2), pp. 408-418.

Digitalization and IT Backsourcing: Towards a Transformational Model for the German Automobile Industry

Kerstin Felser and Martin Wynn
School of Business and Technology
University of Gloucestershire
Cheltenham, UK
Email: kerstinfelser@connect.glos.ac.uk
Email: MWynn@glos.ac.uk

Abstract – **Many organisations are now confronted with the new phenomenon of digitalization and are faced with the challenge of formulating and implementing a company-wide digital transformation strategy. Digitalization is associated with significant and extremely rapid change, and, in some cases, even the replacement of established business models. In manufacturing companies, this transformation is part of what is often termed Industry 4.0 and, in large companies, where the provision of information technology (IT) has hitherto been outsourced (in whole or in part), the introduction of these new technologies may be the catalyst for IT backsourcing. This entails bringing previously outsourced activities back in-house to regain ownership and control, in order to be more flexible and respond more effectively to rapidly changing demands. This study reviews the extant literature to assess existing thinking on the motivation for backsourcing, and then examines the potential role of digitalization in driving IT backsourcing in the German automotive industry. A provisional conceptual framework for subsequent research is put forward, using a knowledge-based view of the firm. The study is in its initial stages, but the model is being developed through more in-depth interviews to provide operational guidance for practitioners and subsequent research studies.**

Keywords – Backsourcing; digitalization; digital transformation; German automotive industry; conceptual model.

I. INTRODUCTION

A company's IT management must constantly review how it can deliver its services most effectively and efficiently [1]. This includes an on-going assessment of whether IT services are provided by the company's own resources or whether external resources are used. In the latter case, an outsourcing decision is made and a company delegates all or part of its IT services through contractual outsourcing agreements to one or more external vendor [2]. Many different forms of IT outsourcing have emerged, all associated with expectations that the company can better concentrate on its core business, focus on innovation, reduce costs and increase the effectiveness of IT services [3].

As and when such outsourcing agreements expire or the activity is reviewed, the decision has to be made as to whether to continue the agreement, to switch to another vendor, or to backsource the activities. Backsourcing is generally defined as bringing previously outsourced activities back in-house [4]. This definition also implies that the decision on backsourcing was taken after considering the possibility of renewing or renegotiating the existing contract or switching the vendor [5].

Significant change in the external technology environment - such as digitalization and new automation technologies - can be the catalyst for IT backsourcing. The German automotive industry is the most affected of all industries by digitalization in the German economy [6], and has been chosen as the business environment within which to undertake this research. The aim of the study is to assess current understanding of IT backsourcing and determine what impact digitalization may have in the German automotive industry regarding IT backsourcing. The study explores a relatively unknown field and will contribute to both research and practice, providing new knowledge for researchers and operational guidance for practitioners.

This article has five sections. Following this Introduction, Section 2 looks at the main concepts under study, briefly discusses relevant background issues and sets out three main research questions. Section 3 then outlines the research methodology, which to date has comprised a systematic literature review. Section 4 addresses the three research questions and makes an initial attempt to establish a conceptual framework for the continuation of the research project. Finally, Section 5 provides a summary of the ground covered in the paper to date.

II. BACKGROUND & CONCEPT DEFINITIONS

It is useful to first establish an understanding of the terminology and definitions associated with this study, as certain terms are not used in a consistent way. This applies above all to the terms "IT Backsourcing" and "Digitalization". Backsourcing is one part of the IT-sourcing cycle which can be summarized as "insourcing + outsourcing – outsourcing = backsourcing" [7]. Backsourcing has been defined by Lacity and Willcocks [4] as bringing previously outsourced activities back in-house. "Insourcing" is sometimes used as a general term for performing activities in-house and the literature does not distinguish between insourcing and backsourcing [8]. Many different forms of IT outsourcing have emerged, which can be combined in many ways and lead to a high degree of complexity, there being many possible dimensions to the outsourcing process. The same variety and complexity also applies to backsourcing.

Terms, such as backshoring, reshoring, onshoring or relocating, are sometimes used synonymously with backsourcing. However, Nujen et al. [9] underlined that these terms imply a change in location and, therefore, backsourcing is the only term that determines a change in ownership. A distinction can also be made between total and selective outsourcing/backsourcing. Lacity and Hirschheim [10] defined total outsourcing as being when more than 80% of IT budgets are outsourced to an external provider. Similarly, total insourcing occurs when more than 80% of the IT budget remains within the company. Finally, selective sourcing describes a degree of outsourcing of between 20% and 80% of the IT budget. Selective outsourcing has been the most popular and the most successful outsourcing strategy [11]. This study applies the same definitions to backsourcing, which can be both the backsourcing of a single IT service, such as a datacenter, or a bundle of applications, and the partial or complete backsourcing, where a company rebuilds the previously outsourced IT organization.

There is some overlap in the literature of the terms "digitization", "digitalization" and "digital transformation". Digitization is a more technical interpretation and refers to the conversion of information from an analog to a digital storage medium [12]. It also equates to the transfer of tasks to the computer that were previously performed by humans. Thus, digitization also refers to a special form of automation. The focus is on digital technologies, for which the term "SMACIT" (social, mobile, analytics, cloud, and Internet of Things) has been coined [13]. This has been widened by some authors to also encompass Big Data, artificial intelligence, digital twin, 3-D-Printing, augmented and virtual reality, and robotics. Many of the technologies mentioned are not new or revolutionary on their own. Rather, their innovative potential stems from their significantly enhanced efficiencies, their intensive networking possibilities and their increasingly widespread use [14].

The term digitalization is more broadly defined and is intended to express the fact that digitalization now affects all economic and social areas [12]. Riedl et al. [15] define digitalization as "the process of introducing digital technologies, which essentially deal with changes caused by information technologies". Koch, Ahlemann and Urbach [16] define four conditions for this. First, the technologies used do not have to be new, rather the newness is created in the context of business and value creation models; second, digitalization is data-driven and is based on an increased generation, processing and analysis of often new types of data; third, digitalization means that the character of the value added or the business model changes significantly as a result; and fourth, that there is an association with a clear strategic dimension, as companies expect competitive advantages from it.

Digital transformation is a result of digitalization and describes the development steps towards new, disruptive business and value creation models [17]. For Singh and Hess [18], this requires a company-wide digital transformation strategy to guide a company through the transformation process. However, there is no uniform definition of this term to date. Vial [19] reviewed 282 digital transformation related academic publications and found 23 different definitions. Based on the existing definitions, he developed a conceptual definition of digital transformation as "a process that aims to improve an entity by triggering significant changes to its properties through combinations of information, computing, communication, and connectivity technologies" [19].

Industry 4.0 can be viewed as part of digitalization, encompassing the entry of complex digital technologies and architectures into manufacturing processes. A generally accepted definition has not yet been established in the literature, but the definition of Roth [20] is used in the context of this research. "Industry 4.0 comprises the networking of all human and machine actors along the entire value chain as well as the digitalization and real-time evaluation of all relevant information with the aim of making processes and value creation more transparent and efficient in order to optimize customer benefits with intelligent processes and services." Industry 4.0 is also sometimes called the "fourth industrial revolution" or Industrial Internet of Things (IIoT), where the focus is on the strong integration of Internet-based information and communication technology (cyber-physical systems) into industrial processes [20].

Industry 4.0 has its roots in the concept of the Smart Factory and this is viewed as the starting point and main purpose of Industry 4.0 [21]. People, machines and products to be manufactured are connected in a network. The aim of this network is to achieve the overall optimization of quality, lead time and utilization of resources. It is considered a decisive innovation that all data are available in real time, providing a permanently up-to-date, virtual image of reality which allows complex manufacturing processes to be better controlled [21]. The Smart Factory represents an adaptable system in which flexible production lines automatically adjust their processes to different types of products and changing conditions [22].

In recent years, digitalization has become one of the most important topics in social, scientific and economic life [12]. Digital technologies are regarded as major technical changes or breakthroughs and the associated digital transformation is seen as a driver for significant and extremely rapid change, in some cases even leading to the replacement of established business models [23]. The term "transformation" reflects the variety and complexity of the measures that may need to be taken when companies are confronted with these new and disruptive technologies [18]. Some companies may see this as requiring a company-wide digital transformation strategy, which can encompass all business areas as well as products, processes and organizational structures.

If pre-existing IT strategy is aligned with the business, IT can be seen as an enabler for digital transformation [24]. Companies may review their IT sourcing strategies and governance models and consider alternatives for existing outsourcing arrangements [25]. This in turn may lead to a move towards IT backsourcing. Many companies have already established innovation labs, digital factories or technology accelerators in recent years in order to keep up with the increased demands of digitalization [26]. Volkswagen, for example, strengthened its IT department with 1,000 new IT employees from various disciplines [27]. At Daimler, too, there are signs of a part move away from the IT sourcing strategy that has been pursued for years, aimed at increasing its own contribution to IT from 25% to 35% [28].

The significance of digitalization as a factor in the backsourcing of IT provisions has received little attention in the scientific literature so far. In contrast to insourcing and outsourcing, IT backsourcing generally lacks scientific studies [29]. The literature that does exist deals mainly with the reasons and decision-making processes for IT backsourcing in relation to contract problems that have led to failure [30]. Internal or external organizational changes are only explained using individual examples of high profile / large-scale events, which have received press attention but cannot support generalization [31].

The German automotive industry consists of the Original Equipment Manufacturers (OEMs) and a three-tier supplier network. The industry is facing serious external organizational changes, which are leading to four megatrends in the automotive industry: Connectivity, Autonomous Driving, Shared & Services, Electric [32], for which the acronym C.A.S.E. is often used.

Each of the C.A.S.E. elements has the power to radically change the industry and undermine existing business models. The challenge will be to combine them in a way that delivers a comprehensive and seamless package to the customer. Digitalization and Industry 4.0 and the associated connection of the physical with the digital world, as well as the networking of the entire value chain, are the drivers of this change [33].

Digitalization and digital transformation affect all areas of a company. The aim of the study is to analyze to what extent digitalization has influenced the German automotive industry's strategy regarding IT backsourcing and provide new insights concerning the decision making and values created by IT backsourcing. The current study addresses three Research Questions (RQs):

RQ 1: What does the extant literature reveal regarding current thinking on the rationale for IT backsourcing?

RQ 2: To what extent has digitalization influenced the German automotive industry's strategy regarding IT backsourcing and what are its potential benefits?

RQ 3: How can an operational framework be developed and applied to aid practitioners in backsourcing IT in the German automotive industry?

This article presents initial findings from the study that are now being pursued through in-depth interviews with industry practitioners. In general, current evidence for IT backsourcing, as presented in the existing literature, brings only partial answers the research questions of this study.

III. Research Methodology

To date, a systematic literature review has been undertaken. The search for existing and relevant literature was carried out in three stages. As the selection of search terms (keywords) has a significant impact on the search results [34], an initial exploratory search was undertaken in April 2019 in order to ascertain key terminologies and concepts used in the literature. A combination of keywords was used in the search string when identifying relevant literature.

A second systematic search was carried out in May 2019 using complex combinations of keywords, and a third search was undertaken in July/August 2019, after reformulating the research questions. Keyword searches were conducted in the Science Direct, IEEExplore, Business Source Complete (EBSCO), AIS Electronic Library and Google Scholar databases, restricting the publication dates to be within the year 2008 and after, because the topic of digitalization was not a current issue before 2008.

A practical screening was performed [35], and after deleting duplications and separating all non-relevant ones, 22 publications were selected. Backward and forward searches based on references and authors were performed to uncover seminal publications on the subject of IT backsourcing [36]. The backward search showed no further results. The forward search resulted in 5 more articles from Sage journals, SpringerLink, Emerald insight and Researchgate. Of the 27 articles in total, 13 are peer reviewed. Practice-oriented publications such as the frequently published magazines MIT-Technology report, CIO magazine or reports from the Association of German Automobile Manufacturers (VDA) as well as from international IT consulting and supplier organizations were also reviewed.

IV. Preliminary Findings

RQ1: What does the current literature reveal regarding current thinking on the rational for IT backsourcing?

The reasons for individual backsourcing decisions are a focus in both the academic and practitioner literature. The practitioner literature highlights cost savings, quality improvements, and increase in control and flexibility as the three most important reasons [37]. The academic literature looks at a broader picture and distinguishes between the three important categories: contract problems, internal organizational changes and external environmental changes, to which individual reasons are assigned [2]. Contract problems emerges as the main reason for backsourcing until now (Table I).

As regards contract problems, one of the main motivators for backsourcing is dissatisfaction with the quality of services provided by the vendor. Moe et al. [38] state a lack of communication between client and vendor, the inability to provide the necessary knowledge and skilled resources, a high turnover of employees on the vendor side and cultural problems such as different understandings of responsiveness and punctuality. Gorla and Lau [39] have analyzed how negative experiences in outsourcing affect future outsourcing decisions. They conclude that competence and coordination problems with the vendor have a stronger influence on backsourcing and future outsourcing decisions than unexpected costs. According to Kotlarsky and Bognar [40] low service quality is typically linked to poor responsiveness or a lack of professionalism on the vendor's side. The relationship between client and vendor, as well as trust, also plays a significant role in either changing vendors or taking backsourcing into account [41]. The gap between expected and actual cost reductions through outsourcing is another important driver for backsourcing. As Kotlarsky and Bognar [40] point out, cost savings through outsourcing tend to be overestimated and hidden costs such as transition costs, rising wages in the outsourcing destination country or staff turnover are not sufficiently taken into account. Another critical factor is losing control over the vendor's activities or over certain functions [8]. This can be risky if security or intellectual capital is involved, or if it turns out that outsourced systems have a strategic value.

Kotlarsky and Bognar [40] stated that a knowledge mismatch is one reason for loss of control if the vendor knows more about the systems than the client does or the vendor only barely understands the client's business. One more factor for backsourcing is when the vendor does not respond to the latest technologies which deliver the best value to the customer [42]. Losing control also leads to limited flexibility for the client compared to in-house operations [43]. Benaroch et al. [44] contend that in times of increased demand uncertainty, there is a tendency among clients towards backsourcing or insourcing decisions, as opposed to vendors' view that these situations would be motivators for outsourcing. They also claim that companies would prefer the flexibility of contracts in increased demand uncertainty, e.g. the possibility to pay a lump sum as a penalty to ease backsourcing. However, without the flexibility built into the original outsourcing contract, the probability of backsourcing is limited.

The most recent studies show, however, that contract problems and the resulting operational difficulties are no longer major drivers of backsourcing. Könning, Westner and Strahringer [31] analyzed over 1,000 sourcing deals in Austria, Switzerland and Germany between 2006 and 2017 and show that the companies are able to manage a large number of IT vendors. They also mention that companies use international sourcing consultancies (e.g. ISG, Accenture, BCG, Deloitte, KPMH, PwC) to design tenders and contracts, support the transition process, the provision of global delivery models and advise on the processes for the constant monitoring of the various vendors and services. A review of the German automotive industry shows that, on the one hand, the depth of service in the in-house provision of IT services is generally between 20% and 30% of the overall IT budget [28], while at the same time companies have employed thousands of IT employees worldwide [45]. These IT organizations have also developed and implemented comprehensive process models to minimize contractual and operational risks in outsourcing [46]. However, Solli-Saether and Gottschalk [47] refer to the Sourcing Circle and the stages-of-growth model to determine whether a formerly in-house function has a higher degree of maturity when it comes back after years of outsourcing. They argue that the outsourcing phase is not a waste of time, "it is not a return to the beginning, but something that has been altered" [47].

The literature on internal organizational factors for IT backsourcing focuses on the discussion of strategic reorientation in the company, the intensive debate about the value of IT and internal power-political behaviour, which are more subjective and therefore more difficult to assess [48]. In this context, the role of IT and the sourcing strategy of IT are repeatedly reassessed. According to Butler [48], the proper alignment between business and IT strategy is the link to re-position IT from commodity to IT as strategic and leads to appropriate backsourcing decisions. He also points out that not all IT functions are core business or non-core business, but the challenge is to categorize IT functions as either commodity or strategic in order to adjust the IT sourcing strategy. Qu, Oh and Pinsonneault [49] also emphasize that companies should make more efforts to assess the strategic value of IT, rather than considering IT as a non-core activity. Benaroch et al. [50] add that strategic considerations play an important role in transaction- and information-intensive processes with volatile demand and that backsourcing increases the capabilities for innovation and competitive advantages.

Thakur-Wernz [51] combined the two theoretical lenses - Transaction Cost Economics (TCE) and Resource Based View (RBV) - and concluded that companies decide backsourcing for two reasons: short-run total costs and internal capabilities. She contradicts earlier research, which assumes that costs and capabilities play a complementary role and are intertwined, especially in the long run. Based on a backsourcing topology, however, Thakur Wernz [51] claims that costs and capabilities are independent of each other, especially in the short-term. The reason for this assumption is that companies would not be in a position to change or expand their capabilities at short notice. She concludes that companies are less likely to undertake backsourcing when the total short-term costs of backsourcing are higher, and more likely to go for backsourcing when internal reintegration capabilities are higher.

Oshri et al. [52] stated that dissatisfaction with an outsourcing agreement is an even stronger driver for backsourcing decisions than cost considerations. They used the behavioral theory as a lens, which is based on realistic assumptions about human cognition and relationships. The theory suggests that decision making in companies is characterized by the limited rationality and organizational politics of decision makers. The assumption is that problem-driven managers tend to make irrational decisions rather than based on a systematic assessment of long-term opportunities and risks. The transition from outsourcing and especially from offshoring to backsourcing means a radical change of strategy with significant economic consequences. Those responsible would do well to first consider a detailed feasibility study.

Qu et al. [49] postulate, from the knowledge-based view, that IT backsourcing would create value and competitive advantage. Best practice processes require the integration of IT and business knowledge and this interaction increases the alignment between IT and business objectives. Shared knowledge and smooth coordination between IT and business is not a commodity, which can be bought on the market. This in-house knowledge only evolves over many years and is part of the corporate culture.

External environmental changes such as economic cycles with volatile demand, financial crises, changes in the structure of the industry that redefine the overall business strategy of the company are identified by some authors as the catalyst for backsourcing [52]-[54]. Regarding mergers and acquisitions, several authors cited the example of how JP Morgan Chase terminated its large-scale outsourcing contracts after the merger with Bank One or Bank of Scotland merged with or Halifax Building Society because the mergers gave rise to new internal capabilities to provide in-house IT services more effectively. In addition, changes on the vendor side are triggers for backsourcing, when the vendor redefines its business strategies or its organizational structure, which is often the result of mergers and acquisitions between vendors. German companies have been affected by the wave of concentration on the vendor side, which can also be assumed as a reason for backsourcing.

Thakur-Wernz [51] refers to the bandwagon effect mentioned by Lacity and Hirschheim [10]. Outsourcing was widespread, many companies did it and therefore more companies followed suit. There was significant increased risk that the outsourcing decision was not adequately researched and assessed, and backsourcing is the correction of outsourcing failures. Ironically, the bandwagon effect could now also happen with backsourcing. Finally, and most significantly for this study, Wong [43] and Von Bary [55] state that new and disruptive technologies, lead to a repositioning of the value of IT and trigger backsourcing decisions.

TABLE I. SUMMARY OF REASONS FOR IT BACKSOURCING BASED ON LITERATURE REVIEW

Contract Problems: Outsourcing agreement did not meet expectations
• Higher than expected costs • Poor service quality • Poor transition planning • Loss of control over the core business • Loss of flexibility • No benefits from outsourcing • Disagreement with vendor • Loss of know-how • Incompetence of the vendor (e.g. missing innovations on the vendor side hinders the client's business success)
Internal Organizational Changes
• New or changed executive management • Structural changes in the company (e.g. new business line, new corporate entity) • New business strategies • Recognition of IT as business enabler • New/changed importance of outsourced activities • Changes in IT strategy due to mergers and acquisitions • Power and politics
External Environmental Changes
• Changes in the environment of the company • Economic cycles • Bandwagon effect • Changes in vendor organization • Technology changes ("break-through" technologies)

RQ2: To what extent has digitalization influenced the German automotive industry's strategy regarding IT backsourcing and what are its potential benefits?

Germany is the second largest outsourcing market in the western world [56] but is under-represented in the academic literature, although online sources provide evidence of a number of failures in large outsourcing deals in German industry. In addition, digital technologies are regarded as major technological changes, and the associated digital transformation is seen as potentially leading in some cases to the replacement of established business models. The German automotive industry as a manufacturing industry and the most important German industrial sector is particularly affected by these changes. New digital business models are becoming the starting point for the future competitiveness of the German automotive industry on the world market [57]. According to Veltri et al. [2] and others, external environmental changes are seen as motivators for IT backsourcing because the core competencies of a company need to be redefined. These dependencies and effects have not yet been specifically investigated by researchers using the example of an entire industry in Germany.

Researchers have applied various theories, such as TCE, RBV or Knowledge-Based View (KBV), to explain and demonstrate the benefits of IT backsourcing. However, there is some debate concerning the extent to which these theories are useful in evaluating IT backsourcing decisions and providing practical guidance. According to Wernerfelt [58] and Barney [59], the RBV considers an organization from the inside and the central thesis of the RBV is that companies generate sustainable competitive advantage by introducing strategies that exploit their internal strengths. The RBV was later enhanced by contributions from various authors to the KBV and it has been argued that competitive advantages are achieved not only on the basis of physical or financial resources, but also through knowledge-based capabilities [60]. Teece, Pisano and Shuen [61] published the theory of Dynamic Capabilities (DC) in 1997, which extends the internal view to the market and defined the DC as "the firm's ability to integrate, build, and reconfigure internal and external competences to address rapidly changing environments" (p. 516).

According to Teece, Pisano and Shuen [61] markets can be divided into moderate and highly dynamic markets. Moderate dynamic markets are characterized by continuous changes. These are relatively easy to predict. Moderate markets are transparent and stable. Resources, organizations and processes are generally based on existing skills, knowledge and abilities. Highly dynamic markets, on the other hand, are characterized by rapid changes, have unstable structures and the resources of a company are based less on existing skills than on situation-specific knowledge, skills and abilities that can be quickly developed and newly created. The static approach of the RBV is not suitable for this field of operation [62]. The RBV would only apply to firms in predictable environments.

Since the German automotive industry is in a highly dynamic market because of the digital transformation, the theories applied to answer the question of whether IT backsourcing contributes to a sustainable competitive advantage or not should be extended to include the DC approach. A review of the existing literature shows that there is no analysis and evaluation with the DC theory on IT backsourcing.

Previous research on IT backsourcing deals with IT technology and IT systems in general. In the context of the strategic alignment between business and IT, there is a need to examine which outsourced IT functions, technologies or applications are brought back in-house, particularly against the background of digital transformation, in order to achieve sustainable competitive advantages. There is clearly a link to the core production process as many manufacturing companies have outsourced parts of their production, especially to offshore locations such as China. It is to be expected that digitalization and Industry 4.0 will lead to backsourcing of production to some extent [63]. The new technologies provide opportunities for production to be more flexibly and cost-effectively re-located in the home country again because the cost advantages that originally resulted in offshoring can be neutralized and, secondly, the application of Industry 4.0 technologies then increase flexibility in the production process. This would also have implications on outsourced IT services for manufacturing processes. Backsourcing does not necessarily mean that the affected functions and capacities are locally returned to the headquarters of the mother organization. The German automotive industry has worldwide access to resources and know-how and has the opportunity to network resources and knowledge with modern forms of agile cooperation [27].

RQ3: How can an operational framework be developed and applied to aid practitioners in backsourcing IT in the German automotive industry?

The existing literature partly shows in individual case studies the challenges of knowledge transfer during outsourcing and provides overviews of the requirements for knowledge re-integration during backsourcing or switching vendors. An overall framework that offers guidance to practitioners involved in backsourcing in the German automotive industry is missing.

The proposed conceptual framework (Figure 1) represents the theoretical basis for answering the research questions in this study. It uses the theory of dynamic capabilities to investigate the value of IT backsourcing. The concept of dynamic capabilities can be divided into the ability to identify and shape opportunities and threats, the ability to seize opportunities and the ability to maintain competitiveness by improving, combining, protecting and reconfiguring the assets of the business [64]. Therefore, sensing, seizing, reconfiguring and transforming are the main components of dynamic capabilities. This theory is combined with the knowledge-based view of the firm, since it is assumed that digital transformation requires significant change in the knowledge-base of the company to increase its innovative capacity [65]. However, in combining these theoretical perspectives, three main dimensions of change relating to the new digital technologies, the change in processes relating to IT backsourcing and the necessary enhancement of people skills and capabilities will be used as an operational model to identify critical success factors and a staged action plan to achieve competitive advantage from the backsourcing process. This aligns with other studies of change and innovation relating to the introduction of new technologies into organizations [66]. IT backsourcing may thus be viewed as a strategic decision of a company to respond to the rapidly changing external environment and provide a source of sustainable competitive advantage. This is especially the case when this enables important innovation, increases flexibility to respond very effectively to new business requirements, introduces emerging technologies to achieve new capabilities and facilitates the rapid placement of new digital business models, products or services in the marketplace.

The knowledge-based view has received a great deal of interest in the literature because it recognizes the fundamental economic changes that have resulted from the accumulation and availability of knowledge over the last two decades [67]. The economy has undergone a structural change in the productive paradigm. The transition from production to service in most developed economies is based on the manipulation of information and not on the use of physical products [68]. Knowledge has become one of the most important assets for creating a sustainable competitive advantage [69].

This trend becomes even more pronounced with digitalization. The digital future means everything is expressed in terms of data. A central element of digitalization and of Industry 4.0 is the generation of huge amounts of data with cyber-physical systems and the storage and linking with technologies such as Big Data. However, data itself are of little value. The data from many different sources are only transformed into valuable information through comprehensive analyzes and correlations to become a strategic value. Therefore, what matters is the management of information and the intelligent usage of this information for new business models and processes, interlinking the company with its ecosystems, for cognitive solutions, virtual reality, predictions and robotics. New core competencies and unique knowledge becomes the critical success factor.

The conceptual framework and underlying philosophy of the study is therefore based on the author's belief that the digital transformation of a company is an eminently knowledge-based issue. The theory of the knowledge-based view of the firm assumes that a company exists because it has advantages in the market through the generation of knowledge and innovations [70]. In addition to the dynamic capabilities, in responding to changes in the external environment, knowledge is also a key resource for achieving sustainable competitive advantage.

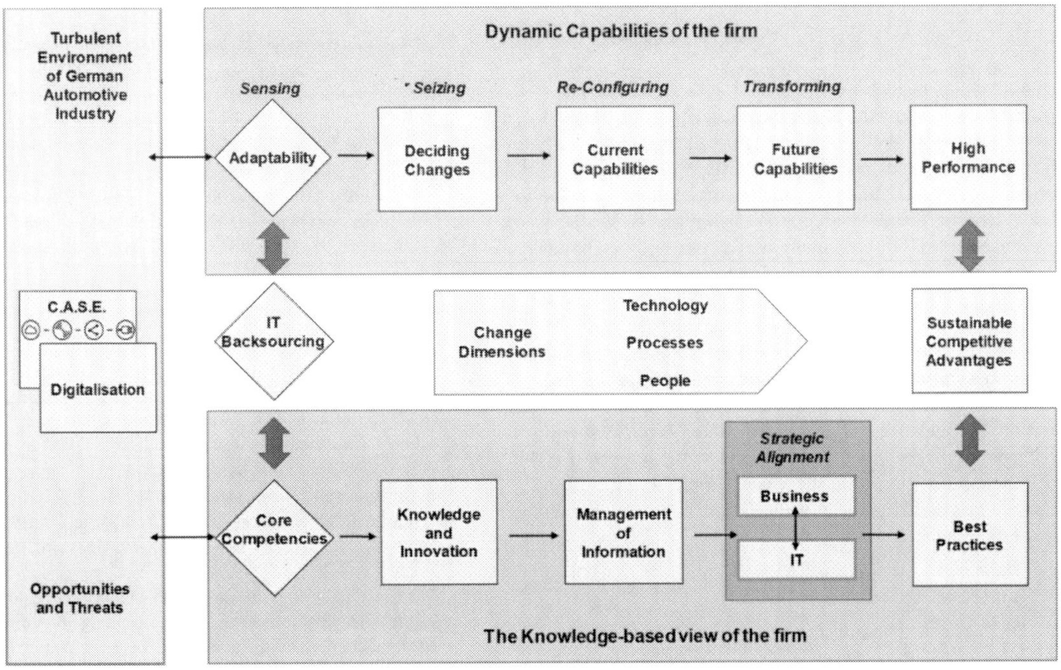

Figure 1. Provisional Conceptual Framework

As outlined above, the provisional conceptual framework (Figure 1) constitutes an initial model for addressing the research questions and provides the basis for discussion in expert interviews. Interview findings will help determine if digitization is encouraging IT backsourcing, and to what extent this can be seen as a source of competitive advantage. Any such correlations and conclusions will need to take account of other influencing entrepreneurial factors. The underlying logic is that digitalization leads to extremely rapid change, in some cases even the replacement of established business models. The German automotive industry must demonstrate appropriate capabilities in two directions. They must have dynamic capabilities to react flexibly to the accelerating changes in the external environment. At the same time, they must have the internal capabilities in terms of resources and knowledge in order to drive and support the necessary innovation. This can provide the basis for a company-wide digital transformation strategy, encompassing possible repositioning in the marketplace, reworking of sourcing agreements, and implementation of necessary change in terms of technologies, processes and people competencies.

V. CONCLUSION

The literature review indicated that there are three main motivations for IT backsourcing: unsolvable contractual problems, internal organizational changes and external environmental changes, with the advent of digitalization being a potentially significant driver in future in the last named category. Digitalization has the potential for new, disruptive business and value models and requires companies to shape the digital transformation process.

In particular, the German automotive industry is affected by four megatrends due to serious external changes, for which digitalization is one of the main triggers. Given these developments, and drawing on a combination of existing theories, a provisional conceptual framework was devised to determine the context in which IT backsourcing should be seen, and which will now be applied to identify critical success factors and key actions for the successful adoption of a backsourcing strategy.

IT backsourcing arguably creates better conditions for the interaction between IT and business and for sharing and integrating IT and business knowledge, which can underpin the adoption of best practice [49]. Through IT backsourcing, mission critical knowledge can be brought back in-house; the protection of intellectual property and security issues are taking on a new significance in the context of digitalization and may be seen as driving IT backsourcing.

The contribution of this research to theory has several aspects. First, it will provide an informed view on whether digitalization is encouraging IT backsourcing – currently a gap in the extant literature. Second, it will explore and explain how companies in the German automotive industry justify decisions for IT backsourcing within the framework of a company-wide digital transformation strategy. This will allow key issues regarding IT backsourcing to surface - for example, the need to develop dynamic capabilities and redefine core competencies in order to achieve sustainable competitive advantages in the so-called digital age. Research results will also establish the methods used by companies to forge a strategic link between digitalization and IT backsourcing and to determine the resulting value.

In terms of contribution to practice, the project aims to provide decision makers with operational guidance to assess the scenarios of IT backsourcing as part of a digital transformation strategy. This will improve knowledge for practitioners about the various factors to be considered for identifying the strategic value contribution of IT backsourcing. The study will provide illustrative examples of the practices, procedures and organizational change needed for re-establishing IT services in-house. Finally, an operational framework and associated strategy checklist will provide practitioners with the tools to assess the impact of IT backsourcing decisions on the overall performance of a company, and guide priority-settings for IT backsourcing projects as an enabler for digitalization.

References

[1] H. Krcmar, "Informationsmanagement [in English: Information Management]", 6th ed., München: Springer Verlag, 2015, ISBN: 978-3-662-45862-4.

[2] N. F. Veltri, C. S. Saunders, and C. B. Kavan, "Information systems backsourcing: correcting problems and responding to opportunities," California Management Review, vol. 5, no. 1, pp. 50-76, 2008, doi: 10.2307/41166468.

[3] J. Barthelemy, "The seven deadly sins of outsourcing," Academy of Management Perspectives, 17(2), vol. 17, no. 2, pp. 87-98, 2003, doi: 10.5465/ame.2003.10025203.

[4] M. C. Lacity and L. P. Willcocks, Outsourcing: A Stakeholder Perspective in Framing the Domains of IT Management Research: Glimpsing the Future through the Past, R. Pinnaflex: Cincinnati, OH, 2000.

[5] D. McLaughlin and J. Peppard, "IT backsourcing: from make or buy to bringing IT back in-house," European Conference on Information Systems (ECIS 2006), Proc. 117.

[6] F. Pfeil, "Megatrends und die dritte Revolution der Automobilindustrie: Eine Analyse der Transformation der automobilen Wertschöpfung auf Basis des Diamantmodells [in English: Megatrends and the third revolution in the automotive industry: an analysis of the transformation of automotive value creation based on the diamond model]", 2018, ISSN: 978-3-00-059102-0.

[7] H. Oshri, "ComputerWeekly," 2013. [Online]. Available: https://www.computerweekly.com/blog/Investigating-Outsourcing/Insourcing-outsourcing-outsourcing-backsourcing-the-academics-view. [retrieved: January, 2020].

[8] C. Salge, "Pulling the Outside In: A Transactional Cost Perspective on IT Insourcing.," Proceedings of the 21th Americas Conference on Information Systems, Puerto Rico, pp. 1-11, 2015.

[9] B. Nujen, L. Halse, and H. Solli-Saether, "Backsourcing and knowledge re-integration: a case study," IFIP International Conference on Advances in Production Management Systems (APMS), Sep 2015, Tokyo, Japan, pp. 191-198, doi:10.1007/978-3-319-22759-7_22

[10] M. C. Lacity and R. Hirschheim, "Information Systems Outsourcing: Myths, Metaphors and Realities," in Chichester: Wiley, 1993, ISBN: 978-0-471-93882-8.

[11] D. Whitten, S. Chakrabarty, and R. Wakefield, "The strategic choice to continue outsourcing, switch vendors, or backsource: Do switching costs matter?," Information & Management, vol. 47, no. 3, pp. 167-175, 2010, doi: 10.1016/j.im.2010.01.006.

[12] T. Hess , "Digitalisierung [in English: Digitalization]," 2016. [Online]. Available: http://www.enzyklopaedie-der-wirtschaftsinformatik.de/lexikon/technologien-methoden/Informatik--Grundlagen/digitalisierung. [retrieved: January, 2020].

[13] N. Urbach et al., "The Impact of Digitalization on the IT Department," Business & Information Systems Engineering, vol. 61, no. 1, pp. 123-131, 2018, doi: 10.1007/s12599-018-0570-0.

[14] N. Urbach and F. Ahlemann, "Die IT-Organisation im Wandel: Implikationen der Digitalisierung für das IT-Management [in English: The IT Organization in Flux: Implications of Digitalization on IT Management]," HMD Praxis der Wirtschaftsinformatik, vol. 54, no. 3, pp. 300-312, 2017, doi: 10.1365/s40702-017-0313-6.

[15] R. Riedl, A. Benlian, T. Hess, D. Stelzer, and H. Sikora, "On the relationship between information management and digitalization," Business & Information Systems Engineering, vol. 59, no. 6, pp. 475-482, 2017, doi: 10.1007/s12599-017-0498-9.

[16] P. Koch, F. Ahlemann, and N. Urbach, "Die innovative IT-Organisation in der digitalen Transformation [in English: The innovative IT organization in digital transformation]," in Managementorientiertes IT-controlling und IT-governance, pp. 177-196, Springer Gabler, Wiesbaden, 2016, doi: 10.1007/978-3-658-07990-1_11.

[17] A. Bharadwaj, O. A. El Sawy, P. A. Pavlou, and N. Venkatraman, "Digital business strategy: toward a next generation of insights," MIS quarterly, vol. 37, no. 2, pp. 471-482, 2013, ISSN: 0276-7783.

[18] A. Singh and T. Hess, "How Chief Digital Officers Promote the Digital Transformation of their Companies," MIS Quarterly Executive, vol. 16, no. 1, pp. 1-17, 2017, ISSN: 1540-1960.

[19] G. Vial, "Understanding digital transformation: A review and a research agenda," The Journal of Strategic Information Systems, vol. 28, pp. 118–144, 2019, doi: 10.1016/j.jsis.2019.01.003.

[20] A. Roth, "Industrie 4.0 - Hype oder Revolution? [in English: Industry 4.0 - Hype or Revolution?]," in Einführung und Umsetzung von Industrie 4.0, pp. 1-15, Springer Gabler, Berlin, Heidelberg, 2016, doi: 10.1007/978-3-662-48505-7_1.

[21] H. Kagermann, J. Helbig, A. Hellinger, and W. Wahlster, "Recommendations for implementing the strategic initiative INDUSTRIE 4.0: Securing the future of German manufacturing industry; final report of the Industrie 4.0 Working Group," Forschungsunion, 2013.

[22] A. G. Frank, L. S. Dalenogare, and N. F. Ayala, "Industry 4.0 technologies: Implementation patterns in manufacturing companies," International Journal of Production Economics, vol. 210, pp. 15-26, 2019, doi: 10.1016/j.ijpe.2019.01.004.

[23] S. Berghaus and A. Back, "Gestaltungsbereiche der Digitalen Transformation von Unternehmen: Entwicklung eines Reifegradmodells [in English: Design areas of the digital transformation of companies: development of a maturity model]," Die Unternehmung, vol. 70, no. 2, pp. 98-123, 2016, doi: 10.5771/0042-059X-2016-2-98.

[24] A. Yeow, C. Soh, and R. Hansen, "Aligning with new digital strategy: A dynamic capabilities approach," The Journal of Strategic Information Systems, vol. 27, no. 1, pp. 43-58, 2018, doi: 10.1016/j.jsis.2017.09.001.

[25] IDG, "Studie Sourcing 2018 [in English: Sourcing Study 2018]," IDG Business Media GmbH, München, 2018.

[26] S. Kahl, N. Urbach, M. Gschwendtner, and A. Zimmer, "IT-Outsourcing im Zeitalter der Digitalisierung [in English: IT outsourcing in the age of digitalization]," Wirtschaftsinformatik & Management, vol. 9, no. 6, pp. 48-55, 2017, doi: 10.1007/s35764-017-0132-0.

[27] Automobilwoche, "Digitalisierung: VW stellt 1000 IT-Experten ein [in English: Digitalization: VW hires 1000 IT experts]," 2016. [Online]. Available: https://www.automobilwoche.de /article/20161228/ Nachrichten/161229894. [retrieved: January, 2020].

[28] J. Hackmann, "Daimler holt ausgelagerte SAP zurück [in English: Daimler brings back outsourced SAP]," 2013. [Online]. Available: https://www.cio.de/a/daimler-holt-ausgelagerte-sap-zurueck,2918732. [retrieved: January, 2020].

[29] B. Von Bary and M. Westner, "Information systems backsourcing: A literature review," Journal of Information Technology Management, vol. 29, no. 1, pp. 62-78, 2018, ISSN: 1042-1319.

[30] A. Nicholas-Donald and K. M. Osei-Bryson, "The Economic Value of Back-sourcing: An Event Study," International Conference on Information Resources Management (CONF-IRM 2017), Proc 31, pp. 1-9, 2017.

[31] M. Könning, M. Westner, and S. Strahringer, "Multisourcing on the Rise–Results from an Analysis of more than 1,000 IT Outsourcing Deals in the ASG Region," Multikonferenz Wirtschaftsinformatik, March 2018, Lüneburg, Germany, pp. 1813-1824.

[32] C. Berlin et al., "Automobil Produktion, IAA Sonderheft [in English: Automobil Production, IAA Special Issue]," Media Manufactur, Pattensen, 2019.

[33] Daimler, "Annual Report 2018," 2018. [Online]. Available: https://www.daimler.com/investors/reports-news/annual-reports/2018/. [Retrieved: September, 2019].

[34] B. Kitchenham et al., "Systematic literature reviews in software engineering–a systematic literature review," Information and Software Technology, vol. 51, no. 1, pp. 7-15, 2009, doi: 10.1016/j.infsof.2008.09.009.

[35] C. Okoli and K. Schabram, "A guide to conducting a systematic literature review of information systems research.," Sprouts: Working Papers on Information Systems, vol. 10, no. 26, 2010, ISSN: 1535-6078.

[36] Y. Levy and T. J. Ellis, "A systems approach to conduct an effective literature review in support of information systems research," Informing Science, vol. 9, 2006.

[37] B. Von Bary, M. Westner, and S. Strahringer, "Do researchers investigate what practitioners deem relevant? Gaps between research and practice in the field of information systems backsourcing," IEEE 20th Conference on Business Informatics (IEEE 2018), vol. 1, pp. 40-49, doi: 10.1109/CBI.2018.00014.

[38] N. B. Moe, D. Šmite, G. K. Hanssen, and H. Barney, "From offshore outsourcing to insourcing and partnerships: four failed outsourcing attempts," Empirical Software Engineering, vol. 19, no. 5, pp. 1225-1258, 2014, doi: 10.1007/s10664-013-9272-x.

[39] N. Gorla and M. B. Lau, "Will negative experiences impact future IT outsourcing?," Journal of Computer Information Systems, vol. 50, no. 3, pp. 91-101, 2010, ISSN: 0887-4417.

[40] J. Kotlarsky and L. Bognar, "Understanding the process of backsourcing: two cases of process and product backsourcing in Europe," ournal of Information Technology Teaching Cases, vol. 2, no. 2, pp. 79-86, 2012, doi: 10.1057/jittc.2012.7.

[41] M. Olzmann and M. G. Wynn, "How to switch IT service providers: recommendations for a successful transition," International Journal on Advances in Intelligent Systems, vol. 5, nos. 1&2, pp. 209-219, 2012, ISSN: 1942-2679.

[42] B. Martens and F. Teuteberg, "Bewertung von Backsourcing-Entscheidungen im Umfeld des Cloud Computing [in English: Evaluation of backsourcing decisions in the context of Cloud Computing]," MKWI 2010 – IT Performance Management/ IT-Controlling, pp. 267-279, 2010.

[43] S. F. Wong and P. Jaya, "Drivers of IT backsourcing decision," Communications of the IBIMA, vol. 2, no. 14, pp. 102-108, 2008.

[44] M. Benaroch, Q. Dai, and R. J. Kauffman, "Should we go our own way? Backsourcing flexibility in IT services contracts," Journal of Management Information Systems, vol. 26, no. 4, pp. 317-35, 2010, doi: 10.2753/MIS0742-1222260411.

[45] International Data Corporation, "Jahrbuch 2019: Prognosen zur Zukunft der IT [in English: Yearbook 2019: Outlook for the future of IT]", München: IDG Business Media GmbH, 2018.

[46] C. Brautsch and M. Wynn, A New Process Model for Optimising IT Outsourcing Operations in the German Automotive Industry, SERVICE COMPUTATION 2013, The Fifth International Conference on Advanced Service Computing, 2013, ISBN: 978-1-61208-270-7.

[47] H. Solli-Sæther and P. Gottschalk, "Stages-of-growth in outsourcing, offshoring and backsourcing: back to the future?," Journal of Computer Information Systems, vol. 55,

no. 2, pp. 88-94, 2015, doi: 10.1080/08874417.2015.11645760.

[48] N. P. Butler, Stay, switch or back: Evaluating the IT sourcing cycle, Doctoral dissertation, Sheffield Hallam University, UK, 2011.

[49] W. G. Qu, W. Oh, and A. Pinsonneault, "The strategic value of IT insourcing: an IT-enabled business process perspective," The Journal of Strategic Information Systems, vol. 19, no. 2, pp. 96-108, 2010, doi: 10.1016/j.jsis.2010.05.002.

[50] M. Benaroch, S. Webster, and B. Kazaz, "Impact of sourcing flexibility on the outsourcing of services under demand uncertainty," European Journal of Operational Research, vol. 219, no. 2, pp. 272-283, 2012, doi: 10.1016/j.ejor.2011.12.007.

[51] P. Thakur-Wernz, "A typology of backsourcing: short-run total costs and internal capabilities for re-internalization," Journal of Global Operations and Strategic Sourcing, vol. 12, no. 1, pp. 42-61, 2019, doi: 10.1108/JGOSS-01-2018-0004.

[52] I. Oshri, J. S. Sidhu, and J. Kotlarsky, "East, west, would home really be best? On dissatisfaction with offshore-outsourcing and firms' inclination to backsource," Journal of Business Research, vol. 103, pp. 644-653, 2019, doi:10.1016/j.jbusres.2017.11.008.

[53] B. Von Bary, "How to bring IT home: Developing a common terminology to compare cases of IS Backsourcing," in Twenty-fourth Americas Conference on Information Systems (AMCIS 2018), New Orleans.

[54] C. Leyh, T. Schäffer, and T. D. Nguyen, "Information System Backsourcing: A Systematic Literature Analysis," 2018 Federated Conference on Computer Science and Information Systems (FedCSIS 2018), pp. 779–788, 2018, doi:10.15439/2018F333

[55] B. Von Bary, What Makes Companies Backsource IT Services? Exploring the Influence of Decision Makers' Preferences, Technische Universität Dresden, 2019, ISBN: 978-0-9966831-8-0.

[56] ISG-Index, "Market Trends and Insights 2018 Annual Report," 2019. [Online]. Available: http://www.prnewswire.com/news-releases/isg-index-digital-tailwinds-likely-to-keep-global-sourcing-on-strong-growth-trajectory-in-2019-300777653.html. [retrieved: January, 2020].

[57] T. Heeg and J. Jansen, "Wir wollen nicht hirnamputiert werden [in English: We don't want to become brain-damaged]," 2019. [Online]. Available: https://www.faz.net/aktuell/wirtschaft/ diginomics/daimler-chef-zetsche-wollen-nicht-hirnamputiert-werden-16066850.html. [retrieved: January, 2020].

[58] B. Wernerfelt, "A resource-based view of the firm," Strategic Management Journal, vol. 5, no. 2, pp. 171-180, 1984, doi: 10.1002/smj.4250050207.

[59] J. Barney, "Firm resources and sustained competitive advantage," Journal of management, vol. 17, no. 1, pp. 99-120, 1991, doi: 10.1177/014920639101700108.

[60] A. Zimmermann, I. Oshri, E. Lioliou, and A. Gerbasi, "Sourcing in or out: Implications for social capital and knowledge sharing," The Journal of Strategic Information Systems, vol. 27, no. 1, pp. 82-100, 2018, doi: 10.1016/j.jsis.2017.05.001.

[61] D. J. Teece, G. Pisano, and A. Shuen, "Dynamic capabilities and strategic management," Strategic Management Journal, vol. 18, no. 7, pp. 509-533, 1997, doi:10.1002/(SICI)1097-0266(199708)18:7<509:AID-SMJ882>3.0.CO;2-Z.

[62] I. Barreto, "Dynamic capabilities: A review of past research and an agenda for the future," Journal of Management, vol. 36, no. 1, pp. 256-280, 2010, doi: 10.1177/0149206309350776.

[63] B. Dachs, S. Kinkel, and A. Jäger, "Bringing it all back home? Backshoring of manufacturing activities and the adoption of Industry 4.0 technologies," Journal of World Business, vol. 54, no. 6, 2019, doi: 10.1016/j.jwb.2019.101017.

[64] M. Augier and D. J. Teece, "Dynamic capabilities and the role of managers in business strategy and economic performance," Organization science, vol. 20, no. 2, pp. 410-421, 2009, doi: 10.1287/orsc.1090.0424.

[65] R. A. Teubner and D. Ehnes, "The Corporate IT/IS Function: Competences and Organization for a (Digital) Future," Multikonferenz Wirtschaftsinformati (MKWI 2018), Lüneburg, Germany, pp. 1825-1836.

[66] M. Wynn, University-Industry Technology Transfer in the UK: Emerging Research and Future Opportunities, Advances in Knowledge Acquisition, Transfer, and Management (AKATM). IGI-Global, Hershey, USA, 2018; ISBN: 9781522574088, ISSN: 2326-7607.

[67] C. Curado, "The knowledge based-view of the firm: from theoretical origins to future implications," Department of Management Working paper Series, ISEG, Lisboa, 2006, ISSN: 0874-8470.

[68] J. Fulk and G. DeSanctis, "Electronic communication and changing organizational forms," Organization science, vol. 6, no. 4, pp. 337-349, 1995, doi: 10.1287/orsc.6.4.337.

[69] K. Umemoto, "Managing existing knowledge is not enough," The Strategic Management of Intellectual Capital & Organizational Knowledge, Oxford University Press, pp. 463-476, 2002.

[70] R. M. Grant, "Toward a knowledge-based theory of the firm," Strategic management journal, vol. 17, Winter Special Issue, pp. 109-122, 1996, doi: 10.1002/smj.4250171110.

Application of Data Mining in Industry in the Transition Era to Industry 4.0: Review

Khaoula Sahraoui, Samia Aitouche, Karima Aksa,
Laboratory of Automatics and manufacturing
Industrial engineering department, University Batna 2, Batna, Algeria
e-mail: sahraouikhaoula12@gmail.com, s.aitouche@univ-batna2.dz, k.aksa@univ-batna2.dz

Abstract— **The era of Industry 4.0 has already begun, however, several improvements should be achieved concerning this revolution. Data mining is one of the modest and efficient tools. Based on a specific query entered in Scopus, related to Industry 4.0, data mining (DM) and logistics, selected documents were studied and analyzed. A brief background of Industry 4.0 and DM are presented. A generic analysis showed that the attentiveness for the cited subject area by countries, universities, authors and especially companies and manufacturers increased through the years. Content analysis reveals that the improvement in quality of the technologies used in manufacturing was noticed, concluding that DM would give Industry 4.0 a leap forward, yet research is dealing with several challenges.**

Keywords-Industry 4.0; data mining; data mining techniques; data mining in Industry 4.0.

I. Introduction

Technological innovation and customer demands for sophisticated technology and services promote the emergence of new challenges, which make an increasingly changing industry [1]. Many companies have started to use Internet of Things (IoT) to have their devices interact with each other. They succeed in the usage of smart devices, RFID (Radio Frequency IDentification) technology, programmed robots and other technologies to automate many orders, make decisions and solve problems [2], with real-time interactions between people, products and devices during the production process. Hence, it was the beginning of the fourth revolution of industry. The concept of Industry 4.0 (I4.0) appeared first in an article published by the German government in November 2011 [2]. At this point, it is the intersection of different technologies at a different level. In addition to IoT, it includes the Cyber-Physical systems, cloud computing, smart factories, self-organization, smart product, etc. (Fig.1).

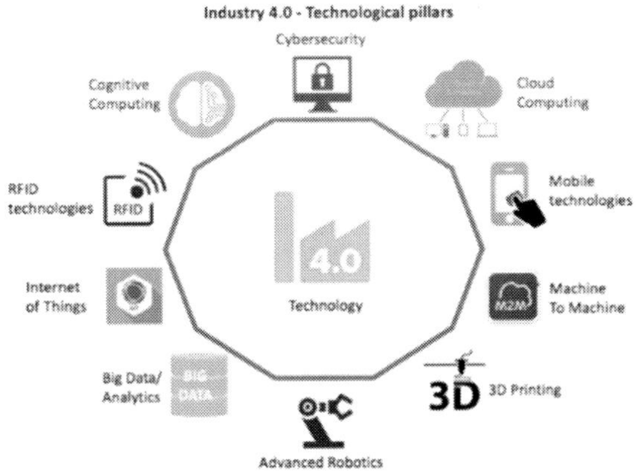

Figure 1. Industry 4.0 technologies pillars [3]

In today's competitive business environment, companies are facing challenges in dealing with big data issues of rapid decision-making for improved productivity. Many manufacturing systems are not ready to manage big data due to the lack of smart analytic tools [4]. Hence, the DM, with its methods and algorithms, was the best solution for the enormous volume of data. DM is the extraction of knowledge from a large volume of data, found its place in the research area, because of its importance in using the wasted data that could support decision-making, chosen from several directions and solve many problems. With the help of DM techniques, computers are no longer limited to passively store or collect data. They can also help the users to actively excerpt the key points from huge amounts of data, and make use of analysis or prediction [5]. This concept was used for the first time in the 1990s. It was developed across the years and many methods and algorithms were offered to science, prove their efficiency in many fields.

In industry, precisely logistics, the tremendous volume of data in the industrial environment has increased; therefore, the use of DM as an analytical tool [6] was necessary. The concept of big data and considerations of how to deal with such large datasets is an intrinsic challenge of any system operating in an I4.0 environment [6].

In this paper, we aim to reveal the location of research and researchers in using DM for I4.0 in logistics and industry field generally. We start with a brief background of both industry and DM. A general statistical analysis was done, by using documents from Scopus database after entering a specific query; also a content analysis was discussed. After that, we present a discussion and challenges that this area is facing, finishing with a conclusion.

II. Background

A. Industry 4.0

The industry began simple and easy, and it depended mostly on human work and simple machines. The first mechanical loom was in 1784, to witness the assembly lines; they used water, hydraulics and steam power. The second revolution came at the end of the 19th century with the introduction of electric powered mass production based of the division of labor. This development made the emerging automatic way of dealing with the processes possible. The improvement and the novelty of technologies, led the industry to a new era. The processes of the production were totally automated using electronic, IT systems and developed machines. The interaction of human in the production process arrived to its end, but it was limited to program the orders and deal with intelligent machines, leading to the third revolution in the early 1970s. The I4.0 or the fourth industrial revolution was a consequence of the introduction of high levels of technologies especially cyber-physical systems [7], where physical and software components interpenetrate on different spatial and temporal scales, having multiple and distinct behaviors and interacting in ways that change the context of the whole system. We can also cite: IoT, cloud computing and smart factory [8]-[9].

B. Data mining

The aim of DM is extracting the needed knowledge (knowledge discovery) supporting decision making. The terms knowledge discovery and DM first appeared in late eightieths and have been used ever since [10]. DM appeared basically from the development of statistic science where Bayes' theorem helped in understanding composite realities based on predictable probabilities. It was presented in 1763 in addition to regression analysis in 1805 [11] consisting in a learning function that maps a detail of data onto a real variable used for prediction. After that, Neural Networks, generic algorithms, databases and clustering, Knowledge Discovery in Databases (KDD) took place in 1989, and conducted to introduce the term data science in 2001. Today, DM is emerging by the novelty and high quality of technologies and the sophisticate demands of clients [12][13][14].

III. Methodology

Aiming at identifying the recent and relevant research on DM, I4.0 and logistics, a complex query was performed on 01/19/2020 in the scientific database Scopus. The query was too complex to improve the relevance and to limit the number of documents; it touched Industry 4.0, DM and logistics in titles and keywords. Twenty-eight documents were found, 75% were a conference paper (21), 17.9% were a journal article (5) and only 7.1% were a review (2). One conference paper was omitted because its content is duplicated in a journal paper, one was omitted because it is written in Russian. We processed then to descriptive (quantitative) analysis and content (qualitative) analysis.

IV. Descriptive Analysis

By observing the number of articles in this subject, it is noticed from Fig. 2 that in the beginning of Industry 4.0, the researchers interact DM with I4.0 and logistics systematically in analyzing big data by using one or more of its methods or algorithms. Then after, the volume of data had been increased, researchers began have more attention to apply DM's methods and algorithms in controlling and analyzing big data in some technologies of the Industry 4.0. In 2019, a considerable number of articles compared to the previous years, reveals the strong relationship of I4.0 and logistics with DM. Even though 2020 is at the beginning, two articles were published according to our request.

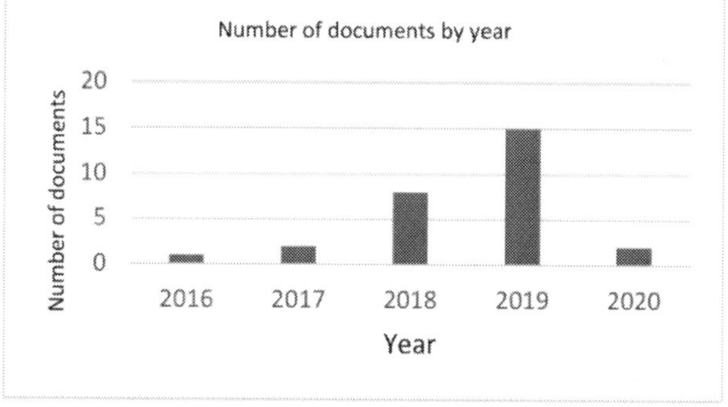

Figure 2. Histogram of the number of articles by year.

While Germany was the first to announce the era of Industry 4.0, it was the leader by 4 articles in this chosen group of articles. Russian Federation comes next with 3 articles. Two articles were the outcomes for each of Colombia, Finland, India, Italy, Netherlands, Spain and Turkey and 1 article for each of the rest of countries, as it is presented in Fig. 3.

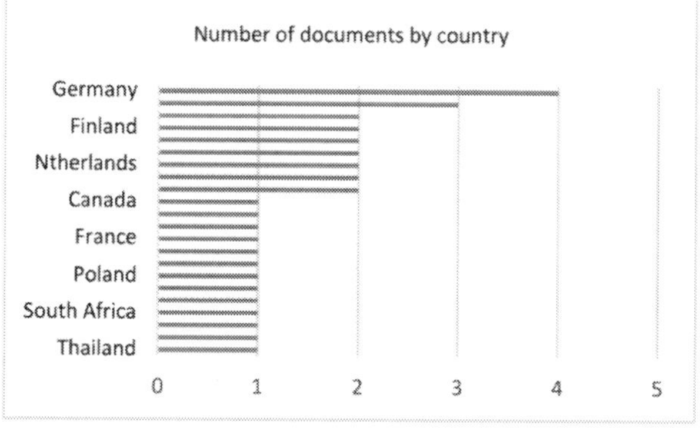

Figure 3. Histogram of the number of documents by country.

Fig. 4 shows that the controller of this group of documents in terms of the subject area was computer science with 30.6% since applying DM is totally dependent on programing languages and computers, while engineering was next with 22.6%, considering that we are in the field of industry. As mathematics is required in some problems along with the integration of DM methods, mathematic has 11.3%. The energy got 6.5% while each of business management and accounting, decision science, earth and planetary sciences, environmental science have 4.8%. Medicine, physics and astronomy each of them has 3.2%, materials science and social sciences have 1.6%. Those percentages prove the involvement of DM in variant fields.

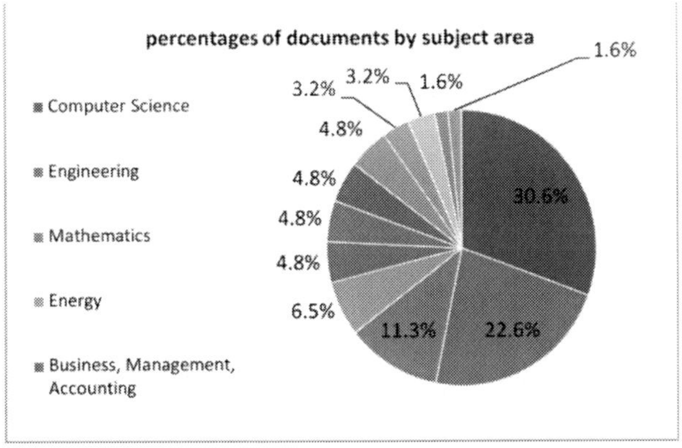

Figure 4. The subject areas of the selected documents.

Binder C., Schiemann R. and Kabugo J.C. each one wrote two documents in this subject area, while the other authors have one for each (Table1).

TABLE 1. NUMBER OF DOCUMENTS BY AUTHOR.

Author's name	Number of documents
Binder, C.	2
Kabugo, J.C.	2
Schiemann, R.	2
Other authors	1 to each author

Index keywords also have been analyzed. The most used keyword was I4.0 (Fig. 5) because it was specified in the title of papers, while DM was placed next, digital storage and learning systems were equal in term of usage as keywords. While many keywords of methods and concepts appeared, it was not expected to be relevant to this subject. Fig. 6 shows a sample of used keywords and their frequency in these documents.

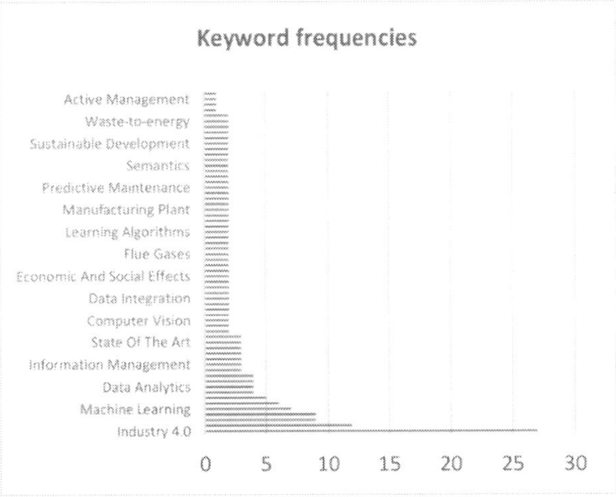

Figure 5. Keyword frequencies

The analysis of author's keywords showed a different frequency in comparison with the filtration by keywords of Scopus (Table 2), even though in three documents from the selected ones, the author's keywords weren't found.

TABLE 2. FREQUENCY OF SIMPLE OF AUTHOR'S KEYWORDS.

Keywords	Frequency	Keywords	frequency
Industry 4.0	19	Manufacturing	3
Enterprise	3	Supply chain	2
Manufacture	9	Industrial	4
Business	1	Data	14
Management	2	Machine learning	7
IoT or internet of things	4	Artificial intelligence	1
Data mining	5	Analytics + analysis	5

V. CONTENT ANALYSIS

A. *Content analysis in 2016*

The objective of this analysis is to identify the improvement that could hint to Industry 4.0 by using different technologies and methods particularly those ones dealing with data sets. K. Sakornsathien [15] develops a valuable framework for some organizations particularly the individuals who purpose to execute I4.0 or the individuals who previously incorporated it in their ventures. This connection of information mining with I4.0 advances assisted with improving the production network, to arrange the market and to fulfill the customers.

B. *Content analysis in 2017*

R. Frischer et al. [16] clarify the changes that must touch the metallurgical engineering to keep abreast of I4.0 and to be compatible with "other world" systems. They pointed out that, although the change already started along with putting into practice new approaches to human resource management, automation, data networks interconnections, data storage, DM and much more in the context of Industry 4.0, the implementations and human stance to new ideas will take decades.

M. Gokalp et al. [17] propose a framework handling collection of data from IoT and Web based data sources, implementation of big data analytics applications containing machine learning and DM components, translation of visually designed programs to platform specific ones, management of jobs among processing units, and delivery of results to people and services. It facilitates the integration of big data analytics with business processes encouraging by that the adoption of big data techniques as part of I4.0 vision in future enterprises.

C. Content analysis in 2018

The validation is necessary to data management, measurement, retrieving, storage, organization, data processing and their presentation. G. DeMilia et al. [18] present a practical case study related to a sensor-based condition monitoring application for validation techniques at the post-processing stage of the data management flow to realize a better feature extraction for the classification algorithm. It is applied in a complex mechanical system of an automatic production with a set of sensors of displacement.

K. Villalobos et al. [19] present a system called I4TSRS1, available as a Web Application, that efficiently guides a data engineer in the task of obtaining industrial time-series data reduced representations that preserve their main characteristics to reduce data storage and transmission costs, without limiting the future exploitation of the data in different processes. I4TSRS recommends the best techniques to achieve a reduced representation of time-series captured in industrial settings.

Several works focus on application of DM and I4.0 in logistics. E. Sternberg and M. Atzmueller [20] apply knowledge-based data analysis in logistics to model background knowledge in the form of knowledge graphs to discover subgroup for identifying exceptional patterns. Overall, the process and the results are well accepted by the domain experts. In the same context, J.I.R. Molano et al. [21] study the relation between I4.0 and supply chain in Colombia and, propose a strategy based on I4.0 for small and medium-sized companies to diagnose their needs and solve them. The work of K. Chaudhary et al. [22] presents a machine learning based adaptive framework for logistics planning and digital supply chain growing, acclimate and expand as its knowledge grows to provide a generalized solution to all kinds of logistics and supply chain activities

J.I. Rodríguez-Molano et al. [23] analyze the man-things-software communication and propose a metamodel of integration (IoT, social networks, cloud and Industry 4.0) for generation of applications for the Industry 4.0, and the manufacturing monitoring prototype implemented with the Raspberry Pi microcomputer, a cloud storage server and a mobile device for controlling an online production.

D. Content analysis in 2019

The year 2019 was rich in this topic because of its improvement and its quick spread in the mining field transportation with the use of belt conveyors allows cost reductions and increased range. It also allows fully automatic operation as well as remote monitoring and control from the centralized control room. L. Jurdziak et al. [24] introduce diagnostic systems and integrate data from a number of sources in order to include the idea of conveyor belt 4.0 into the digitally controlled conveyors 4.0. It is reliant on several technologies, for example, it is depending on a lot of information given by an expanding number of sensors and identified with the activity of machines and devices.

M. Kebisek et al. [25] focus on the utilization of neural networks for paint errors classification in the area of automotive industry, utilizing hypothesis, that outdoor weather has significant impact on the number of paint errors, as a basis for comparison of neural network algorithms. Deep learning was from the used methods. They concluded that neural networks algorithms are suitable for this kind of analyses and data sets. While D. Penumuru et al. [26], with the use of machine vision and machine learning techniques, develop a novel generalized methodology based on Support Vector Machine (SVM) to accurately identify and classify flat materials being machined in a typical manufacturing environment. They saw that the proposed methodology will be applied to machine tools and robots commissioned in smart manufacturing set up and that these results will be made available in future communications. M.D. Anuşlu et al. [27] used DM differently; they cluster countries using cluster analysis and group them within the scope of significant impact areas of I4.0 using global innovation index. They observed that the most important supporting elements of I4.0 are creativity and innovation. C.C. Osman et al. [28] introduced the difficulties that meet up with I4.0 and proposed process mining procedures as another methodology for business process examination to help organizations to quickly adjust to advertise changes by offering modified answers for clients. The study affirms that the digitization is a key factor in I4.0 changing business forms.

The study of J. Stentoft et al. [29] was based on 270 valid answers to a questionnaire-survey distributed among Danish manufacturers. The study identifying potential drivers and barriers for I4.0 and how to deal with respecting different technologies such as data processing and big data. L.A. Rodríguez et al. [30] propose a new architecture for a web platform for management and inference of information based on machine learning. The experimental part was obtained from simulator of a hydrogen production biorefinery. The designed platform uses methods and algorithms of automatic learning and DM to receive process and analyze large amounts of data that generates a biorefinery which produces hydrogen from wastewater. The authors mentioned that improving the platform's architecture is worthwhile to use it in other complex systems to support decision making and for the good reception and storage of data in addition to displaying the results. A. Edirisuriya et al. [31] identify gaps in the field of logistics in applying lean and green concepts in the context of I4.0. They develop a conceptual framework enhancing operational performance of logistics operations by applying lean and green concepts with special reference to I4.0 technologies mentioning that realizing I4.0is becoming critical for almost all the manufacturing industries existing in the world.

A. Mayr et al. [32] compare different generic approaches for identifying, selecting and implementing I4.0 use cases. They present also a methodical approach in order to tap the numerous I4.0 potentials within the electric motor production although that they see that the application of I4.0 technologies in this domain has hardly been examined yet. They presented the DM and machine learning from the fundamental relevant I4.0 technologies, as tools for intelligent data analyses. S. Cho et al. [33] propose semantic-driven architecture to facilitate the real-time update/control of incoming data together with the runtime module and distribution of computers resources without direct active management by users. The proposed approach provides a novel method to open an efficient way to manage/integrate data in I4.0 applications through the semantic technology.

J. Para et al. [34] suggest a new methodology ASPPID for efficiently selecting sensing equipment in industrial processes and machinery essentially capitalizing on a predominant role of the data scientist along the entire decision workflow, not only within the stages where the captured data are exploited. All decisions through the proposed methodology are made towards minimizing the costs and fulfilling the target benefit of the overall project. F. Galati et al. [35] use text mining methodologies, to discuss technological solutions at the core of I4.0. 'Work and skills' stream of literature attempts to under the human element lurking behind the scene of I4.0 regarding opportunities and implications. J. Piest et al. [36] discussed the problem of limited usage of real time data originating from I4.0 technologies by Small Medium Enterprises (SMEs) in the logistics industry. SMEs benefit from such data and help them streamline their operational processes and overall performance, by developing an intelligence amplification framework in the context of SMEs in logistics and overall performance of supply chain. The used methods (KDD, SEMMAn CRISP-DM) could be limited therefore a technical knowledge and extensiveness of the methods are required.

K. Bertayeva et al. [37] studied the I4.0 concept in the field of mining and suggested that research and development should be carried out to constantly support projects such as "Virtual Mine of the Future", "Virtual Section of the Future", aimed at optimizing the combination of promising technologies, organizational, economic and other solutions. In their opinion, implementation of the I4.0 project involves the creation of a smart industry that has evolved evolution from the use of integrated information and communication control systems to cyber physical systems. Moreover, to achieve the positive effects of the formation of innovative systems in the long term, it is necessary to strategically plan the system of government regulation measures, develop a set of measures combining elements of industrial and innovation policies that stimulate the innovative development of not only the mining industry, but also related sectors and industries.

E. Content analysis in 2020

During the current year (2020), J. P. UsugaCadavid et al. [38] contributed to the definition of a methodology to implement machine learning for production planning and control and proposed a mapping to classify the scientific literature in order to identify further research perspectives. In their opinion, classical methods like simulation and Enterprise Resource Planning (ERP) perform poorly at the operative level therefore the implementation of smart manufacturing is required. J. C. Kabugo et al. [39] developed a concept of a process monitoring platform aiming at highlighting the use of the state-of-the-art machine learning methods coupled with big-data processing tools and cloud computing technologies in process data analytics. They applicate the developed platform on a waste-to-energy plant as a study case to better predict of both syngas heating value and flue gas temperature in this process.

VI. DISCUSSION AND CHALLENGES

It appeared after analyzing the selected documents that a remarkable attentiveness head towards using DM techniques aiming to implement, develop and improve I4.0 in the industrial field generally or even know barriers and the constraints in front of this objective, and it is increasing from year to another. Logistics and supply chain have also benefited from DM and its technologies. The research reveals also that relying I4.0 with DM makes it featuring more technological systems and smart methods.

I4.0 faces different challenges and difficulties involving many aspects, including scientific, technological, and economic challenges, in addition to social problems and political issues [2]. The increase of using DM in the context of I4.0 is a main challenge that can eliminate or even reduce the previous challenges in different levels. Even though, due to the complexity of I4.0 with various types, volumes and uncertainty of data [8], it is well known that the simple use of DM algorithms will not produce good results; very complicated and efficient algorithms and methods need to be used in order to catch the desired results using a high quality and strong potency machines that would be expensive. Furthermore, it is difficult to generalize the integrated DM in all the technologies of Industry 4.0; each technology requires a specific algorithm or method.

VII. CONCLUSION

The aim of this paper was to define where research is in the field of applying DM in I4.0 and logistics. A quick review about the background of I4.0 and DM was presented. A complicated query was entered in Scopus database to do a generic analysis on the resulting documents; furthermore, the contents had to be analyzed to distinguish what was the novelty given by each one. Through this research, different challenges were observed and have been presented.

The analysis of the documents shows the interest in this subject area increased through the years, and as it was expected, Germany was the leader in the number of the selected documents. The variant branches articulating this subject confirms that the application of DM is touching numerous fields and has the attention of many researchers. The content of those documents showed the rapidly spread of using DM in Industry 4.0, improving by that the supply chain management and logistics industry. From the two analyses, the improvement quality of the technologies that are used in logistics and industry was noticed, concluding that DM would give logistics and I4.0 a leap forward.

This group of documents was chosen according to the query that was written to limit the search to our domain of research; however, many other articles have discussed this subject which could be analyzed and treat. Future research may focus on dealing with the faced challenges; also other challenges could appear by consulting other articles in this field.

REFERENCES

[1] L. Barreto, A. Amaral, and T. Pereira, "Industry 4.0 implications in logistics: an overview,", Procedia Manufacturing, vol. 13, 2017, pp. 1245-1252, doi: 10.1016/j.promfg.2017.09.045.

[2] K. Zhou, T. Liu, and L. Zhou, "Industry 4.0: Towards future industrial opportunities and challenges,", Proc. 12 th International conference on fuzzy systems and knowledge discovery (FSKD), Aug. 2015, pp. 2147-2152, doi: 10.1109/fskd.2015.7382284.

[3] https://www.researchgate.net/publication/319944621 Proposal_of_an_automation_solutions_architecture_for_Industry_40/figures?lo=1.

[4] J. Lee, H. A. Kao, and S. Yang, "Service innovation and smart analytics for industry 4.0 and big data environment,", Proc. Procedia Cirp, vol. 16 (1), May 2014, pp. 3-8, doi: 10.1016/j.procir.2014.02.001.

[5] C. F. Chien, and L. F. Chen, "Data mining to improve personnel selection and enhance human capital: A case study in high-technology industry,", Expert Systems with applications, vol. 34 (1), 2008, pp. 280-290, doi: 10.1016/j.eswa.2006.09.003.

[6] H. Oliff, and Y. Liu, "Towards industry 4.0 utilizing data mining techniques: a case study on quality improvement,", Procedia Cirp, vol. 63, 2017, pp. 167-172, doi: 10.1016/j.procir.2017.03.311.

[7] A. Stăncioiu, "The fourth industrial revolution industry 4.0,", Fiability & Durability/Fiabilitate si Durabilitate, 1(19), 2017, pp. 74-78.

[8] Li Da Xu, Eric L Xu., and Ling Li, "Industry 4.0: state of the art and future trends,", International Journal of Production Research, vol. 56 (8), 2018, pp. 2941-2962, doi: 10.1080/00207543.2018.1444806.

[9] M. Gabriel, and E. Pessl, "Industry 4.0 and sustainability impacts: Critical discussion of sustainability aspects with a special focus on future of work and ecological consequences,", Annals of the Faculty of Engineering Hunedoara - International Journal of Engineering, Vol. 14 Issue 2, May2016, pp. 131-136.

[10] K.J. Cios, W. Pedrycz, and R.W. Swiniarski, "Data mining and knowledge discovery", Data mining Methods for Knowledge Discovery, The Springer International Series in Engineering and Computer Science, 1998, Springer, Boston, MA, vol 458, pp 1-26, doi: 10.1007/978-1-4615-5589-6_1, ISBN: 978-1-4613-7557-9.

[11] J. He, "Advances in data mining: History and future", Proc. Third International Symposium on Intelligent Information Technology Application, vol. 1, Nov. 2009, pp. 634-636, IEEE, doi: 10.1109/IITA.2009.204. ISBN: 978-0-7695-3859-4.

[12] https://www.javatpoint.com/history-of-data mining. Consulted in the 20/01/2020.

[13] https://hackerbits.com/data/history-of-data mining/. Consulted in the 20/01/2020.

[14] https://www.exastax.com/big-data/the-history-of-data mining/. Consulted in the 20/01/2020.

[15] K. Sakornsathien, "Ingenious product form co-design system for the industry 4.0,", Proc. Lecture Notes in Computer Science (including subseries Lecture Notes in Artificial Intelligence and Lecture Notes in Bioinformatics), 9992 LNAI, Dec. 2016, pp. 682-688, Springer Verlag, doi: 10.1007/978-3-319-50127-7_60

[16] F. Robert, G Ondrej, and H Robert, "Concept industry 4.0 in metallurgical engineering,", Proc. 26th International Conference on Metallurgy and Materials (METAL), Brno, Czech Republic, Jan. 2017, pp. 2122-2126, TANGER Ltd.

[17] M. O. Gokalp, K. Kayabay, M. A. Akyol, P. E Eren, and A. Kocyigit, "Big data for industry 4.0: A conceptual framework,", Proc. 2016 International Conference on Computational Science and Computational Intelligence (CSCI), Dec. 2016, pp. 431-434, doi: 10.1109/CSCI.2016.0088.

[18] G. D'Emilia, and A. Gaspari, "Data validation techniques for measurements systems operating in an industry 4.0 scenario a condition monitoring application,", 2018 Workshop on Metrology for Industry 4.0 and IoT, 16-18 April 2018, IEEE, pp. 112-116, doi: 10.1109/METROI4.2018.8428317.

[19] K Villalobos, B. Diez, A. Illarramendi, A. Goñi, and J.M. Blanco, "I4tsrs: A system to assist a data engineer in time-series dimensionality reduction in industry 4.0 scenarios,". In Proceedings of the 27th ACM International Conference on Information and Knowledge Management, Oct. 2018, pp. 1915–1918, doi: 10.1145/3269206.3269213.

[20] E. Sternberg, and M. Atzmueller, "Knowledge-based mining of exceptional patterns in logistics data: approaches and experiences in an Industry 4.0 context". In: Ceci M., Japkowicz N., Liu J., Papadopoulos G., Raś Z. (eds) Foundations of Intelligent Systems. ISMIS 2018. Lecture Notes in Computer Science, vol 11177. Springer, Cham, Oct. 2018, pp. 67-77, doi: 10.1007/978-3-030-01851-1_7 , ISBN: 978-3-030-01850-4.

[21] J. I. R. Molano, S. J. G. Moncada, and K. D. L. Parra, "Impact of implementing industry 4.0 in Colombia's supply chains,". In: Tan Y., Shi Y., Tang Q. (eds) Data Mining and Big Data. DMBD 2018. Lecture Notes in Computer Science, vol 10943. Springer, Cham, June. 2018, pp. 704-713, doi: 10.1007/978-3-319-93803-5_66, ISBN978-3-319-93802-8.

[22] K. Chaudhary, M Singh, S. Tarar, D. K Chauhan, and V. M. Srivastava, "Machine learning based adaptive framework for logistic planning in Industry 4.0,". In: Singh M., Gupta P., Tyagi V., Flusser J., Ören T. (eds) Advances in Computing and Data Sciences. ICACDS 2018. Communications in Computer and Information Science, vol 905. Springer, Singapore, Oct. 2018, pp. 431-438, doi: 10.1007/978-981-13-1810-8_43, ISBN978-981-13-1809-2

[23] J. I. Rodríguez-Molano, C. A. López-Bello, and L. E. Contreras-Bravo, "Modeling and implementation data architecture for the internet of things and industry 4.0,". In: Figueroa-García J., Villegas J., Orozco-Arroyave J., Maya Duque P. (eds) Applied Computer Sciences in Engineering. WEA 2018. Communications in Computer and Information Science, vol 916. Springer, Cham, Sep. 2018, pp. 214-222,

doi: 10.1007/978-3-030-00353-1_19, ISBN: 978-3-030-00352-4.

[24] L. Jurdziak, R. Blazej, and M Bajda, "Conveyor belt 4.0". In: Burduk A., Chlebus E., Nowakowski T., Tubis A. (eds) Intelligent Systems in Production Engineering and Maintenance. ISPEM 2018. Advances in Intelligent Systems and Computing, vol 835. Springer, Cham, Aug. 2018, pp. 645-654, doi: 10.1007/978-3-319-97490-3_61, ISBN: 978-3-319-97489-7.

[25] M. Kebisek, L. Spendla, P Tanuska, G. Gaspar, and L. Hrcka, "Neural network comparison for paint errors classification for automotive industry in compliance with industry 4.0 concept". In: Silhavy R. (eds) Artificial Intelligence Methods in Intelligent Algorithms. CSOC 2019. Advances in Intelligent Systems and Computing, vol 985. Springer, Cham, May. 2019, pp. 353-359, doi: 10.1007/978-3-030-19810-7_35, ISBN978-3-030-19809-1.

[26] D. P. Penumuru, S. Muthuswamy, and P. Karumbu, "Identification and classification of materials using machine vision and machine learning in the context of industry 4.0", Journal of Intelligent Manufacturing, Nov. 2019, doi.org/10.1007/s10845-019-01508-6.

[27] M. D. Anuşlu, and S. Ü. Fırat, "Clustering analysis application on Industry 4.0-driven global indexes,", Procedia Computer Science, vol 158, Oct. 2019, pp. 145-152, doi: 10.1016/j.procs.2019.09.037.

[28] C. C. Osman, and A. M Ghiran, "When industry 4.0 meets process mining,", Procedia Computer Science, vol 159, Oct, 2019, pp. 2130-2136, doi: 10.1016/j.procs.2019.09.386.

[29] J. Stentoft, and C. Rajkumar, "The relevance of industry 4.0 and its relationship with moving manufacturing out, back and staying at home". International Journal of Production Research, Sep. 2019, doi: 10.1080/00207543.2019.1660823.

[30] L.A. Rodriguez, C.J. Vadillo, J.R Gómez, and I. Torres, "Education + Industry 4.0: Developing a web platform for the management and inference of information based on machine learning for a hydrogen production biorefinery". In: Nguyen N., Chbeir R., Exposito E., Aniorté P., Trawiński B. (eds) Computational Collective Intelligence. ICCCI 2019. Lecture Notes in Computer Science, Springer, Cham, vol 11684, Aug. 2019, pp. 603-613, doi: 10.1007/978-3-030-28374-2_52, ISBN978-3-030-28373-5.

[31] A. Edirisuriya, S. Weerabahu, and R. Wickramarachchi, "Applicability of lean and green concepts in logistics 4.0: A systematic review of literature". International Conference on Production and Operations Management Society (POMS), IEEE, 2018, doi: 10.1109/POMS.2018.8629443. ISBN: 978-1-5386-9514-2.

[32] A. Mayr et al, "Electric Motor Production 4.0 – Application potentials of industry 4.0 technologies in the manufacturing of electric motors", 8th International Electric Drives Production Conference (EDPC), IEEE, 2018, doi: 10.1109/EDPC.2018.8658294, ISBN: 978-1-7281-0149-1.

[33] S. Cho, G. May, and D. Kiritsis, "A semantic-driven approach for industry 4.0". 15th International Conference on Distributed Computing in Sensor Systems (DCOSS), IEEE, 2019, doi: 10.1109/DCOSS.2019.00076, ISBN: 978-1-7281-0571-0.

[34] J. Para, J. Del Ser, A. J. Nebro, U. Zurutuza, and F. Herrera, "Analyze, Sense, Preprocess, Predict, Implement, and Deploy (ASPPID): An incremental methodology based on data analytics for cost-efficiently monitoring the industry 4.0". Engineering Applications of Artificial Intelligence, vol 82, June. 2019, pp. 30–43, doi: 10.1016/j.engappai.2019.03.022.

[35] F. Galati, and B. Bigliardi, "Industry 4.0: Emerging themes and future research avenues using a text mining approach", Computers in Industry, vol 109, Aug. 2019, pp. 100–113, doi: 10.1016/j.compind.2019.04.018.

[36] J. P. S. Piest, "A platform architecture for industry 4.0 driven intelligence amplification in logistics", 23rd International Enterprise Distributed Object Computing Workshop (EDOCW), IEEE, 2019, doi: 0.1109/EDOCW.2019.00038, ISBN: 978-1-7281-4599-0.

[37] K. Bertayeva, G. Panaedova, N. Natocheeva, T. Kulagovskaya, and T. Belyanchikova, "Industry 4.0 in the mining industry: global trends and innovative development". E3S Web of Conferences, vol 135, (04026) 2019, doi: 10.1051/e3sconf/201913504026.

[38] J. P. UsugaCadavid, S. Lamouri, B. Grabot, R. Pellerin, and A. Fortin, "Machine learning applied in production planning and control: a state-of-the-art in the era of industry 4.0", Journal of Intelligent Manufacturing, 2020, doi: 10.1007/s10845-019-01531-7.

[39] J. C. Kabugo, S.L. Jämsä-Jounela, R. Schiemann, and C. Binder, "Industry 4.0 based process data analytics platform: A waste-to-energy plant case study", International Journal of Electrical Power & Energy Systems, vol 115, Feb. 2020, 105508, doi: 10.1016/j.ijepes.2019.105508.

Analysis of Human Skills in Industry 4.0

Djouggane Fadhila, Samia Aitouche, Karima Aksa,
Laboratory of Automatics and manufacturing
Industrial engineering department, University Batna 2,
Batna, Algeria
e-mail : djouggannefadila@yahoo.fr, s.aitouche@univ-batna2.dz, k.aksa@univ-batna2.dz

***Abstract*—This paper presents a state-of-the-art of recent research work analyzing the requirements of Industry 4.0, particularly related to the competences issue. Over the last few years, the fourth industrial revolution has attracted researchers worldwide to find suitable solutions. However, there are still many gaps related to the Industry 4.0, particularly related to the humans competences issue. Among the many challenges facing companies in this paradigm, one of the most important is the qualification of employees with the necessary skills to succeed in a transformed work environment. To cope with knowledge and competence challenges related to new technologies and processes of Industry 4.0, new strategic approaches for holistic human resource management are needed in manufacturing companies. The main objective of the presented research is to investigate the importance of employee competences, key to the development of Industry 4.0.**

Keywords-Human Competences; Skills; Industry 4.0; human resource management; Fourth Industrial revolution.

I. INTRODUCTION

In industrial companies that are subject to constant competitive pressure [4], changes are coming faster and are more unpredictable [5]. This has considerable consequences on their investments and their competitiveness, which are highly dependent on knowledge, skills, competences and creativity of its workforce. Today, we are on the cusp of the Fourth Industrial Revolution [35], or Industry 4.0, expected to deeply change the future manufacturing and production processes, and which leads to smart factories and networked industrial environments that will benefit from its main design principles. The adoption of new technologies and production processes undoubtedly implies more qualified workforce. Thus, the biggest challenge for industrials would be to adapt their workforce to be able to follow the current revolution. Fig.1 [8] provides a global view of enabling technologies for Industry 4.0 and the organizational requirements in terms of technical and management problems for successful implementation. In recent years researchers have been very interested in Industry 4.0 and have published a large number of works in this field. Some works focused on the challenges that companies face in qualifying employees with the necessary skills, while others emphasize new learning approaches to adapting Engineering Education to Industry 4.0 Vision,

Certain researchers are particularly interested in specific modules to integrate them into teaching programs and adapt them to Industry 4.0. By contrast, other articles are also focused on the transformation of education itself according to the needs of Industry 4.0. Finally, a sequence of works demonstrates new concepts of learning factories and responds to the growing demand of future skills of production staff and laboratories to allow students to discover production environments type 4.0.

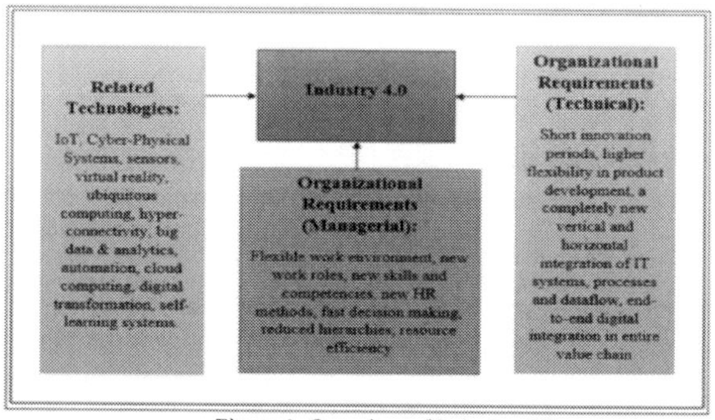

Figure 1. Overview of Industry 4.0

In Section 2, we will discuss the challenges and new technologies facing business workers in Industry 4.0. Section 3 presents the required competencies in Industry 4.0. Section 4 finds the challenges facing the new technologies to respond to Industry 4.0 requirements. Section 5 illustrates the role of training in the formation of Industry 4.0 skills. Section 6 explains the requirement of skills approach and finally, Section 7 concludes the paper.

II. THE ISSUES AND CHALLENGES RELATED TO SKILLS FACE INDUSTRY 4.0

In a globalized world with highly interconnected processes, companies are faced with an increasing number of challenges to be met [1], especially in terms of adapting their skills to the automation and digitalization in progress. In this context, research work of great importance and surveys have been carried out in search of solutions to face the challenges of Industry 4.0. [29] presents a case study of an Estonian ICT company, Proekspert, where the authors define the necessary skills in the context of Industry 4.0 to explore how workers can be included in the future planning process. It is based on the creation of a prototype instrument to map the perceived skills gap. It will help to inform the design and development of a unified platform for defining and planning the skills around which a fruitful dialogue of all stakeholders can take place. In [8], a job that meets one of the challenges of Industry 4.0 which is the qualification of future employees with the skills necessary to act and work in the transformed work environment. To meet this challenge and to have a successful implementation of new Industry 4.0 systems in organizations, the authors combine three approaches: sociotechnical system theory; competence-based view; competence models of the Evolute approach, with a revision and update of the latter.

Often technical skills help people to succeed in an interview, but they need general skills to keep a job and achieve professional development. The authors of [26], describe a methodology, centered on a mapping of the skills and personal qualities necessary to assess the specificity required by the industrial environment 4.0, after the application of a complex psychological evaluation system Abcd-M based on a psycho-lexical approach system compatible with the Big Five personality traits (OCEAN model) on successive series of students from Politechnica University in Bucharest. A map of the capacities necessary for the assessment and selection of human resources able to work in the environment of Industry 4.0 was conceived. Continuing on this path, and towards developing ethical leaders, in a survey [31], young workers indicate that the top four skills employers need to ensure long-term success are interpersonal skills, confidence/motivation, ethics/integrity and critical thinking. In [30], qualitative information is provided from an ongoing collaborative research project involving a variety of manufacturing stakeholders in Northern Italy, to meet the challenges of changing technical skills in the context of Industry 4.0. The results help to shed light on manufacturing skills needs related to Industry 4.0, to prepare the ground for future research on the subject.

The authors of [10] have chosen to help SMEs to cope with the Industry 4.0 trend and prosper in the future, to provide it with technological support that can help them plan, direct and monitor the transition process, as well as develop their employees. This fact belongs to the objective of the Adaption project. In this article, the authors describe the work in progress, in particular on the tool using the newly created models of progress and maturity, but also on the associated skills development approach. A huge effort is now required in manufacturing companies in order to constantly update the skills of workers. In this context, the question of the evaluation of the training provided to workers is increasingly critical, since increasingly complex data must be collected in real time and correctly analyzed in order to define the skill level of workers and to introduce in case the necessary corrective actions.

[27] aims to present a training data evaluation tool based on the integration of a training evaluation ontology with a training analysis model to define the skill levels of workers. [3] presents an initial competence model and describe the dimensions of knowledge and skills necessary to Industry 4.0. This model can be used to create individuals for the training proposal or to assess the knowledge gaps existing in a company. The skills identified are classified as technical, behavioral and contextual. To define the educational needs, the authors propose to use six different dimensions namely technology, industrial sector, software life cycles, transversal skills, skills and job profiles. By combining factors of these dimensions, it should be able to provide a skill set at the individual or enterprise level.

III Investigation to Unveil the Required Skills by Industry 4.0

Predictions of future skill requirements in the manufacturing sector vary widely, depending on occupational requirements across sectors, regional variations and the degree of digitization [33]. Based on these requirements, surveys are carried out to find out the skills necessary for Industry 4.0. [30] is a research based on a qualitative methodology, aimed to achieve a double objective. On one hand, it identifies the latest manufacturing needs in terms of Industry 4.0 skills. On the other hand, it is an attempt to anticipate the needs of businesses in the near future. The results of this research also help to provide business, government and education with new perspectives relevant to the identification of the needs for recycling, improvement and development of future industrial human capital. Despite the limits of this study, it advances research and practice by providing a precise set of technical skills related to Industry 4.0.

Another survey was carried out on a group of companies selected randomly [32]. In order to diagnose the willingness of Polish companies to implement the concept of Industry 4.0, a questionnaire-based study focusing on individual employee skills, the authors adopted their approach that employee skills are one of the main challenges for the development of Industry 4.0. Based on the results of the German research conducted on the key skills of employees for the development of the concept of Industry 4.0, the most important skills, respondents indicated problem solving (69.84%) and personal responsibility for decision making (65.08%). The authors draw as a result that the essential general skills of employees in a modern enterprise will be mainly focused on understanding the problems and concepts of other disciplines and on openness to change and novelty, they argued that communication skills that are also cross-cultural, often with the use of virtual tools, will be more important. The authority of Engineer 4.0 will still rest mainly on solid technical knowledge, but the importance of general skills will continue to grow. The lack of importance of these skills is interpreted by researchers as a lack of willingness on the part of Polish employees to develop a new era.

[6] describes the results of a research carried out by its authors at the Polytechnic University of Peter the Great Saint Petersburg with the main aim of determining the status of use of digital technologies and advanced means of communication by students during their studies and their

preparation to work for the future digital industry. According to the research results, 30 to 35% of trainees do not actively use the latest means and communication skills of information technology. To address this challenge, it was proposed a number of measures reasonable to implement, additional training of university professors in the field of IT, as well as the development of more mobile applications, practical to use by students during their studies.

[9] makes a contribution to two important challenges currently affecting the industry and the companies: the definition of skills and the development of a skill model for Industry 4.0, the study focuses on three areas: Information System, Computer Science and Engineering which require academic training and will play a crucial role in the Industry 4.0, where the authors propose a skills model for the professions and develop a curriculum with content that can be applied in these areas of education. A skills-based program was developed, following a structured didactic approach, for this purpose, the SHL skill framework was used, therefore, 69 assessed skills were extracted. [17] considers that the main asset of the Industry 4.0 framework is the staff. The authors would like to determine what skills and expertise are necessary for young engineers to be ready for the framework of Industry 4.0. A questionnaire was developed at the level of three Italian universities, Brescia, Udine and Cassino, to analyze this situation. The questions aimed to investigate certain key problems of Industry 4.0, as well as the digital beliefs and behaviors of students when they entered the system university education. Answering a fundamental question: "Are our engineering students and educators effectively ready for the Industry 4.0 framework?". The results of the survey suggest the need to create a broader and better structured knowledge of the basic concepts linked to this new industrial revolution. Then, this knowledge should be improved and integrated, taking into account the revision of the educational content of the courses, in particular with regard to technical subjects.

For the same reason, in [25], data were collected from 85 manufacturing companies in the cross-border cooperative region of Lubuskie / Poland and Brandenburg / Germany. Respondents were managers and general managers. They were asked to rate the characteristics of employees in terms of the most important for Industry 4.0. They stated that they had sufficient knowledge of the assumptions of the idea for Industry 4.0. In this article, the authors are confronted to challenges from industry 4.1 which are the evaluation of the qualitative factors in the basic skills for Industry 4.0 in manufacturing companies, and the selection of employees with the appropriate skills to undertake business projects. The proposed approach, presenting the weighting of basic skills, makes it possible to assess a potential employee in manufacturing companies.

IV. New Technologies Facing the Challenges of Industry 4.0

With the advent of Industry 4.0 and its components: Cyber-physical systems, Internet of Things, big data and cloud computing, robotics, systems based on artificial intelligence and additive manufacturing [26], companies will not only have difficulties in implementing new technologies, but some other challenges related to the adaptation of these technologies to have a highly qualified workforce. As Industry 4.0 takes shape, human operators experience greater complexity in their daily tasks: they must be very flexible and demonstrate adaptability in a very dynamic work environment. [12] emphasized the need for tools and approaches that could be easily integrated into daily practice and capable of combining complex methodologies with high usage requirements. For this reason, the authors offer a multi-layered modular solution, Sophos-MS, based on augmented reality content and an intelligent personal digital assistant with voice interaction capabilities. After deploying the approach and studying its potential through field experiments, the results of the experimental campaign were first checked to ensure their statistical relevance, then evaluated analytically to show that the proposed solution has a real impact on operators' learning curves and can make the difference between who uses it and who does not.

In [19], the authors present the aspects and limits of Virtual Reality (VR) technology to help VR developers create VR industrial environments that produce reliable / achievable simulations of the behavior of machines and real processes and stable operation of real processes afar. Industry 4.0 relies on virtual reality in order to reduce design and production costs, maintain product quality and overcome several technical compromises such as reducing the complexity of rendering while keeping rates high refresh rates or increasing resolution while providing a stable VR experience. [28] provides a first shared vision on how Augmented Reality (AR) can tackle four different challenges related to handling complexity in a Cyber-Physical Systems (CPS) environment: develop intelligent assistance systems for learning and performance assessment at the workplace, adapt job profiles accordingly, and address also the issue of work-life balance. The provision of such a technology will help to improve employability in a sustainable way by providing access to better paid jobs. It will also have a positive effect on well-being, enabling more people to keep their jobs through up-skilling, while job performance requirements increase.

V. The Course Towards Adapting Human Skills to Industry 4.0

The 4th revolution aims to push the industry to mutate towards connected factories where humans and machines collaborate throughout the production process. The digitization of the industry requires the rehabilitation of the infrastructure and the invention of new methods and processes. For these reasons, the industry makes call university teaching and researches to help them to adapt and qualify their workers according to the needs of Industry 4.0.

The rise of new digital industrial technologies and the diffusion of the Industry 4.0 framework have also led academia to be interested in possible changes that could involve the academic education of young people in general and, the learning of technical and engineering topics in particular [17]. An important part of the tasks of preparation for Industry 4.0 is the adaptation of higher education to the requirements of this vision, in particular the training of engineer, for which, [13] introduce a roadmap made up of three pillars describing the changes / improvements to be made in the areas of curriculum development, laboratory concept and student club activities. In order to bring about changes in behavior, attitudes and knowledge, a circular four-step experiential learning cycle model developed by Kolb is used. This model is selected as the most appropriate learning theory to adapt engineering education to the vision of Industry 4.0. Preliminary results from this implementation of this framework at the Turkish German University showed that it was possible to apply such framework and the underlying theory adopted from Kolb to adapt engineering education to the vision of Industry 4.0. [23] presents a concept on the development of an information system in order to formalize the reflections of the experts via business scenarios by input-output model and to verify the influence of sectors with high labor intensity-work on related professions and skills. The dynamic collection of input-output and labor market data via the internet is new to the system, where it provides an opportunity to test future scenarios on the effects of technological change on the labor market and determines the sets of skills for analysis. It helps to rethink the skill sets provided by training programs in the light of business scenarios derived from the business climate of Industry 4.0. The educational process has experienced difficulties in reaching national standards of competence in specific teaching tools and the best way to solve this problem is to compare different approaches, to study all the factors and to find the best practical tool in education, like in [21] where a questionnaire-based survey was conducted at the level of the Korean University of Technology and Education with the aim of carrying out a comparative study of two university courses of engineering to present the difference between the effect of education based on virtual reality (VR) and traditional education on learning robotics. An expert method, interviews with focus groups and a comparative study are used by the authors to achieve this objective. The authors studied the impact of different teaching methods on the development of students' skills. They also analyzed the effect of VR training in the classroom and found that there is a significant impact of the report CQI (Channel Quality Indication) on the performance of the teacher's teaching system. [22] is a part of the Erasmus + project "Approach to training in the workplace in the field of Industry 4.0 for a competitive European industry" - iNduce 4.0, it presents a state-of-the-art analysis of the knowledge and skill gaps on Industry 4.0 and the workplace learning requirements (WBL), using a large-scale survey of 6 European countries. The researchers defined the key points concerning the development of the iNduce 4.0 training course and the iNduce 4.0 practical methodology for the WBL. It provides awareness of the subject Industry 4.0, the training modules developed, the necessary skills and the proportion of theory and practice. [15] focuses on the facilitation of mobile learning processes in technical vocational education and engineering as well as its integration in learning about employment scenarios in Industry 4.0. The need of mLearning (mobile learning) applications that support learning in the real work process was motivated by two areas of application: laboratory courses, Industry 4.0 where in the latter, learning processes can be triggered by data cyber-physical systems of work processes. This allows mobile training on work scenarios. The author proposed the use of competence extracts instead of complete documents easily accessible via QRCodes, NFC or process data.

VI. SKILLS APPROACH

All these challenges require continuous innovation and learning, which is dependent on people and enterprise's capabilities. Appropriate management approaches can play a vital role in the development of dynamic capabilities, and effective learning and innovation climate. [2] stresses the important role of a learning factory (LeanLab) to improve university education, company training and practical research in the fields of industrial engineering and logistics. The authors present the current state of LeanLab and illustrate the next concrete steps towards an Industry 4.0 learning factory. [11] describes the design of a learning factory for Industry 4.0 that meets the growing demand for future skills of production personnel. But it focuses on soft skills such as decision making, group work and performance monitoring. [7] presented a learning model based on serious games, thought for industrial production plants, as a viable alternative for the development of professional skills. [14] presents a structured integrated vision of computer-aided applications (CAx) and Product Lifecycle Management (PLM) tools and their learning, for this purpose the author to propose Learning by project (PDB) as an approach to provide a learning experience that facilitates the development of skills and competences of Industry 4.0. It uses the Fusion 360 applications from Autodesk and DExperience from Dassault Systems, which have functionalities adapted to the implementation of collaborative learning based on a project. To enable future executives and workers of a factory to meet the challenges of an increasingly digitalized production system, other skills must also be addressed according to future production scenarios in the sense of Industry 4.0. [16] makes the abstract vision of Industry 4.0 more tangible using a Learning Factory approach in combination with scenario-based learning. The TU Wien Industry 4.0 pilot plant served as the basic infrastructure for the implementation of this concept. In order to supervise all the skills required, the authors have developed a preliminary skills catalog in which they have distinguished skills according to the skills framework of Rosenstiel and Erpenbeck and according to the typical roles in production. They are based on the RAMI4.0 architecture model, to create a "problem skills cube" serving as a reference for the targeted development of problem-specific skills and educational formats. This theoretical approach is intended to be a first step towards a more tangible vision of Industry 4.0 in collaboration with the pilot plant of Industry 4.0.

[18] presents a generative method led by a model used to adapt and reuse a set of learning components for the delivery of a skills development program concerned with a given learning objective and which serves a specific educational context, t describes a generative (IE) Instructional Engineering method used to create and adapt Competence Development Programs (CDPs). Such adaptations can be made at the time of conception or at the time of learning, which complicates the task of educational design. The generative framework of the work consists of a functionality model, a set of learning components and a transformational approach based on the meta-model to eventually generate the learning artifact. Another learning space presented in [20], the makerspace, a type of Science, Technology, Engineering, and Mathematics (STEM) creation space, where students must combine skills and knowledge in the fields of science, technology, engineering and mathematics to create, build and review a product, the Maker space in is different from project-based learning because these products do not necessarily have to take the form of projects such as tools, prototypes or designs. The model developed was called Heat STEM Makerspace and from analysis and discussion, the authors concluded that the Heat STEM creation space could be used to stimulate creative thinking, critical thinking and problem solving. The design model could guide the teacher to help students explore their best STEM potential. Students also learn better because the model develops not only their 21st century skills, but also their STEM literacy in physics so that the model can promote higher order thinking skills. In industries, workers may use different types of machinery or have to perform manual tasks that require a specific sequence of actions. In both cases, they may be faced with unexpected events, which require great expertise, for these reasons.

[24] presents a concept of gamification suitable for application in Industry 4.0 environments in the context of knowledge sharing, thanks to this platform, workers can raise discussions on certain problems, such as solutions to execution failures of automation systems, publish multimedia content related to training on certain procedures or cases of solution errors and also answer questions from other colleagues. Other learning and knowledge-sharing environments are cited in [29]: IntelLEO, an ICT research project was initiated with the aim of developing intelligent technologies that support Learning and Knowledge-Building (LKB) activities in Intelligent Learning Extended Organization (IntelLEO). An example of real lifelong learning that prepares for a career and not a job, eDidaktikum environment initially intended only for teacher training in order to facilitate the exchange and collection of didactic information within universities and between them. To achieve this, the main aspects are the systematization of information, cooperation and social learning, as well as personal development and evaluation.

VII. Conclusion

The industrial revolution represents an issue of competitiveness for all industrial companies. Their objective is to overturn paradigms and make industry more communicative and more interactive in order to simplify all operations. Whether in terms of training, maintenance or production, using new technologies must be thought out in conjunction with other aspects of competitiveness, and in particular the rise in skills of human capital to all levels of the company. In this article, we have presented some research work which presented the human skills necessary to face Industry 4.0. This aspect is often displayed as a central concern by public policies, but few are the concrete devices to have emerged. Admittedly, many uncertainties about the development of the industry make it difficult to accurately anticipate skill needs. Howeevr, effective support for employees affected by the changes will be the key to the successful transition to the industry of the future.

References

[1] F. Hecklaua, M. Galeitzkea, S. Flachsa, and H. Kohlb "Holistic approach for human resource management in Industry 4.0", Proc. 6th CLF - 6th CIRP Conference on Learning Factories. Procedia CIRP 54, 2016 , pp. 1 – 6, doi: 10.1016/j.procir.2016.05.102.

[2] H. Karre, M. Hammera, M. Kleindiensta, and C. Ramsauera "Transition towards an Industry 4.0 State of the LeanLab at Graz University of Technology", Proc. 7th Conference on Learning Factories, CLF, Jan. 2017, Pages 206-213 doi.org/10.1016/j.promfg.2017.04.006.

[3] P. Fitsilis, P.Tsoutsa, and V. Gerogiannis, "Industry 4.0: required personnel competences", international scientific journal "Industry 4.0", vol. 3 (3), 2018, pp. 130-133.

[4] F. Pellerin, M-L.Cahier "Organization and skills in the factory of the future: Towards a work design?" Paris, Presses des Mines, 2019, ISBN : 978-2-35671-583-8; ISSN : 2495-1706

[5] K. Grzybowska, and A.Łupicka "Key competencies for Industry 4.0,", Economics & Management Innovations (ICEMI), vol. 1 (1), 2017, pp. 250-253, ISBN: 978-1-948012-02-7.

[6] A. Kozlov, A. Kankovskaya, and A.Teslya "The investigation of the problems of the digital competences formation for ndustry 4.0 workforce", Proc. IOP Conference Series: Materials Science and Engineering, vol. 497 (01), pp. 1-5, Apr. 2019, doi:10.1088/1757-899X/497/1/012011

[7] M. Contreras, D. Bonilla, and A. Negrón "Proposal of a model for the development of labor competencies based on serious games in the context of Industry 4.0", Proc. 7th International Conference on Software Process Improvement, (CIMPS), Oct. 2018, pp. 80-87, doi: 10.1007/978-3-030-01171-0_7.

[8] F. Imran, and J. Kantola "Review of Industry 4.0 in the light of sociotechnical system theory and competence-based view: A future research agenda for the evolute approach", Proc. AHFE Advances in Human Factors, Business Management and Society, Jul. 2018, pp. 118-128, doi: 10.1007/978-3-319-94709-9_12.

[9] Loina Prifti, "Professional Qualification in "Industrie 4.0": Building a Competency Model and Competency-Based Curriculum", Ph.D. thesis, 2019, Technical university of Munich, Faculty of Computer Science.

[10] M. Kravcik, X. Wang, C. Ullrich, and C. Igel, "Towards competence development for Industry 4.0", proc. Artificial Intelligence in Education (AIED), Jun. 2018, pp. 442-446 doi: 10.1007/978-3-319-93846-2_83.

[11] B. Schallock, C. Rybski, R. Jochem and H. Kohl, "Learning factory for Industry 4.0 to provide future skills beyond technical training", Proc. 8th International CIRP Conference on Learning Factories (CLF), Apr. 2018, pp. 27-32. doi: 10.1016/j.promfg.2018.03.156.

[12] F. Longo, A. Padovano, and L. Nicoletti, "Smart operators in Industry 4.0: A human-centered approach to enhance operators' capabilities and competencies within the new smart factory context", Computers & Industrial Engineering, Elsevier, 2017, doi: 10.1016/j.cie.2017.09.016.

[13] S. Coskun, Y. Kayıkcı, and E. Gençay "Adapting engineering education to Industry 4.0 vision", Technologies, Vol. 7 (1), 2019, pp. 1-13, doi: 10.3390/technologies7010010.

[14] C. Vila, D. Ugarte, J. Ríos, and J.V. Abellán, "Project-based collaborative engineering learning to develop Industry 4.0 skills within a Product Lifecycle Management (PLM) framework", Manufacturing Engineering Society International Conference (MESIC), Jun. 2017, pp. 1269-1276, doi: 10.1016/j.promfg.2017.09.050.

[15] S. Jaschke, "Mobile learning applications for technical vocational and engineering education: The use of competence snippets in laboratory courses and Industry 4.0", Proc. International Conference on Interactive Collaborative Learning (ICL), Jan. 2014, pp. 605-608, doi: 10.1109/ICL.2014.7017840.

[16] S. Erola, A. Jäger, P. Hold, K. Ott, and W. Sihn, "Tangible Industry 4.0: a scenario-based approach to learning for the future of production", Proc. 6th CIRP Conference on Learning Factories, Jun. 2016, pp. 13-18, doi: 10.1016/j.procir.2016.03.162.

[17] B. Motyl, G. Baronio, S. Uberti, and D. Speranza, "How will change the future engineers' skills in the Industry 4.0 framework? A questionnaire survey", Proc. 27th International Conference on Flexible Automation and Intelligent Manufacturing (FAIM), Jun. 2017, pp. 1501-1509, doi: 10.1016/j.promfg.2017.07.282.

[18] J.M. Dodero, T. Zarraonandia, C. Fernández, and D. Díez, "Generative adaptation and reuse of competence development programmes", Journal of Interactive Media in Education, 2007, pp. 1-13, doi: 10.5334/2007-4.

[19] V. Liagkou, D. Salmas, and C. Stylios, "Realizing virtual reality learning environment for Industry 4.0", Proc. 12th CIRP Conference on Intelligent Computation in Manufacturing Engineering, Jul. 2018, pp. 712-717, doi: 10.1016/j.procir.2019.02.025.

[20] A. Abdurrahman, "Developing STEM learning makerspace for fostering student's 21st century skills in the fourth industrial revolution era", Proc. 1st Young Scholar Symposium on Transdisciplinary in Education and Environment (YSSTEE), Nov. 2018, pp. 1-6, doi:10.1088/1742-6596/1155/1/012002.

[21] J. H. Lee, and O. A. Shvetsova, "The impact of VR application on student's competency development: A comparative study of regular and VR engineering classes with similar competency scopes", Sustainability, 2019, vol. 11 (8), pp. 1-26, doi:10.3390/su11082221.

[22] L. Moldovan, "State-of-the-art qnalysis on the knowledge and skills gaps on the topic of Industry 4.0 and the requirements for work-based learning", Proc. 12th International Conference Interdisciplinarity in Engineering, Oct. 2018, pp. 294-301, doi: /10.1016/j.promfg.2019.02.217.

[23] A. Gabor, F. Ahmed, and I.B. Szabó, "Systematic analysis of future competences affected by Industry 4.0", Proc. 11th IFIP WG 8.9 Working Conference on Research and Practical Issues of Enterprise Information Systems, Oct. 2017, pp. 91-103, doi: 10.1007/978-3-319-94845-4_9.

[24] M. Tsourma et al, "Gamification concepts for leveraging knowledge sharing in Industry 4.0", International Journal of Serious Games, vol. 6 (2), pp. 75-87, 2019, doi: 10.17083/ijsg.v6i2.273.

[25] J. Patalas, M. zewska, and S. Kłos, "An intelligent system for core-competence identification for Industry 4.0 based on research results from German and Polish manufacturing companies", Proc. Intelligent Systems in Production Engineering and Maintenance (ISPEM), Sep. 2017, pp. 131-139, doi: 10.1007/978-3-319-64465-3_13.

[26] G.B. Cotet, B.A. Balgiu, V.C.Z. Negrea, "Assessment procedure for the soft skills requested by Industry 4.0", Proc. 8th International Conference on Manufacturing Science and Education: Trends in New Industrial Revolution (MSE), Jun. 2017, pp. 1-8, doi: 10.1051/matecconf/20171210 7005.

[27] S. Perini, D. Arena, M. Taisch, and D. Kiritsis, "An ontology-based model for training evaluation and skill classification in an Industry 4.0 environment", Proc. IFIP International Federation for Information Processing, Sep. 2017 doi: 10.1007/978-3-319-66923-6_37.

[28] E. Ras, F. Wild. C. Stahl, and A. Baudet, "Bridging the skills gap of workers in Industry 4.0 by human performance augmentation tools - Challenges and roadmap", Proc. 10th ACM International Conference on PErvasive Technologies Related to Assistive Environments (PETRA), Jun. 2017, pp. 428-432, doi: dx.doi.org/10.1145/3056540.3076192.

[29] K-L. Kusmin, T. Ley, and P. Normak, "Towards a data driven competency management platform for Industry 4.0", Proc. 2017 International Conference on Knowledge Technologies and Data-Driven Business Workshop (i-Know-WS), Oct. 2017, pp. 1-8, Semantic Scholar.

[30] M. Pinzone et al, "Jobs and skills in Industry 4.0: An exploratory research", Proc. IFIP International Federation for Information Processing, Sep. 2017, pp. 282-288, doi: 10.1007/978-3-319-66923-6_33.

[31] J. Foutty, "Aspire to lead in Industry 4.0? Hone your soft Skills", The Wall Street Journal, 2009, https://deloitte.wsj.com/cio/2019/01/23/aspire-to-lead-in-industry-4-0-hone-your-soft-skills/, consulted the February 4th 2020.

[32] A. Grzelczak, M. Kosacka, and Werner-Lewandowska K., "Employees competences for Industry 4.0 in Poland– preliminary research results", Proc. 24th International Conference on Production Research (ICPR), Jul. 2017, pp. 139-144, doi:10.12783/dtetr/icpr2017/17598.

[33] "Défi de l'industrie 4.0 et recherche de nouvelles réponses" IndustriALL Global Union, Geneva Switzerland, http://www.industriall-union.org/sites/default/files/uploads/documents/2018/industry_4_fr_web.pdf

[34] L.D. Xu, E.L. Xu, and L. Li, "Industry 4.0: state of the art and future trends" International Journal of Production Research, vol. 56 (8), 2018, pp. 2941-2962, doi: 10.1080/00207543.2018.1444806.

Semantic Visual Query Answering on Heterogeneous Territorial Data

Loris Bozzato, Giulia Bruscagin, Gaetano Calabrese, Luciano Serafini, Cesare Furlanello

Fondazione Bruno Kessler,
Trento, Italy
Email: <surname>@fbk.eu

Abstract—**With the growing availability of administrative data in digital form, one of the current challenges of local municipalities is to manage and integrate information coming from different sources and formats with the aim of recognizing irregularities derived from the combination of such data. In this paper, we present our experience in the context of a local project for the semantic integration of real estate and associated tributes data. The integrated access to these data should support semantic visual analytic, and query formulation and geo-visualization. The data integration is based on an ontology that has been specifically developed to represent the main concepts and relations on this domain. This ontology is populated with the data available in different repositories, such as the cadastre, municipal registry, and household utilities. The ontology has been populated with the available data, which need to be normalized, completed and, in some cases, disambiguated. Finally, we developed a system for the visual formulation and execution of queries over the integrated knowledge base.**

Keywords*–*Cadastral Information System; Semantic Knowledge Integration; Visual Query Formulation.

I. Introduction

With the growing availability of administrative data in digital form, the local municipalities are nowadays faced with the problem of managing this data coming from different sources and putting it to good use. In particular, one of the advantages of having such data is the possibility to link the different sources and reason on the resulting combined knowledge in order to recognize irregularities and analyze the overall trends of the merged data.

Solving these problems was the aim of the *Geo@Reporter project*, a local project developed in the Trentino region (Italy). The project proposed an integration of real estate and associated tributes data in a common semantic repository, with the support of visual data analytics on cadastrial maps and guided semantic query formulation over the integrated data. The goal of the project was thus to provide municipalities with a comprehensive system for the analysis of the integration of the local cadastral and tax-related information. The choice of defining our system on semantic technologies allowed us to integrate data coming from heterogeneous sources and provide an unified model for the formulation of complex queries. It is interesting to present our experience on this project because, other than the interest in the developed knowledge and software resources, it provides an insight on what are the challenges and possible solutions for the management of geo-indexed semantic data and the development of a visual system for *SPARQL Protocol and Query Language (SPARQL)* query formulation and execution. The contributions of this paper can be summarized as follows:

- We present (in Section III) the structure and development of the Geo@Reporter base ontology. The ontology represents the main objects of the project (cadastral units, subjects and their relations) and their related information (e.g., energy tributes, rents, etc.). The structure of the ontology is derived from the analysis of the different sources to be merged.
- In Section IV, we present the system we developed for the integration and cleaning of the information coming from different sources. One interesting aspect is the management of geographical entities recognition, where an external geographical service is used as reference.
- We describe (in Section V) the system for visual analysis and query for the understanding of the integrated data. The interface for geographical analysis integrates different visual tools for the representation of data over the cadastral maps. The visual query system provides an intuitive way of composing a semantic query that is then executed as a SPARQL query over the semantic knowledge base.

II. Related Work

As we introduced in previous section, in the Geo@Reporter project we aimed at developing a comprehensive system for the analysis of integrated data on cadastral and local tribute data based on semantic technologies. This implies that the system has to provide a combination of different solutions for the semantic representation of (cadastral) data, data import and integration, data analysis and formulation of semantic based queries. As we briefly discuss in the following, to the best or our knowledge, no one of the currently available solutions for these aspects could cover all of the features we needed for the realization of our system.

With respect to the model for representation of cadastral data and related information, different local initiatives in Italy have explored the possibility to use ontologies for its representation, but there is still no agreement on a reference model. For example, in [1] ontology matching is used to map different schemas related to tax and revenues in the Province of Trento in order to integrate new data sources in the local knowledge bases. In [2], semantic technologies and ontologies are used to publish the contents of a territorial information system as Linked Open Data. However, these works do not aim at using their semantic representations to provide a general system for the management of cadastral and tributes data. Moreover, we highlight that, in the case of the Trentino province, the cadastre records have a slightly different structure from the Italian records, historically inherited from the Austrian cadastre. We note that a current effort to standardize ontologies and vocabularies for the Italian public administration is ongoing under the *OntoPiA* initiative [3].

In order to populate ontology based knowledge bases from different data sources, there are currently solutions to convert (mostly tabular) data in *Resource Description Framework (RDF)* format. A relevant example is *OpenRefine* [4], a Java-based tool to define and apply transformations on data files which is commonly used to publish (tabular) data in RDF format. Related approaches include mapping languages like *RDB to RDF Mapping Language (R2RML)* [5], which allow for the definition of transformations of data stored in a relational database for their exposition as RDF data. In our case, however, these approaches are not enough: first of all, the format of some data sources (specially in the case of cadastral data) is not strictly in a tabular format (i.e., records are positional and have multiple record formats depending on some of the fields) and thus the manipulation of such sources needs more freedom. The type of data formats we need to import is also different, thus our need is to provide a single (but extensible) tool to integrate all of the sources.

Different solutions for implementing web based dashboards for data analysis exist. Among the currently available open source solutions, two major proposals are *Superset* [6] and *Kibana* [7]. The objective of these environments is to facilitate the realization of web interfaces with views and graphical indicators over a given database, in order to provide users with insights on their datasets of interest. With respect to query composition, there exist libraries that can be promptly included in web interfaces, as for example *jQuery Builder* [8]. An advantage of such solutions is that they facilitate the definition of complex queries to non expert users. On the other hand, in our project we need to adapt and combine the current available tools to the specific case of representation of cadastral maps and building structures. Also, the current web libraries for query composition are not intended to work with SPARQL queries, so further work is needed to compose such queries, interact with the RDF knowledge base and represent the returned results.

III. Ontology Structure and Development

In this section, we detail the modelling activity and resulting structure of the *Geo@Reporter ontology*, which defines the base schema for the representation of the semantic information of the project. The ontology has been developed following the common guidelines and methods for ontology engineering (see, e.g., [9]). In particular, given the goal of integrating specific knowledge sources, the modelling has been guided by the form and contents of the initial data.

A. Ontology specification

The goal of the realization of the ontology is the formalization and schematization of the aggregated data in the Geo@Reporter Knowledge Base (KB). In particular, the ontology aim is to represent the central objects of the project knowledge base, i.e., buildings, their cadastral subdivisions together with their owners and their associated features. The ontology will be formalized and implemented in *Web Ontology Language (OWL 2)* [10], which allows us to take advantage of the available tools for modelling and reasoning in the standard ontology language. The formal definition of the ontological model is thus oriented towards the definition of the relations across the imported data sources, so to permit the successive population of the knowledge base, and the primitives for access to the main objects of the project, so to facilitate the formulation of relevant semantic queries on the integrated data.

B. Contents

The specification of the contents of the ontology, that is the extraction of the domain objects to be included in the ontology representation, has been driven by the need for the integration of the available data sources. The identification of the domain objects to be represented began with the analysis of the initial data sources and their structure. The interpretation of this data has been supported by meetings with domain experts (developers of cadastral related systems, knowledgeable about the details of data sources and interests of municipalities), who guided the modelling decisions in this developement phase by recognizing the most important objects and properties. The modelling of the ontology was driven by the initial data sources motivated by the heterogeneous nature of the sources and the need to recognize connections across the integrated information related to the represented objects. This analysis is also functional to the identification of the format of the different information pieces that need to be integrated in the final KB, thus it is preliminary to the design of the KB integration system.

The initial data over which we based our modelling consisted of an extraction relative to one year of two specific municipalities in the Trentino region. The following sources of data were identified:

Cadastral data: the source includes land and real estate cadastral information; the geographic information about boundaries and shape of the parcels are stored separately in the visualization interface system. This data has been provided in a proprietary format in form of pipe-separated text files (together with documentation for interpretation of fields). Cadastral data contains the principal objects of the discourse, thus will represent the central objects of the model. Principal objects from this data source are land and real estate units, owner subjects and their onwership relation with cadastral units.

Civil registry data: this source provides complete information about family units from the municipalities' registry data. This data is provided as *comma-separated values (CSV)* format files for individuals and families units. Main objects of this sources are resident individuals and family units.

Real estate tributes: this data includes all information from the municipality about real estate tributes for the specific year. The data is provided as a spreadsheet export of the administrative software of the municipality. The central content of this source is the information about municipalities taxes to be linked to local real estate units.

Utility and rent contracts: similarly, data about rents and utility contracts for waste collection, gas, electricity and water were provided by the municipality. These data is extracted as spreadsheets from the *Sistema Interscambio Anagrafe Tributarie Enti Locali (SIATEL)* system for exchange of tributary data in the Italian public administration. The main objects of interest are contracts (and their related information) for the different utilities linked to specific real estate units.

As it can be noted, the sources are heterogeneous for format and structure of the data, while also overlapping on some of the represented objects.

C. Application

Parallel to this activity of knowledge sources analysis, we identified the intended users and uses of the model. The ontology will be used mostly by two "users" (i.e., components of the system):

(1). Data analysis interface: the visualization interface has to allow the user to visualize data in the KB and permit different kinds of aggregations and query over the integrated data, with the goal of analyzing the connections and possible anomalies across the different sources. The interface will not modify the KB, but allow both simple retrieval of objects in the KB (e.g., for their visualization on a map) and complex queries that require interaction of objects from different data sources.

(2). Population and integration system: the system has the objective of inserting (or updating) in the KB the objects derived form the different data sources, with the creation (or update) of new instance data in the form specified by the ontology. The system is typically to be used at the "setup" of a new instance of the system with the import of data relative to a specific municipality to be analyzed or, in a later time, with the addition of new updated data. The integration system has the goal of uniforming the different sources of data to the RDF format used in the KB; during insertions, the system can use query services exposed by the KB to retrieve references to existing objects that need to be linked to the new objects.

D. Conceptual modelling

From the analysis of the presented data sources and use cases, we then proceeded to the conceptual modelling of the ontology schema. In Figure 1, we show an overview of the resulting conceptual schema. The conceptual modelling started from the analysis of the structure of cadastral data, given that it contains the central objects to be represented, and then completed by developing the sub-models for each of the related data sources. Figure 1 displays the main classes of the model (where the larger labels are the main objects of the model) and the main object properties across them. Gray boxes mark the classes of the sub-schemas for *cadastral, contracts, tributes and utilities* and *civil registry* information. Note that, by the integration of such schemas, many of the shared concepts like e.g., *Indirizzo* (address) or *IdentificativoCatastale* (cadastral identifier) become hubs for the access to information extracted from different sources.

E. Implementation

The resulting schema has been realized as an OWL ontology implementing the conceptual model. This schema will constitute the schema at the base of the project KB for the semantic representation of the integrated data. Intuitively, the physical modelling of the conceptual schemas is realized by translating to OWL class inclusion axioms the hierarchy of classes described in the conceptual model; similarly relations across classes are modelled as object properties while data fields associated to each object are modelled as a distinct data property. In the implementation of the ontology further features of the properties (e.g., functionality, transitivity) can be specified and hierarchies across properties have been defined. We report in Table I some metrics about the final version of the Geo@Reporter ontology. The rather small number of classes is due to the limited number of object types to be represented, while the larger number of datatype properties is related to the quite extended set of (mostly numerical and textual) information associated to such objects. Property axioms are mainly composed of domain and range assertions on object and data properties.

TABLE I. GEO@REPORTER ONTOLOGY METRICS

DL expressivity	$\mathcal{ALUHF}(D)$
Classes	29
Object / datatype properties	28 / 230
Annotations	284
SubClass axioms	12
Object / datatype p. axioms	63 / 462

The current version of the ontology is available for download in [11].

IV. KNOWLEDGE BASE INTEGRATION SYSTEM

After the realization of the ontological schema, we developed a system for importing the data from the different sources and integrating this information as semantic objects of the KB. Figure 2 shows the architecture of the integration system. The architecture has been designed with the goal of providing independence between the management of the format of input data and their information content to be integrated in the KB.

Intuitively, the import process is divided in two steps. In the first, the *input wrapper* component works on the format of the input files to apply data cleaning operations and to recognize relations across entities. In the second step, different *update services*, implemented as *Representational State Transfer (REST)* interfaces, allow to interact with the KB in order to add to the KB (or update) the information derived from input files in terms of the structure of the ontology. In the first step, the data cleaning and entity definition operation are kept separated in the input wrapper implementation so to facilitate their maintainability in case of the integration of new data formats.

In the first phase of the import, every input wrapper (designed for a specific data source) takes as input the data files containing the objects to be integrated in the KB together with a *mapping file* and *headers file* if required by the input data format. The mapping files, implemented as *JavaScript Object Notation (JSON)* textual files, define the correspondence between the fields in the input records and the ontology properties of the object to be created in the KB. By representing this information as a file external to the implementation, the mapping files ensure a better adaptability of the import procedure to the changes in the format of input files. For some of the input formats (in particular, for the cadastral data), the fields' headers are not specified in the input files but are documented externally. For such data formats, the input wrapper also needs a further support headers file containing the fields' interpretation.

During the data import, the system implements some base operations for cleaning and uniforming the data (e.g., by uniforming the format of dates, numbers and person names). These data refinement procedures have been developed during the analysis of the data sources, contextually to the development of the wrappers, with the aim of uniforming the data contents of the KB and thus facilitate the query operations on the integrated data. In particular, in order to facilitate the identification of elements on the map visualization of data, the data related to objects of type *Indirizzo* (address) has been normalized and completed with an external service. On the base of the data available on an address, the external service

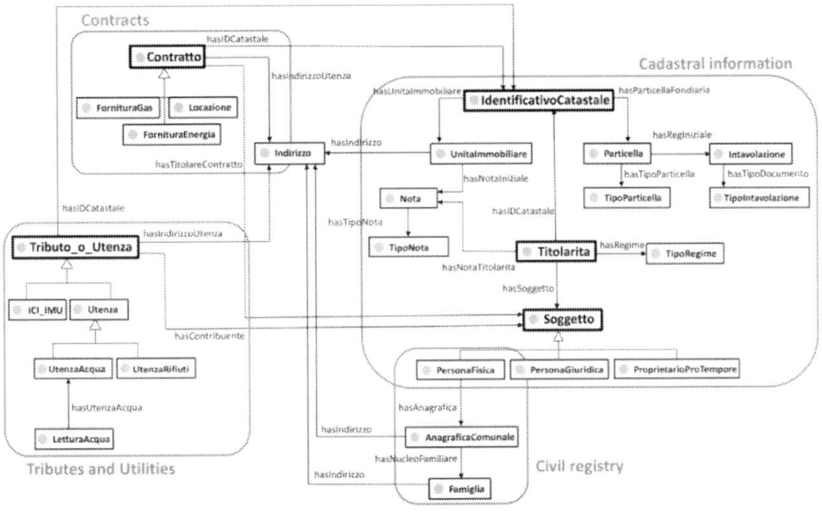

Figure 1. General schema of the Geo@Reporter ontology.

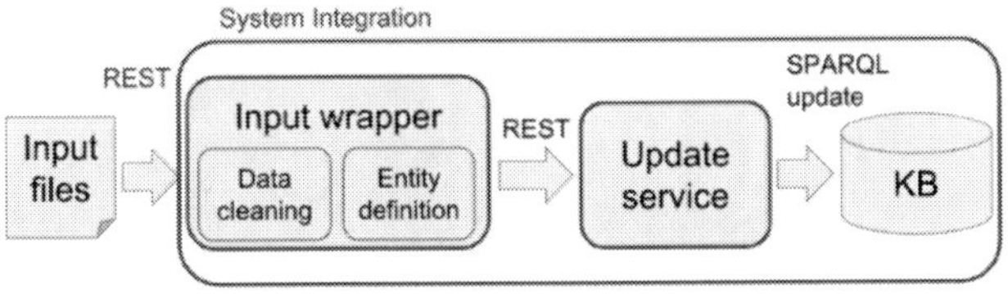

Figure 2. Integration system architecture.

Google GeoCode [12] (based on GoogleMaps API) is used to retrieve a normalized address string and its geographic coordinates. This new data is added (in post processing) to the address objects in the KB by distinct data properties. Similarly, to facilitate the recognition of links across elements of the KB, a post processing procedure has been developed that recognizes the possible relation across utility contracts and their associated cadastral units. The (one-to-many) association is derived by computing the proximity between the address specified for a contract and the addresses of cadastral identifiers.

Once the objects to be added to the KB have been defined by the first step, the actual creation of the objects in the KB is executed in the second step of the architecture (*Update service*). This is realized as calls to REST operations (for each kind of object) providing the interface for SPARQL based insertion queries on the RDF store implementing the knowledge base (in our case, *Eclipse RDF4J* [13]). In this phase, REST interfaces implementing the query services are used to recognize and retrieve entities that need to be linked to the new objects. Actually, both the *update services* and *query services* on the KB are implemented as REST interfaces. They define the access interface to the KB by allowing to abstract from the details of the (SPARQL based) interaction on the RDF store.

The integration system implementation has been completed with respect to the initial data sources, by realizing the necessary wrappers and mapping files for the import and cleaning of the initial data files. To simplify the import process, a simple Web interface has been realized to facilitate the access to the import services.

To verify and validate the work on the integration system and the ontology implementation (and for assessing the visualization components), the system has been tested on the initial data from the Trentino municipalities. An integrated KB for each of the two municipalities has been successfully obtained.

V. Visual Query Answering System for Data Analysis

The main purpose of the research activity of this project is to provide a Web-based instrument that can make affordable the analysis of heterogeneous data through one visual interface. In public administrations, there are usually various pieces of software dedicated to managing different data sources. The analysis between these datasets is difficult and problematic and is vulnerable to ambiguities, inaccuracies, and inconsistencies. In order to solve this problem, we developed an innovative visual system that can guide the user to explore and combine different data sources with flexibility, consistency, and intuitivity. We developed three main visualizations tools for Geo@Reporter:

- *Smart Query Builder*: a visual-based system for complex semantic query building on the KB;
- *Logic Tree*: a visual representation of the query results, highlighting the existing relationship between the different ontology elements;
- *Hybrid 2D/3D Geographic Information System (GIS)*: a multi-level visualization that combines 2D and 3D environments to describe and inspect geo-referenced entities from a high level to detailed features.

These tools are developed so that they can dynamically display the ontology model and, in case of changes to entities or tables, they can automatically adapt with no additional code modification.

A. Smart Query Builder

Public Administration identifies discrepancies in tax reports or cadastral documents through the comparison of various data sources. This activity is often very demanding in terms of time and resources, since most of the time these analyses are done manually. The chance to overlook some details or to commit some mistakes is very high. Furthermore, the dataset is often incomplete, and the user cannot easily find a way to correlate between two entities.

For this reason, we decided to create a graphic instrument that can guide the user easily and with high flexibility in the search process. We developed *Smart Query Builder* (SQB), a graphical interface that allows the user to easily compose complex queries and display the aggregated results in a table with optional geo-referenced data represented on the cadastral map. This system is highly interactive, with user-friendly user experience and allows to: (i). retrieve all the information from the ontology in a series of easy steps; (ii). query the ontology from different starting points, depending on the objective of the analysis. Smart Query Builder is a *Decision Support System (DSS)*: the tool does not identify problems or inconsistencies, but it is the user, after retrieving the results from the ontology, that can easily judge the investigated situation and decide an action strategy. The graphic design and the logical functionality of Smart Query Builder resemble the standard of *Visual Programming Languages (VPL)* where the user creates a query manipulating the elements graphically rather than specifying it with a procedural language (like, e.g., SPARQL). Therefore, queries and ontology are accessible even by less expert users, with no specific knowledge in programming.

Our Smart Query Builder is built as a customization of the Open Source library *jQuery Builder* [8] and it is developed in JavaScript. jQuery Builder provides a visual interface in order to build complex interrogations and it was the starting point for our research and development activities for this part of the project. The most important features we added were: (i). interoperability with SPARQL (not originally included within the specification list); (ii). query consistency controls (AND/OR/NOT functions are permitted only between entities with effective relations). We developed a specific workflow to enable the following steps:

1) Dynamic and flexible query-building process: the user chooses the first entity, and the SQB progressively suggests only the entities directly or inversely correlated to the previously chosen entity.
2) The set of rules is translated to JSON format and sent to the knowledge base;
3) A dedicated service of the KB translates the JSON dictionary into a SPARQL command, that is sent to the RDF store;
4) The extraction from the KB is returned to the front-end and results are displayed in tables and on the map.

Figure 3 shows the graphical interface developed for Smart Query Builder. After choosing the first entity (i.e., *Contratto Locazione*, rent contract), the list of connected entities is available in a drop-down menu. The user can choose mathematical and logical operators in a dedicated drop-down menu and insert free text in the empty box to complete the query with custom parameters. As long as the Smart Query Builder finds relations with other entities, the user can keep adding new boxes, creating a more complex query. The results can be consulted in tables and on a specific layer on the cadastral map. A donut pie chart is placed on the centroids of the corresponding cadastral parcel on the map, showing the number of real estates present on the parcel, highlighting the ones resulting from the query (Figure 4).

Figure 3. Example of use of Smart Query Builder.

Figure 4. Example of graphical and geo-referenced representation of the results of the query (Map data © OpenStreetMap contributors, CC BY-SA).

B. *Logic Tree*

In order to highlight the association between cadastral parcel, real estate identifier (*Unità Immobiliare*) and personal/services/tax-related data in the ontology, we defined a graphical logic structure to represent the relations between the various entities. For this purpose, we choose a tree representation that we called Logic Tree. This structure can visually represent the connection between cadastral parcel and the various properties of the parcel itself, with a strong hierarchical mark. The structure of the Logic Tree intuitively represents the existing connection between the cadastral elements and the entities referred to them (i.e., tax-related data, rent contracts, services, etc.). The selection of a subset of cadastral parcels with Smart Query Builder triggers the automatic generation of the Logic Tree where the user can interact on its leaves, querying the entities related to the parcel under investigation. The data are organized in the following levels (Figure 5) of the tree:

- *Level 0:* cadastral parcel;
- *Level 1:* real estate units;
- *Level 2:* personal and tributes data, services and contracts.

The graphical structure of Logic Tree is particularly helpful

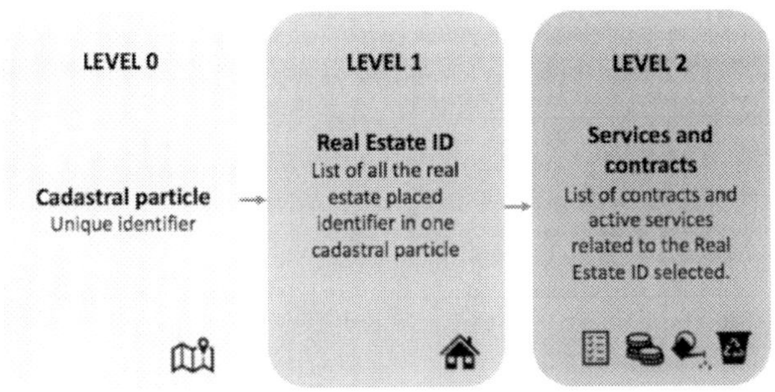

Figure 5. Logic scheme of Logic Tree.

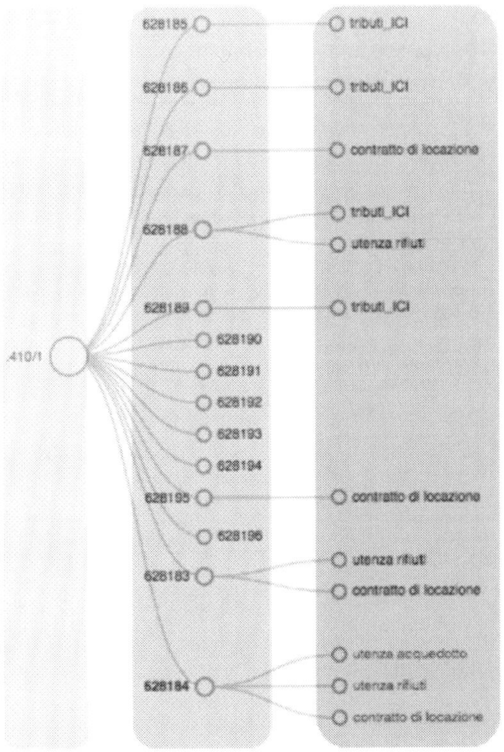

Figure 6. Example of Logic Tree: colors reflect the levels of the structure.

to understand the dependencies between the entities of these kinds of datasets (Figure 6). In particular, Logic Tree highlights the central position of the cadastral data and its structure reflects the ontology structure thanks to the visual aggregation of different data sources through simple graphical connections.

C. Hybrid 2D/3D GIS System

One of the most important data sources of the Geo@Reporter Project is the geo-referenced and geometric descriptions of the real estate properties, that are collected from two different sources: the cadastral data and the documentation inventory report, called *Documenti Catasto Fabbricati (DOCFA)*, officially registered to the *Ufficio del Catasto* (Municipal Building Department). A dedicated GIS module equipped with specific functions was developed for Geo@Reporter software. The GIS module, allows the user to geo-reference and navigate the consulted data in a spatial context.

To empower the user with the best possible data exploitation, we explored and tested different visualization solutions. We took into consideration different visualizations systems ranging from 2D to 3D environments. Considering the type of data involved, we were strongly interested in the use of the 3D representation, in particular, to model real estate data available in 3D for the single cadastral parcel. There are various approaches that allow three-dimensional modeling and that can be more or less suitable depending on the available data. We focused our research activity on two main components of these systems: (i). Modeling and exchanging formats of semantic enriched 3D data; (ii). Web libraries for Dynamic 3D visualization. We evaluated and tested all the main functionalities of several software and formats, considering the benefits and disadvantages, given the requirements of Geo@Reporter. The most suitable stack of software selected for the project was:

- *Leaflet* [14]: an open-source JavaScript library for 2D interactive maps;
- *Three.js* [15]: an open-source JavaScript library used to create and display 3D models in a Web browser;
- *Cesium* [16]: an open-source JavaScript library for world-class 3D globes and maps.

The DOCFA documentation provides most of the information required to reconstruct the three-dimensional representation of the building, but it does not specify the geographical coordinates. Thus, it is possible to generate a 3D reconstruction of the entire building or even just a part of it, but the 3D model cannot always be exactly placed in a geo-referenced map. We conducted several usability tests with Cesium, to check the performances of the library and the representation quality. While very immersive, the overall experience in using Cesium showed several usability concerns. The navigation and the consultation of 3D objects can be confusing and difficult due to the free camera and location movements that, in some cases, the user can find difficult to control. Furthermore, Cesium hides the representation of objects that are located under the road surface (i.e., cellars, basements, parking lots, etc.). For these reasons, we decided to place side by side the bidimensional cadastral map and the three-dimensional building in two separate modules. The cadastral map can be navigated with Leaflet and a connected module is dedicated to the 3D reconstruction of a selected building with Three.js. In this way, the user can navigate the bidimensional map (published with Leaflet) and, when interested in consulting the features of a particular cadastral particle, the 3D model (rendered with Three.js) shows the reconstruction of the whole building placed on the selected particle (Figure 7).

The usability test (performed with the domain experts) showed that this hybrid representation is easier to explore rather than a full 3D environment. In Three.js, the point of view of the visualization is always fixed towards the center of the building and the library allows the reconstruction of those parts that are under the road surface, allowing a complete exploration of the structure.

VI. Conclusion and Future Work

In this paper, we presented our experiences in developing a semantic-based platform for the Geo@Reporter project for

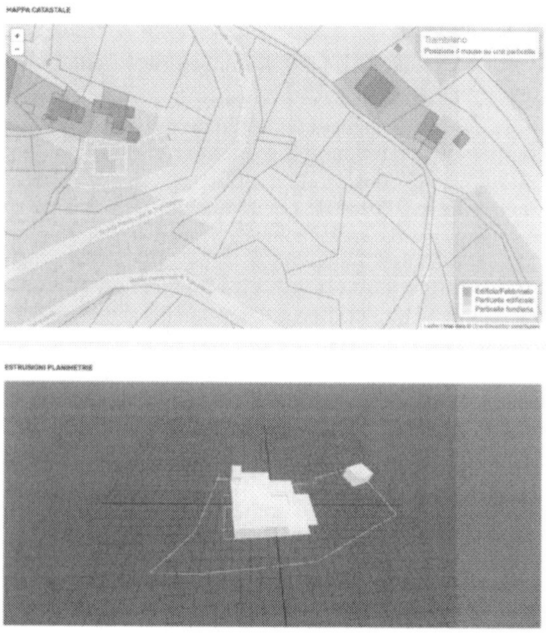

Figure 7. Example of Hybrid 2D/3D GIS Representation (Map data © OpenStreetMap contributors, CC BY-SA).

the representation and analysis of local administrative data. We first detailed the structure and modelling of the project ontology, by showing how the different data sources guided the schema definition. Then, we detailed the integration system of the platform, which allows to clean and map different data formats to the semantic based representation of the project KB. Finally, we presented our solutions for data visualization, providing different tools for data analysis and 2D/3D map navigation.

The project has been currently tested and applied to data for municipalities in the Trentino region. As a future direction, it can be interesting to extend the knowledge model and integration system to allow for additional information and data formats. In particular, a KB currently represents the data relative to a municipality for a specific period of time. It would be interesting to add a structured concept of *context* to sets of such data (see, e.g., [17][18]) to represent "snapshots" of such information and their relations. Similarly, the system can be extended to be applied to other Italian municipalities (but also to local administrations outside of Italy) by generalizing the ontological model and integration system to new sources of data. This can be useful to perform usability tests on the platform and further extend the system data-analysis capabilities.

ACKNOWLEDGMENT

This work has been supported by the *Geo@Reporter* project (*Progetto Di Ricerca Applicata*), funded by the Province of Trento, Italy under L.P. 13.12.1999, n. 6, art. 5.

REFERENCES

[1] S. Brida, M. Combetto, S. Frasson, and P. Giorgini, "Tax and revenue service scenario for ontology matching," in OM, ser. CEUR Workshop Proceedings, vol. 551. CEUR-WS.org, 2009, pp. 242–243.

[2] S. Consoli et al., "D4.1.2. Linked Open Data Arricchimento e pubblicazione dei dati," CNR, PRISMA Project Deliverable D4.1.2, Jan. 2013.

[3] "OntoPiA - la rete di ontologie e vocabolari controllati della Pubblica Amministrazione," 2019, URL: https://github.com/italia/daf-ontologie-vocabolari-controllati [accessed: 2020-03-19].

[4] "OpenRefine," 2019, URL: https://github.com/OpenRefine/OpenRefine [accessed: 2020-03-19].

[5] S. Das, S. Sundara, and R. Cyganiak, "R2RML: RDB to RDF Mapping Language," W3C, W3C Recommendation, Sep. 2012.

[6] "Apache Superset," 2019, URL: https://github.com/apache/incubator-superset [accessed: 2020-03-19].

[7] "Kibana," 2019, URL: https://www.elastic.co/kibana [accessed: 2020-03-19].

[8] "jQuery Builder," 2019, URL: https://querybuilder.js.org/ [accessed: 2020-01-28].

[9] Y. Sure, S. Staab, and R. Studer, "Ontology engineering methodology," in Handbook on Ontologies, ser. International Handbooks on Information Systems. Springer, 2009, pp. 135–152.

[10] W3C, OWL 2 Web Ontology Language Document Overview. W3C Recommendation, 2009.

[11] "Geo@Reporter ontology," 2019, URL: https://github.com/dkmfbk/GeoreporterOntology [accessed: 2020-01-28].

[12] "Google GeoCode," 2019, URL: https://developers.google.com/maps/documentation/geocoding/intro [accessed: 2020-01-28].

[13] "Eclipse RDF4J," 2019, URL: https://rdf4j.org/ [accessed: 2020-01-28].

[14] "Leaflet," 2019, URL: https://leafletjs.com/ [accessed: 2020-01-28].

[15] "Three.js," 2019, URL: https://threejs.org/ [accessed: 2020-01-28].

[16] "Cesium," 2019, URL: https://cesium.com/cesiumjs/ [accessed: 2020-01-28].

[17] L. Bozzato, C. Ghidini, and L. Serafini, "Comparing contextual and flat representations of knowledge: a concrete case about football data," in K-CAP 2013. ACM, 2013, pp. 9–16.

[18] L. Bozzato, L. Serafini, and T. Eiter, "Reasoning with justifiable exceptions in contextual hierarchies," in KR 2018. AAAI Press, 2018, pp. 329–338.

Chance Constrained Portfolio Optimization using Loan

Kiyoharu Tagawa

School of Science and Engineering
Kindai University
3-4-1 Kowakae, Higashi-Osaka, 577-8502, Japan
Email: tagawa@info.kindai.ac.jp

Abstract—**In this paper, portfolio optimization using loan is formulated as a chance constrained problem in which the borrowing money from a loan can be invested in risk assets. Then, the chance constrained problem is transformed into an equivalence problem. Furthermore, the equivalence problem is proven to be a convex optimization problem and solved efficiently by using an interior point method. Experimental results show that the use of the loan depends on acceptable risk and improves the efficient frontier.**

Keywords–Portfolio optimization; risk management; modeling.

I. Introduction

Portfolio optimization is the process of determining the best proportion of investment in different assets according to some objective. Portfolio optimization requires knowledge about the returns of assets. Thereby, the objective typically maximizes factors such as expected return, and minimizes costs like financial risk. Since portfolio optimization is one of the most challenging problems in the field of finance, a large number of works about portfolio optimization have been reported. In these works, according to some precondition, portfolio optimization is formulated as an optimization problem. Then, an appropriate method is used to solve the optimization problem [1].

Optimization methods of mathematical programming have been used to solve portfolio optimization problems based on Markowitz's model [2]. Evolutionary Algorithms (EAs) have been also used to solve portfolio optimization problems recently. Cardinality constraints limit a portfolio to have a specified number of assets. Genetic Algorithm (GA), Tabu Search (TS), and Simulated Annealing (SA) have been applied, respectively, to a portfolio optimization problem that includes cardinality constraints [3]. An extended GA has been proposed to solve a portfolio optimization problem considering the costs for selling and buying assets to change portfolio structures in multiple periods [4]. An Artificial Bee Colony (ABC) algorithm [5] has been proposed for solving a portfolio optimization problem based on the efficient frontier model [3]. Furthermore, in order to predict the future returns of assets from market data for portfolio optimization, an Artificial Intelligence (AI) method based on deep learning has been reported [6].

In our prior work [7], portfolio optimization using bank deposit and loan is formulated as a chance constrained problem in which a non-risk asset called bank deposit is included in the portfolio and the borrowing money called bank loan can be invested in risk assets. The chance constrained problem is transformed into an equivalence problem. The equivalence problem is proven to be a multimodal optimization problem having multiple optimal solutions. Therefore, an Adaptive Differential Evolution using Directed mutation (ADED) is proposed to solve the equivalence problem effectively.

In this paper, the effect of the loan is studied intensively. Portfolio optimization using loan is formulated as a chance constrained problem in which borrowing money from a loan can be invested in risk assets. Then, the chance constrained problem is transformed into an equivalence problem. The equivalence problem is analyzed mathematically. As a result, it is proven that the equivalence problem is a convex optimization problem. Besides, the condition of borrowing money from a loan up to the limit is revealed. An interior point method [8] is used to solve the portfolio optimization problem using loan because the interior point method is effective for convex optimization problems. Experimental results show that the use of the loan depends on acceptable risk and loan interest. If the loan is used properly, the efficient frontier is improved.

The remainder of this paper is organized as follows. Section II defines the portfolio considered in this paper. Besides, the basic models of portfolio optimization are explained. Section III formulates the portfolio optimization problem using loan. Section IV analyzes the optimization problem mathematically. Section V presents and discusses the results of experiments. Section VI concludes this paper and mentions future work.

II. Portfolio Optimization

A. Definition of Portfolio

We invest money in n assets. Let $x_i \in \Re$, $i = 1, \cdots, n$ be the proportion of i-asset normalized by owned capital. A portfolio is defined as $\boldsymbol{x} = (x_1, \cdots, x_n)$. Since $\boldsymbol{x} \in \Re^n$ is a long-only portfolio of single-period, it is constrained as

$$x_1 + x_2 + \cdots + x_n = 1 \tag{1}$$

where $0 \leq x_i$, $i = 1, \cdots, n$.

The unit investment in the i-asset provides return $\xi_i \in \Re$ over a single period operation [3]. Each $\xi_i \in \Re$ is modeled by a random variable following a normal distribution as

$$\xi_i \sim \mathrm{Normal}(\mu_i, \sigma_i^2). \tag{2}$$

Let ρ_{ij} be the correlation coefficient between ξ_i and ξ_j, $i \neq j$. The mean μ_i and the standard deviation σ_i in (2), ρ_{ij} are estimated statistically from historical data.

From (2), the vector of random returns $\boldsymbol{\xi} = (\xi_1, \cdots, \xi_n)$ obeys a multivariable normal distribution as

$$\boldsymbol{\xi} \sim \mathrm{Normal}(\boldsymbol{\mu}, \boldsymbol{C}) \tag{3}$$

where the mean is given as $\boldsymbol{\mu} = (\mu_1, \cdots, \mu_n) \in \Re^n$.

The covariance matrix $\boldsymbol{C}$ in (3) is derived as follows. First of all, the matrix $\boldsymbol{D}$ is defined by using σ_i in (2) as

$$\boldsymbol{D} = \begin{pmatrix} \sigma_1 & 0 & \cdots & 0 \\ 0 & \sigma_2 & \cdots & 0 \\ \vdots & \vdots & \ddots & \vdots \\ 0 & 0 & \cdots & \sigma_n \end{pmatrix}. \tag{4}$$

From the correlation coefficient ρ_{ij} between asset returns ξ_i and ξ_j, the coefficient matrix $\boldsymbol{R}$ is also defined as

$$\boldsymbol{R} = \begin{pmatrix} 1 & \rho_{12} & \cdots & \rho_{1n} \\ \rho_{21} & 1 & \cdots & \rho_{2n} \\ \vdots & \vdots & \ddots & \vdots \\ \rho_{n1} & \rho_{n2} & \cdots & 1 \end{pmatrix}. \tag{5}$$

From $\boldsymbol{D}$ in (4) and $\boldsymbol{R}$ in (5), $\boldsymbol{C}$ in (3) is obtained as

$$\boldsymbol{C} = \boldsymbol{D}\,\boldsymbol{R}\,\boldsymbol{D}. \tag{6}$$

The return of a portfolio $\boldsymbol{x} \in \Re^n$ is defined as

$$r(\boldsymbol{x}, \boldsymbol{\xi}) = \sum_{i=1}^{n} \xi_i\, x_i = \boldsymbol{\xi}\,\boldsymbol{x}^T. \tag{7}$$

From the reproductive property of normal distribution [9], the return in (7) also obeys a normal distribution as

$$r(\boldsymbol{x}, \boldsymbol{\xi}) \sim \text{Normal}(\mu_r(\boldsymbol{x}), \sigma^2(\boldsymbol{x})) \tag{8}$$

where the mean and the variance are given as

$$\mu_r(\boldsymbol{x}) = \sum_{i=1}^{n} \mu_i\, x_i = \boldsymbol{\mu}\,\boldsymbol{x}^T \tag{9}$$

$$\sigma^2(\boldsymbol{x}) = \boldsymbol{x}\,\boldsymbol{C}\,\boldsymbol{x}^T. \tag{10}$$

B. Models for Portfolio Optimization

By using the portfolio $\boldsymbol{x} \in \Re^n$ stated above, we explain basic models used to formulate portfolio optimization.

1) Markowitz's Model [10]: The risk of the portfolio is evaluated by the variance $\sigma^2(\boldsymbol{x})$ in (10). The risk is minimized keeping an expected return $\mu_r(\boldsymbol{x})$ larger than $\gamma \in \Re$ as

$$\left[\begin{array}{ll} \min & \sigma^2(\boldsymbol{x}) = \boldsymbol{x}\,\boldsymbol{C}\,\boldsymbol{x}^T \\ \text{sub. to} & \mu_r(\boldsymbol{x}) = \boldsymbol{\mu}\,\boldsymbol{x}^T \geq \gamma, \\ & x_1 + x_2 + \cdots + x_n = 1, \\ & 0 \leq x_i,\ i = 1, \cdots, n. \end{array}\right. \tag{11}$$

2) Efficient frontier Model [3]: By using the risk aversion indicator $\lambda \in [0, 1]$, Markowitz's model is modified as

$$\left[\begin{array}{ll} \min & \lambda\,\sigma^2(\boldsymbol{x}) - (1-\lambda)\,\mu_r(\boldsymbol{x}) \\ \text{sub. to} & x_1 + x_2 + \cdots + x_n = 1, \\ & 0 \leq x_i,\ i = 1, \cdots, n. \end{array}\right. \tag{12}$$

By changing the value of $0 \leq \lambda \leq 1$, we can obtain the efficient frontier, which is a continuous curve illustrating the tradeoff between expected return and risk (variance).

3) Roy's Model [11]: The risk of portfolio is evaluated by the probability that the return $r(\boldsymbol{x}, \boldsymbol{\xi})$ in (7) falls below a desired value $\gamma \in \Re$. For minimizing the risk α, portfolio optimization is formulated as a chance constrained problem:

$$\left[\begin{array}{ll} \min & \alpha \\ \text{sub. to} & \Pr(r(\boldsymbol{x}, \boldsymbol{\xi}) \leq \gamma) \leq \alpha, \\ & x_1 + x_2 + \cdots + x_n = 1, \\ & 0 \leq x_i,\ i = 1, \cdots, n. \end{array}\right. \tag{13}$$

4) Kataoka's Model [12]: Contrary to Roy's model in (13), the desired value $\gamma \in \Re$ of the return $r(\boldsymbol{x}, \boldsymbol{\xi})$ is maximized for a given risk $\alpha \in (0, 0.5)$. Thereby, portfolio optimization is also formulated as a chance constrained problem:

$$\left[\begin{array}{ll} \max & \gamma \\ \text{sub. to} & \Pr(r(\boldsymbol{x}, \boldsymbol{\xi}) \leq \gamma) \leq \alpha, \\ & x_1 + x_2 + \cdots + x_n = 1, \\ & 0 \leq x_i,\ i = 1, \cdots, n. \end{array}\right. \tag{14}$$

III. Problem Formulation

The Portfolio Optimization Problem using Loan (POPL) is an extended version of Kataoka's Model shown in (14).

A. Portfolio including Loan

The money borrowed from a loan is invested in risk assets. Let $x_0 \in \Re$ be the proportion of the loan used for a portfolio $\boldsymbol{x} \in \Re^n$. Let $m \in \Re$, $m > 0$ be the upper limit of the loan, which is specified by a multiple of owned capital. If the loan is not used, the proportion of the loan is $x_0 = 0$. On the other hand, if the loan is used up to the limit, the proportion of the loan is $x_0 = -m$. Therefore, the constraints of POPL are

$$\left\{\begin{array}{l} x_0 + x_1 + x_2 + \cdots + x_n = 1, \\ -m \leq x_0 \leq 0,\ 0 \leq x_i,\ i = 1, \cdots, n. \end{array}\right. \tag{15}$$

From the first constraint in (15), the proportion of the loan $x_0 \in \Re$ used for a portfolio $\boldsymbol{x} \in \Re^n$ can be evaluated as

$$x_0 = 1 - \mathbb{1}\,\boldsymbol{x}^T \tag{16}$$

where $\mathbb{1} \in \Re^n$ is a vector defined as $\mathbb{1} = (1, \cdots, 1)$.

Let $L \in \Re$ be the interest rate of the loan. The interest rate $L \in \Re$, $L \geq 0$ is a constant value. Considering the loan, the return $r(\boldsymbol{x}, \boldsymbol{\xi})$ of a portfolio $\boldsymbol{x} \in \Re^n$ in (7) is revised as

$$\begin{aligned} g(\boldsymbol{x}, \boldsymbol{\xi}) &= r(\boldsymbol{x}, \boldsymbol{\xi}) + L\,x_0 \\ &= \boldsymbol{\xi}\,\boldsymbol{x}^T + L\,(1 - \mathbb{1}\,\boldsymbol{x}^T) \\ &= (\boldsymbol{\xi} - L\,\mathbb{1})\,\boldsymbol{x}^T + L. \end{aligned} \tag{17}$$

From the reproductive property of normal distribution [9], the return in (17) also obeys a normal distribution as

$$g(\boldsymbol{x}, \boldsymbol{\xi}) \sim \text{Normal}(\mu_g(\boldsymbol{x}), \sigma^2(\boldsymbol{x})) \tag{18}$$

where the mean is given as

$$\mu_g(\boldsymbol{x}) = (\boldsymbol{\mu} - L\,\mathbb{1})\,\boldsymbol{x}^T + L. \tag{19}$$

The variance $\sigma^2(\boldsymbol{x})$ in (18) is also given by (10).

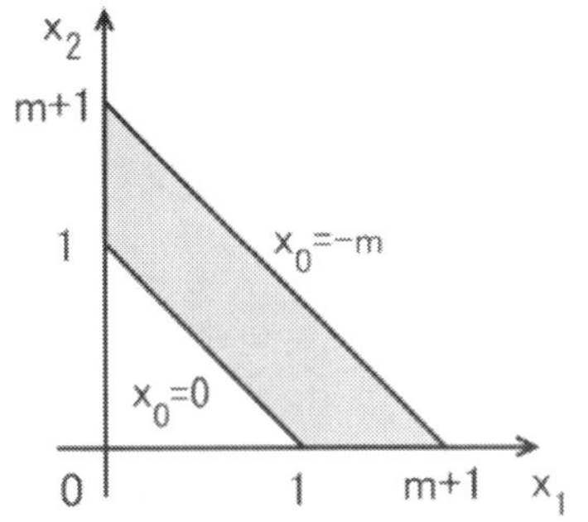

Figure 1. Feasible region of POPL in (23).

B. Portfolio Optimization using Loan

As stated above, POPL is formulated as an extended version of Kataoka's Model in (14). A risk $\alpha \in (0, 0.5)$ is given in advance. From (15) and (17), POPL is also formulated as a chance constrained problem:

$$\begin{bmatrix} \max & \gamma \\ \text{sub. to} & \Pr(g(\boldsymbol{x}, \boldsymbol{\xi}) \leq \gamma) \leq \alpha, \\ & x_1 + x_2 + \cdots + x_n = \mathbb{1}\,\boldsymbol{x}^T \leq m+1, \\ & x_1 + x_2 + \cdots + x_n = \mathbb{1}\,\boldsymbol{x}^T \geq 1, \\ & 0 \leq x_i,\ i = 1, \cdots, n \end{bmatrix} \tag{20}$$

where the proportion of the loan $x_0 \in [-m, 0]$ is eliminated from the constraints in (15) by using the equation in (16).

C. Equivalence Problem

It is hard to solve the chance constrained problem that contains probabilistic constraints [13]. Therefore, we transform the above POPL in (20) into an equivalence problem.

Since the return $g(\boldsymbol{x}, \boldsymbol{\xi})$ follows the normal distribution in (18), we can standardize the chance constraint in (20) as

$$\Pr\left(\frac{g(\boldsymbol{x}, \boldsymbol{\xi}) - \mu_g(\boldsymbol{x})}{\sigma(\boldsymbol{x})} \leq \frac{\gamma - \mu_g(\boldsymbol{x})}{\sigma(\boldsymbol{x})}\right) \leq \alpha. \tag{21}$$

The probability in (21) can be written as

$$\Phi\left(\frac{\gamma - \mu_g(\boldsymbol{x})}{\sigma(\boldsymbol{x})}\right) \leq \alpha \tag{22}$$

where $\Phi : \Re \to [0, 1]$ denotes the Cumulative Distribution Function (CDF) of the standard normal distribution.

From (22), we can derive the equivalence problem of the chance constrained problem in (20) as

$$\begin{bmatrix} \max & \gamma(\boldsymbol{x}) = \mu_g(\boldsymbol{x}) + \Phi^{-1}(\alpha)\,\sigma(\boldsymbol{x}) \\ \text{sub. to} & x_1 + x_2 + \cdots + x_n = \mathbb{1}\,\boldsymbol{x}^T \leq m+1, \\ & x_1 + x_2 + \cdots + x_n = \mathbb{1}\,\boldsymbol{x}^T \geq 1, \\ & 0 \leq x_i,\ i = 1, \cdots, n. \end{bmatrix} \tag{23}$$

Since the equivalence problem in (23) is a deterministic one, we do not need to evaluate the chance constraint in (20). The optimization problem in (23) is also called POPL.

Figure 1 illustrates the feasible region of POPL for the case of $n = 2$. The feasible region is shown by the gray area between two hyper-planes. If a portfolio $\boldsymbol{x} \in \Re^n$ does not use the loan as $x_0 = 0$, it exists on the lower plane: $\mathbb{1}\,\boldsymbol{x}^T = 1$. On the other hand, if a portfolio $\boldsymbol{x} \in \Re^n$ uses the loan up to the limit as $x_0 = -m$, it exists on the upper plane: $\mathbb{1}\,\boldsymbol{x}^T = m+1$.

IV. Problem Analysis

We analyze POPL in (23) mathematically.

Lemma 1: The standard deviation $\sigma(\boldsymbol{x})$ in (10) is convex.

Proof: Since the covariance matrix $\boldsymbol{C}$ in (6) is positive semi-definite, it is decomposed with $\boldsymbol{y} = \boldsymbol{x}\,\boldsymbol{A} \in \Re^n$ as

$$\sigma(\boldsymbol{x}) = \sqrt{\boldsymbol{x}\,\boldsymbol{C}\,\boldsymbol{x}^T} = \sqrt{\boldsymbol{x}\,\boldsymbol{A}\,\boldsymbol{A}^T\,\boldsymbol{x}^T} = \sqrt{\boldsymbol{y}\,\boldsymbol{y}^T}. \tag{24}$$

From (24), $\sigma(\boldsymbol{x})$ is a norm. Therefore, for any $\theta \in [0, 1]$ and $\hat{\boldsymbol{x}} \in \Re^n$, $\hat{\boldsymbol{x}} \neq \boldsymbol{x}$, the triangle inequality holds as

$$\sigma(\theta\,\boldsymbol{x} + (1-\theta)\,\hat{\boldsymbol{x}}) \leq \sigma(\theta\,\boldsymbol{x}) + \sigma((1-\theta)\,\hat{\boldsymbol{x}}). \tag{25}$$

The right side of (25) can be transformed as

$$\sigma(\theta\,\boldsymbol{x}) = \sqrt{\theta\,\boldsymbol{y}\,(\theta\,\boldsymbol{y})^T} = \theta\,\sqrt{\boldsymbol{y}\,\boldsymbol{y}^T} = \theta\,\sigma(\boldsymbol{x}). \tag{26}$$

From (25) and (26), we have

$$\sigma(\theta\,\boldsymbol{x} + (1-\theta)\,\hat{\boldsymbol{x}}) \leq \theta\,\sigma(\boldsymbol{x}) + (1-\theta)\,\sigma(\hat{\boldsymbol{x}}). \tag{27}$$

From (27), $\sigma(\boldsymbol{x})$ in (10) is a convex function. ■

Theorem 1: The objective function $\gamma(\boldsymbol{x})$ of POPL in (23) is concave. In other words, $-\gamma(\boldsymbol{x})$ is convex.

Proof: From (19) and $\gamma(\boldsymbol{x})$ in (23), we have

$$\begin{aligned} &\theta\,\gamma(\boldsymbol{x}) + (1-\theta)\,\gamma(\hat{\boldsymbol{x}}) - \gamma(\theta\,\boldsymbol{x} + (1-\theta)\,\hat{\boldsymbol{x}}) \\ &= \Phi^{-1}(\alpha) \times \\ &(\theta\,\sigma(\boldsymbol{x}) + (1-\theta)\,\sigma(\hat{\boldsymbol{x}}) - \sigma(\theta\,\boldsymbol{x} + (1-\theta)\,\hat{\boldsymbol{x}})). \end{aligned} \tag{28}$$

From Lemma 1 and $\Phi^{-1}(\alpha) < 0$ for $\alpha \in (0, 0.5)$, the right side of (28) is negative. Therefore, we have

$$\gamma(\theta\,\boldsymbol{x} + (1-\theta)\,\hat{\boldsymbol{x}}) \geq \theta\,\gamma(\boldsymbol{x}) + (1-\theta)\,\gamma(\hat{\boldsymbol{x}}). \tag{29}$$

From (29), $\gamma(\boldsymbol{x})$ in (23) is a concave function. ■

Since all constraints of POPL in (23) are linear, the feasible region of POPL is convex. Therefore, from Theorem 1, POPL in (23) is a convex optimization problem [14].

Theorem 2: Let $\boldsymbol{x}^\star \in \Re^n$ be a local optimum solution of a convex optimization problem. Then, the solution $\boldsymbol{x}^\star \in \Re^n$ is a global optimum solution for the optimization problem.

Proof: See arguments in [14]. ■

The gradient of $\gamma(\boldsymbol{x})$ in (23) can be derived as

$$\nabla\gamma(\boldsymbol{x}) = (\boldsymbol{\mu} - L\,\mathbb{1}) + \Phi^{-1}(\alpha)\frac{\boldsymbol{x}\,\boldsymbol{C}}{\sqrt{\boldsymbol{x}\,\boldsymbol{C}\,\boldsymbol{x}^T}}. \tag{30}$$

According to Karush-Kuhn-Tucker (KKT) conditions [14], the optimum solution (portfolio) $\boldsymbol{x}^\star \in \Re^n$ of POPL in (23) satisfies either of the following two conditions.

- $\nabla\gamma(\boldsymbol{x}^\star) = \boldsymbol{0}$ holds.
- Some constraints in (23) are active with $\boldsymbol{x}^\star \in \Re^n$.

Theorem 3: A portfolio $\boldsymbol{x} \in \Re^n$ of POPL borrows money from the loan up to the limit such as $x_0 = -m$ if

$$\gamma(\boldsymbol{x}) > L. \tag{31}$$

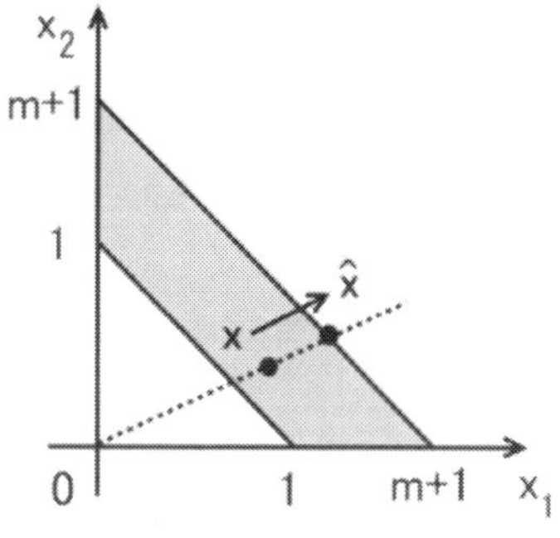

Figure 2. Illustration of Theorem 3.

Proof: Let us consider a new portfolio $\hat{\boldsymbol{x}} = \kappa\, \boldsymbol{x}$, $\kappa > 1$. The portfolio $\hat{\boldsymbol{x}} \in \Re^n$ borrows much money than $\boldsymbol{x}$ as

$$\begin{aligned} \hat{x}_0 &= 1 - \mathbb{1}\, \hat{\boldsymbol{x}}^T = 1 - \kappa\, \mathbb{1}\, \boldsymbol{x}^T \\ &< 1 - \mathbb{1}\, \boldsymbol{x}^T = x_0 \leq 0 \end{aligned} \tag{32}$$

where $\hat{x}_0 \in \Re$ is the proportion of the loan for the new portfolio $\hat{\boldsymbol{x}} \in \Re^n$, while $x_0 \in \Re$ is the proportion of the loan for the current portfolio $\boldsymbol{x} \in \Re^n$.

The objective function value of $\boldsymbol{x} \in \Re^n$ is

$$\begin{aligned} \gamma(\boldsymbol{x}) &= \mu_g(\boldsymbol{x}) + \Phi^{-1}(\alpha)\, \sigma(\boldsymbol{x}) \\ &= (\boldsymbol{\mu} - L\, \mathbb{1})\, \boldsymbol{x}^T + L + \Phi^{-1}(\alpha)\, \sigma(\boldsymbol{x}). \end{aligned} \tag{33}$$

The objective function value of $\hat{\boldsymbol{x}} \in \Re^n$ is

$$\begin{aligned} \gamma(\hat{\boldsymbol{x}}) &= \mu_g(\hat{\boldsymbol{x}}) + \Phi^{-1}(\alpha)\, \sigma(\hat{\boldsymbol{x}}) \\ &= \kappa\, (\boldsymbol{\mu} - L\, \mathbb{1})\, \boldsymbol{x}^T + L + \kappa\, \Phi^{-1}(\alpha)\, \sigma(\boldsymbol{x}). \end{aligned} \tag{34}$$

From (33) and (34), the gap between them is

$$\varepsilon = \gamma(\hat{\boldsymbol{x}}) - \gamma(\boldsymbol{x}) = (\kappa - 1)\, (\gamma(\boldsymbol{x}) - L). \tag{35}$$

From (35) and $\kappa > 1$, if the condition in (31) is satisfied, the new portfolio $\hat{\boldsymbol{x}}$ is better than the current one $\boldsymbol{x}$ as

$$\varepsilon = \gamma(\hat{\boldsymbol{x}}) - \gamma(\boldsymbol{x}) > 0. \tag{36}$$

Since the value of ε increases in proportion to the value of κ, the portfolio $\boldsymbol{x} \in \Re^n$ that satisfies the condition in (31) is improved by borrowing money as much as possible. ■

Figure 2 illustrates the two portfolios in Theorem 3 for the case of $n = 2$. The portfolio $\hat{\boldsymbol{x}} \in \Re^2$ on the upper hyper-plane is better than any portfolios $\boldsymbol{x} \in \Re^2$ within the feasible region of POPL (gray area) if the condition in (31) is satisfied.

V. Numerical Experiment

In order to solve POPL in (23), the interior point method provided by MATLAB [15] is employed. The information of the gradient $\nabla\gamma(\boldsymbol{x}) \in \Re^n$ in (30) is used effectively by the interior point method for improving its performance. As stated above, the optimality of the obtained solution is verified.

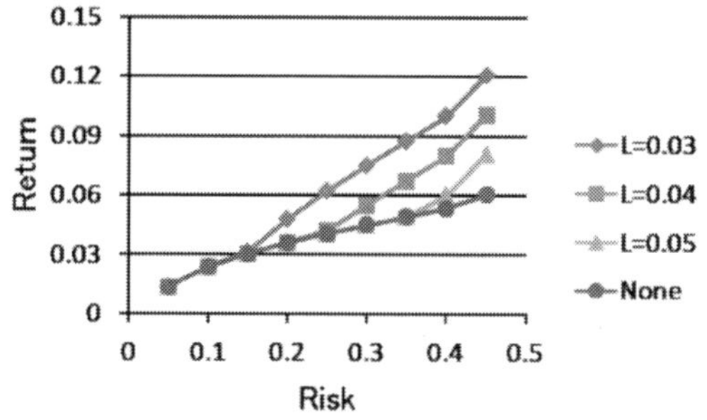

Figure 3. Efficient frontier (port0, $m = 2$).

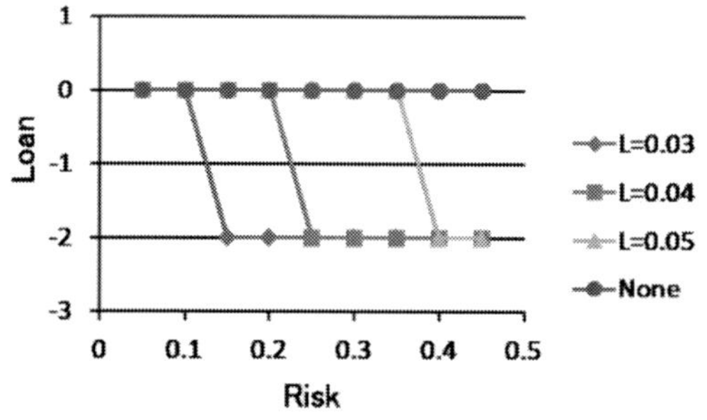

Figure 4. Proportion of the loan x_0 (port0, $m = 2$).

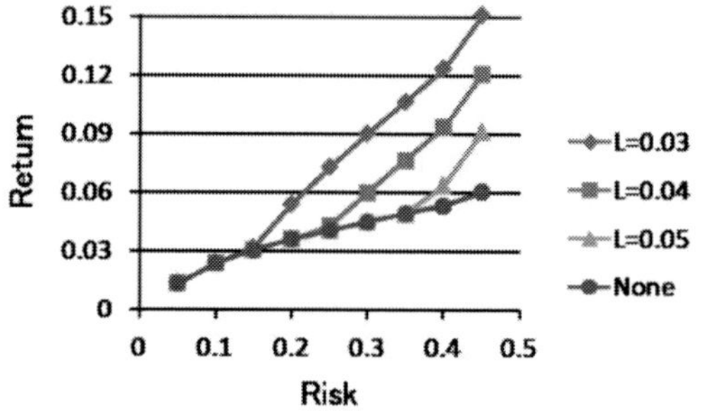

Figure 5. Efficient frontier (port0, $m = 3$).

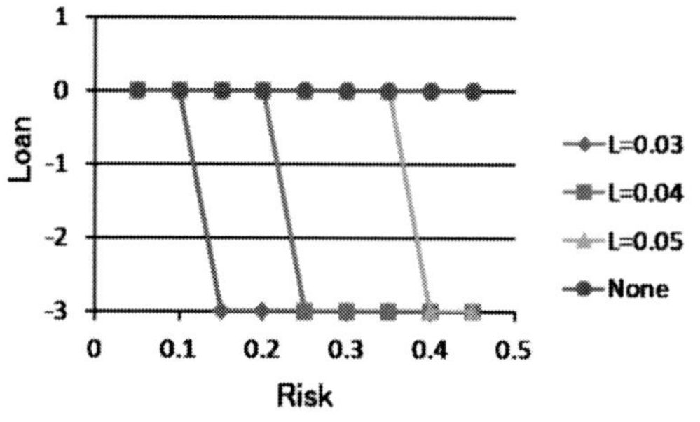

Figure 6. Proportion of the loan x_0 (port0, $m = 3$).

TABLE I. MEAN AND VARIANCE OF ASSET RETURN (PORT0).

ξ_i	ξ_1	ξ_2	ξ_3	ξ_4
μ_i	0.05	0.06	0.07	0.08
σ_i^2	0.10^2	0.20^2	0.15^2	0.25^2

TABLE II. CORRELATION BETWEEN ASSET RETURNS (PORT0).

ρ_{ij}	ξ_1	ξ_2	ξ_3	ξ_4
ξ_1	1.0	−0.7	0.1	−0.4
ξ_2	−0.7	1.0	−0.5	0.2
ξ_3	0.1	−0.5	0.1	−0.3
ξ_4	−0.4	0.2	−0.3	1.0

TABLE III. INDEX OF DATA SET AND NUMBER OF ASSETS.

Data set	Index	n
port1	Hang Seng	31
port2	DAX	85
port3	FTSE	89
port4	S&P	98

A. *Case Study 1*

An instance of POPL called port0 is given by Table I and Table II. The port0 consists of $n = 4$ assets. Table I shows the mean and variance of asset returns $\xi_i \in \Re$, $n = 1, \cdots, n$. Table II shows the correlation coefficient between them.

We evaluate the effect of the interest rate of the loan L on the return $\gamma(\boldsymbol{x})$ of POPL. Figure 3 shows the efficient frontier, or the trade-off between the return $\gamma(\boldsymbol{x}) \in \Re$ and the risk $\alpha \in (0, 0.5)$, when the upper limit of the loan is given as $m = 2$. Three different interest rates of the loan, $L = 0.03$, 0.04, and 0.05, are compared in Figure 3. "None" denotes the efficient frontier when the loan is not used. Figure 4 shows the proportion of the loan $x_0 \in [-m, 0]$ for each portfolio shown in Figure 3. In the case of "None", $x_0 = 0$ always holds.

From Figure 3, the efficient frontier is improved by using the loan. Specifically, the smaller the interest rate of the loan is, the higher the return. Besides, the portfolio $\boldsymbol{x}$ taking a high risk uses the loan even if the interest rate of the loan is high.

From Figure 4, as we have proven in Theorem 3, the loan is always used up to the limit ($x_0 = -m$) when it is used.

Figure 5 shows the efficient frontier when the upper limit of the loan is given as $m = 3$. Figure 6 shows the proportion of the loan $x_0 \in [-m, 0]$ for each portfolio in Figure 5.

From Figure 3 and Figure 5, we can confirm that the efficient frontier is improved by borrowing more money from the loan. From Figure 4 and Figure 6, the loan is always used up to the limit ($x_0 = -m$) regardless of the value of m.

B. *Case Study 2*

Instances of POPL are defined by using the data sets called port1 to port4, which are available from OR-Library [16]. Each of the data sets contains the means, variances, and a coefficient matrix of n asset returns. They are evaluated for real-life data sets, or historical data sets about asset returns. Table III shows the capital market indices and their numbers of assets. By using port1 to port4, we construct the models of asset returns as shown in (3) for the instances of POPL.

For all the instances of POPL, the upper limit of the loan is given as $m = 3$. Thereby, three different interest rates of

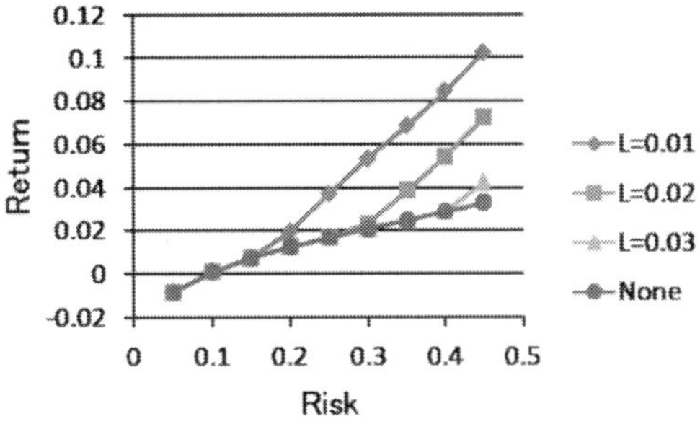

Figure 7. Efficient frontier (port1, $m = 3$).

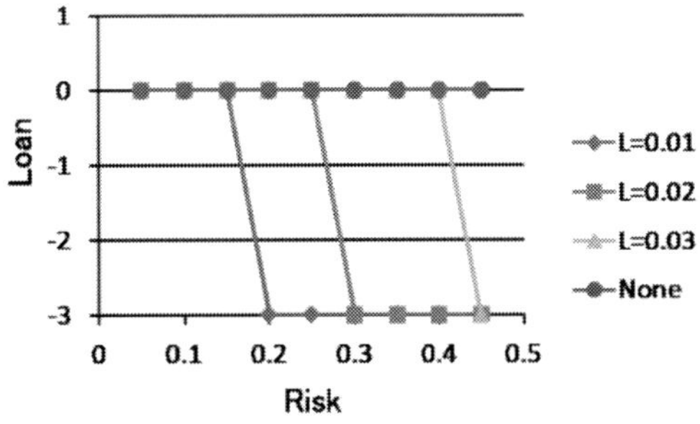

Figure 8. Proportion of the loan x_0 (port1, $m = 3$).

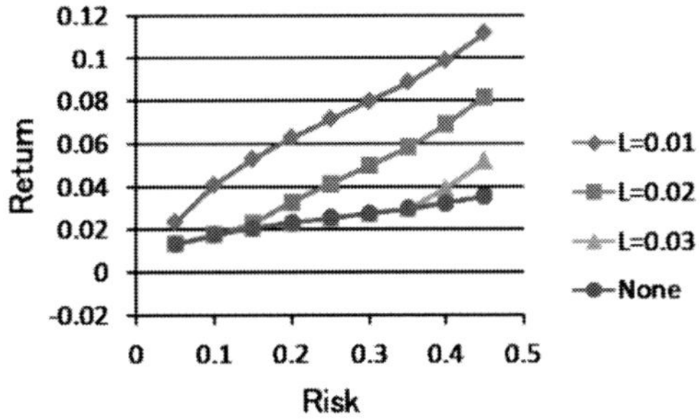

Figure 9. Efficient frontier (port2, $m = 3$).

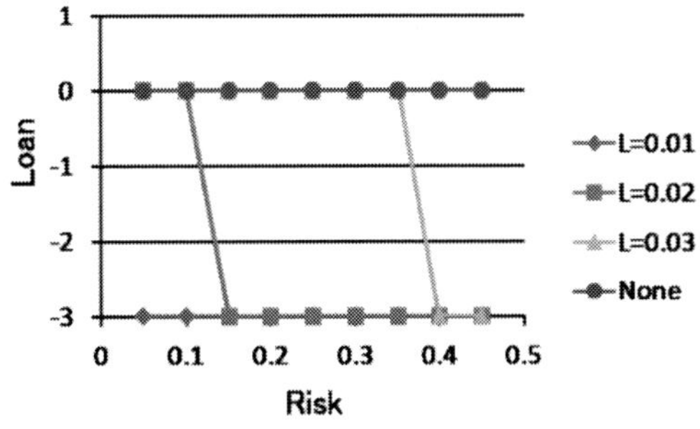

Figure 10. Proportion of the loan x_0 (port2, $m = 3$).

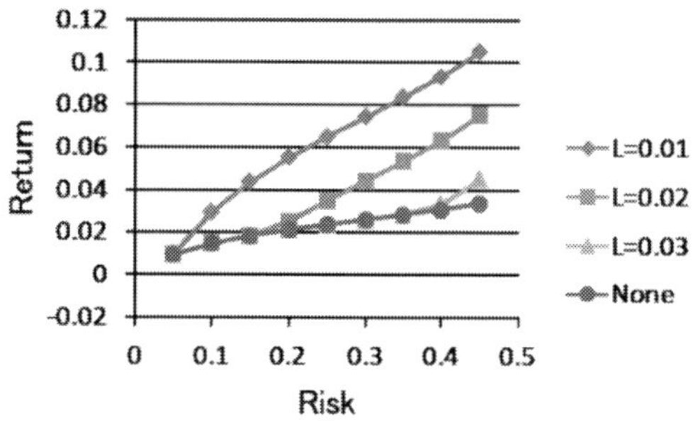

Figure 11. Efficient frontier (port3, $m = 3$).

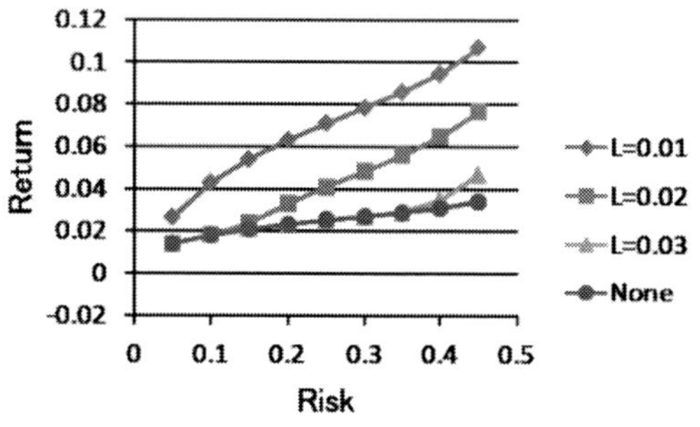

Figure 12. Efficient frontier (port4, $m = 3$).

the loan, namely $L = 0.01$, $L = 0.02$, and $L = 0.03$, are examined in each of the instances of POPL.

Figure 7 and Figure 8 show the results of the experiment conducted on port1. Figure 7 shows the efficient frontier, or the trade-off between the return and the risk, while Figure 8 shows the proportion of the loan for each portfolio shown in Figure 7. As stated above, "None" denotes the result when the loan is not used. Similarly, Figure 9 and Figure 10 show the results of the experiment conducted on port2. Figure 9 shows the efficient frontier, while Figure 10 shows the proportion of the loan for each portfolio shown in Figure 9.

Figure 11 shows the efficient frontier obtained for port3. Figure 12 also shows the efficient frontier obtained for port4. The proportions of the loan for the portfolios shown in Figure 11 and Figure 12 are omitted for want of space. However, the results of the experiments conducted on port1 to port4 are almost the same as the result of the experiment on port0.

From Figure 7 to Figure 12, we can confirm that the use of the loan works well for improving the efficient frontier. Especially, the lower interest rate of the loan provides higher return and benefits borrowers. On the other hand, the higher interest rate of the loan does not benefit lenders because such a loan is not used. Of course, the higher interest rate of the loan does not benefit borrowers, either. Furthermore, as we have proven by Theorem 3, we can see that the loan is always used up to the limit when it is used. From the results of the experiments, the loan seems to be used up to the limit immediately when the condition in (31) is satisfied.

VI. Conclusion

Portfolio optimization using loan is formulated as POPL. The emphasis of our work is on the theoretical characterization of POPL. From the analysis of POPL in (23), it is proven that POPL is a convex optimization problem. Furthermore, the condition of borrowing money from the loan up to the limit is revealed. Through numerical experiments, it can also be confirmed that the risk $\alpha \in (0, 0.5)$ and the interest rate of loan L play an important role in the decision whether the loan is used or not. If the money borrowed from the loan is invested in assets, the efficient frontier is improved by higher return.

For future work, we will think about a suitable interest rate of the loan that benefits both borrowers and lenders. Besides, we would like to include cardinality constraints in POPL.

Acknowledgment

This work was supported by JSPS KAKENHI (17K06508).

References

[1] D. G. Luenberger, Investment Science, International Edition. Oxford University Press, 2009.

[2] M. Mokhtar, A. Shuib, and D. Mohamad, "Mathematical programming models for portfolio optimization problem: a review," International Journal of Mathematical and Computational Sciences, vol. 8, no. 2, 2014, pp. 428–435.

[3] T.-J. Chang, N. Meade, J. E. Beasley, and Y. M. Sharaiha, "Heuristics for cardinality constrained portfolio optimization," Computers & Operations Research, vol. 25, 2000, pp. 1271–1302.

[4] C. Aranha and H. Iba, "Modelling cost into a genetic algorithm-based portfolio optimization system by seeding and objective sharing," in Proc. IEEE Congress on Evolutionary Computation, Singapore, 2007, pp. 196–203.

[5] I. Strumberger, E. Tuba, N. Bacanin, M. Beko, and M. Tuba, "Hybridized artificial bee colony algorithm for constrained portfolio optimization problem," in Proc. IEEE Congress on Evolutionary Computation, Rio de Janeiro, Brazil, 2018, pp. 1–8.

[6] S. Obeidat, D. Shapiro, and M. Lemay, "Adaptive portfolio assets allocation optimization with deep learning," IARIA International Journal on Advances in Intelligent Systems, vol. 11, no. 1&2, 2018, pp. 25–34.

[7] K. Tagawa, "Group-based adaptive differential evolution for chance constrained portfolio optimization using bank deposit and bank loan," in Proc. IEEE Congress on Evolutionary Computation, Wellington, New Zealand, 2019, pp. 1557–1563.

[8] R. Horst and P. M. Pardalos, Handbook of Global Optimization. Kluwer Academic Publishers, 1995.

[9] R. B. Ash, Basic Probability Theory. Dover, Downers Grove, 2008.

[10] H. Markowitz, "Portfolio selection," The Journal of Finance, vol. 7, no. 1, 1952, pp. 77–91.

[11] A. D. Roy, "Safety first and the holding of assets," Econometrica, vol. 20, no. 3, 1952, pp. 431–449.

[12] S. Kataoka, "Stochastic programming model," Econometrica, vol. 31, no. 1/2, 1963, pp. 181–196.

[13] A. Prékopa, Stochastic Programming. Kluwer Academic Publishers, 1995.

[14] G. P. McCormick, Nonlinear Programming. John Wiley & Sons, 1983.

[15] C. P. López, MATLAB Optimization Techniques. Springer, 2014.

[16] J. E. Beasley, "OR-Library: distributing test problems by electronic mail," Journal of the Operational Research Society, vol. 41, no. 11, 1990, pp. 1069–1072, URL: http://people.brunel.ac.uk/ mastjjb/jeb/info.html [accessed: 2020-01-23].

Analyzing Model Element Labels of Business Process Model Examples Provided on the Web

Christian Kop
University of Klagenfurt
Klagenfurt, Austria
e-mail: christian.kop@aau.at

Abstract— **Business process models are important for Information Systems and the digitalization of the workplace. The Business Process Model and Notation (BPMN) is the de-facto standard in this domain. Therefore, creating BPMN business process models that are understandable to all stakeholders is an important task. The Web provides many business process model examples. These examples are provided by enterprises and consultants who offer technical solutions (i.e., business process modeling tools) or consulting services. Since such models are provided on the Web as introductory learning examples, such examples can also influence novice business process modelers. Therefore, it is worth to examine if such examples have the same quality standards as suggested in the literature. Related to the area of business process modeling, this paper, therefore, focuses on the analysis of such BPMN examples. Particularly, it focuses on the labels of model elements since these labels represent the relationship between the process model and a certain domain.**

Keywords-Business Process Model and Notation (BPMN); Business Process Modeling; Quality of Business Process Models; Labels of Model Elements.

I. INTRODUCTION

A good analysis and documentation of business processes is necessary in order to understand the internal behavior of an enterprise and to implement process automation well. The Business Process Model and Notation (BPMN) is the de-facto business process modeling language standard for documenting processes (for the model elements of BPMN, see e.g., the BPMN poster on the Web [16]). It is intended for both high level organizational processes and lower level processes that can be executed by a workflow engine.

For good business process documentation, which is understandable by all stakeholders, skills in business process modeling with BPMN are very relevant. Today, these skills cannot only be obtained by reading books about BPMN or visiting BPMN courses. Instead, it is often much easier and cheaper to click through the Web, looking and reading the diagrams, as well as the enclosed explanations, on a Web site. Thus, Web examples can be taken as surrogates for examples in professional literature (e.g., specialist books). Actually, the BPMN and Process Management (BPM) community (e.g., tool providers and consultants) also have the aim to present BPMN examples on the Web to give either an introduction of the tool features for BPMN modeling or to show modelers how these diagrams look like and how they should be modelled. Hence, a look at such Web examples and their quality for being a standard for novice process modelers can be useful.

There are different aspects of how modeling quality can be defined (e.g., syntactical correctness; adequate drawing of models; adequate color and shape of model elements; adequate labels of model elements, etc.). This work focuses on the labels of model elements. Labels on model elements (e.g., "send application") as a label example of a BPMN Activity are important since they relate the model to the observed reality. They represent the semantic bearing parts of a domain giving the model elements and thus the whole BPMN model a certain meaning in a specific domain. Therefore, if the labels are not well chosen, a model can be more confusing than understandable and this can lead to a wrong interpretation of models. In the literature, which deals with the quality of model element labels, also recommendations are given how certain model elements should be labelled.

The goals of this work, therefore, are to:

- Check if the introductory learning examples provided on the Web by BPMN experts (e.g., enterprises that offer BPMN tools and consultants offering consulting services) follow the label quality guidelines mentioned in literature.
- Examine if in these examples, the labels are at least well chosen. That means that, even if the labels do not exactly match the guidelines, nevertheless, they make sense in a specific context.

In order to answer this, the analysis of the examples on the Web has been done on a sample extracted from the Web.

The paper is structured as follows. In Section 2, an overview of related work is given and labeling styles together with literature recommendations of good labeling styles are presented. Section 3 describes the preparation of the sample of Web examples for this work. Section 4 focuses on the labels of model elements for business process models provided on the Web. It discusses which kinds of labels are used and compares these with literature suggestions. The paper is summarized in Section 5.

II. RELATED WORK

All aspects of the quality of process models are in the focus of the research community. Issues of deficiencies in BPMN are stated in [14] and [15]. In [3], the author of the book describes how good modeling styles of BPMN should look like. A literature survey about business process modeling quality is given in [5]. Seven guidelines for process modeling are proposed and verified with user studies in [6].

Some researchers have thought about automating the labeling process of business process modeling and aggregation of process models to support the comprehension of such process models [7] [8]. It was even analyzed how the style, color and arrangement of label parts on a model element improves readability [9] [10].

A. Related Work with respect to Labels of Model Elements

More detailed work on labels of BPMN model elements itself was done in [11] - [13]. These research works are based on data sets of process models from industry. Good labeling styles of Activities, Events and Gateways for three different natural languages were proposed and recommended in [11]. There, violations of these labeling styles are described.

Activities subsume Sub Processes, Event Sub Processes, Transactions, Tasks and Call Activities. In all cases, the tasks of a person or a system, namely, the working step within a process, are described. For the labels of Activities, the following styles were found in this literature:

- *Verb Object Style*: A label that starts with a verb expressing the activity followed by an object, on which this activity is executed (e.g., "create document").
- *Action Noun Style*: This style has three sub styles: a) A label that has either a nominalized verb only or a compound noun consisting of a verb as the head of this compound noun (e.g., "creation", "document creation"). b) The Noun can also be a noun phrase with the preposition "of" in between (e.g., "creation of document"). c) Finally, the *Action Noun Style* can also start with a gerund followed by a noun (e.g., "creating document").
- The style called "*Descriptive*" is a style consisting of a subject, a verb in 3rd person singular and an object (e.g., "author writes book").

Beside this, there are also labels that do not follow a good style at all. These are labels with nouns only and no verbs at all (e.g., "error"). According to literature [12], the *Verb Object Style* is the most recommended style that should be used for modeling Activities.

With Gateways, a work flow can be divided into several paths, but different paths can also be merged. Most recommended Gateway labeling styles in literature have in common that they should end with a question mark ("?"). Thus, the literature assumes that these kinds of styles are mainly used for XOR and OR Gateways since in these Gateways a decision is made, which can be expressed as a question. On contrary, an AND (parallel) Gateway does not need such a label since no decision is made. Such questions in Gateway labels can be expressed in one of the following styles:

- *Question with Noun and Verb in Past Participle* (e.g., "document created?")
- *Infinitive verb question* (e.g., "approve contract?")
- *Object with adjective question*: A phrase consisting of an object followed by an adjective or an auxiliary and an adjective (e.g., "parts available?" or "parts are available?")
- *Equation question*: A phrase consisting of an object followed by a logical operator and a value (e.g., "amount is greater than $ 200").

Even here, there are labels, which are treated as bad labels. As a counter example for good quality, a noun only (e.g., "result?") is treated, since from this kind of label it is not possible to derive a clear decision. For Gateways, the most recommended label style is: *Question with Noun and Verb in Past Participle* [12].

Finally, events that can occur within a process are modelled with the model element Event.

Labeling styles for Events can be classified as followed:

- *Verb in Past Participle Style*: This can be characterized by an object followed by a verb in past participle or followed by a (modal) auxiliary and a verb in past participle (e.g., "document created", "document has been created", "document is created", "document must be created")
- *Predicative Adjective Style*: Here, a noun together with a predicative adjective is used to label an Event (e.g., "document correct" or "document is correct").
- *Categorization Style*: Two nouns are related with a verb (mainly the verb "is") in order to express that the term specified with the first noun can be categorized according to the term expressed with the second noun (e.g., "person is author").

Modelers also use labels that better should not be used for Events at all, since they do not provide sufficient information to a reader. For instance, they use a noun only (e.g., "inquiry"). The *Verb in Past Participle Style* is the one which is most recommended as a labeling style for Events [12].

Beside simple labels, it has also been examined in literature that modelers use complex phrases and sentences for Activity labels instead of drawing more model elements with simpler, so called canonical labels. Especially in [13], these kinds of inconsistent use of labeling, so called non-canonical patterns, are examined. Three categories of complex non-canonical label patterns were detected:

- *Complex control flow label*: The label of an Activity consists of a sequence of verbs, each describing an Activity, which are concatenated with "or" or "and". This verb sequence, however, implicitly expresses a decision (in the case of "or") or a parallel respectively a sequential execution of several Activities (in the case of "and"). It does not express an atomic working step. Thus, instead of one Activity with a complex label, several Activities with simpler labels together with control flows can also be used. Other complex labels of that kind are phrases, which end with "as required", "as / if needed", as well as sentences or phrases expressing an iteration (e.g., "while .... ", "repeat until ... ", "for each ...").
- *Extra specification of data, resources and time*: In this category, the label of the model element not

only contains the necessary information, but also additional information that is often given in some sorts of brackets (e.g., "clear differences (inventory management)"). Most often, either this extra information should be itself explicitly modelled with a model element like an Event, Activity or Gateway or this extra information is useless.

- *Implicit Action and Decision*: Here, the label and the modelling element do not fit. For instance, the label of an Activity is expressed in terms of a pattern that is typically used for an Event (e.g., "Order received" instead of "Receive Order").

In literature, these categories of non-canonical labels are seen as patterns that can confuse the reader of a model.

B. Focus of this Work with respect to Related Work

In this work, the labels of the model elements are also examined. The focus is on model elements of process diagrams. An explanation of process diagrams can be found at [4]. In addition to previous work in the related literature, the main emphasis of this work can be characterized as follows. Instead of working with data sets from industry, the aim of this paper is to look for BPMN examples on the Web. Existing results of labeling guidelines in literature are taken as a reference. With this as a basis, the Web examples are examined and compared with the given guidelines.

Furthermore, for analyzing the labels, this work does not only consider Activities, Gateways and Events as such, but also explores different types of Activities, Gateways and Events in detail.

III. Preparation of the Work

In order to check how different enterprises, which sell BPMN modelling tools, as well as consultants, provide BPMN diagram examples, the following procedure was executed to get the sample. In the first step, the search term "BPMN" was entered into the search field of Google. This search engine was used as a means to choose the sample. In order to get diagrams first and not descriptions of BPMN, the image result list of the search engine was used. Here, it was expected to get various images of BPMN diagram examples. Once the list of diagram images were generated by the search engine, in the second step the list was manually examined. For each image, it was first of all decided if this image is really a BPMN diagram example in English provided at a Web site or if it is not. If it was indeed such a diagram, then the link to the respective Web site, from which the search engine listed the image, was collected. For this purpose, the link was entered into a file in order to generate a list of Uniform Resource Locator (URL) links. At the end of this URL collection step, a list of URL links, each containing at least one image of a BPMN diagram was collected in the file. In the third step, the file with these links was further examined. For doing this, the file with the URL link list was automatically scanned and each link was grouped to a Web domain.

Afterwards in the fourth step, each link, as well as the additional link to the more general Web domain, was once again examined further. From all these sources, images of BPMN diagram examples were downloaded and collected on the local file system. The aim of this fourth step was to find more BPMN images provided at this Web domain. Much more images were found and collected.

In the fifth step, all these collected images were manually examined and the individual BPMN model elements together with their features and labels for each diagram and domain were transcribed into a database. This data set was then analyzed according to the aim of this work.

In total, 43 Web domains and the BPMN 2.0 by Example document of Object Management Group (OMG) [2] were examined. The BPMN 2.0 by Example document was included, since this is also an important information resource about BPMN on the Web. During this collection phase, images, which were not readable, were filtered out. Images that are used as BPMN counter examples (i.e., how a BPMN diagram should not be modeled) were filtered out too, since the focus is on models that are seen as correct by the provider. The remaining examples, which in total are 346 diagram images of BPMN model examples were used for this work. Furthermore, only distinct labels were analyzed. This should avoid that a certain label pattern appears too often just because the same label (e.g., "order product") is used in many examples.

IV. Labels of Model Elements

In this section, the analyzed distinct labels of Activities, Events and Gateways specified in process model examples on the Web are discussed with respect to the recommendations in literature mentioned in Section II. These model elements are chosen since a) quality guidelines as references already existed in literature and b) introductory examples hardly make sense without them. Especially, this holds for Tasks as a subset of Activity and Events. Gateways on the other hand have to be used as soon as a process model does not have only a single sequence, but the specified process in the process model branches to several paths. Thus, in most process models, except the most trivial once, Gateways are important. Furthermore, these labels are analyzed in detail according to the specific model element, since for different model elements different labeling strategies are needed.

A. Labels of Activities

Activities represent those parts of a process where somebody or something should act in order to progress the process. Therefore, an active verb, which is the best word category for acting, should be used to label these model elements. In literature, the *Verb Object Style* is preferred. An object itself could be a noun (simple ore compound) or a noun phrase.

In the sample, 944 distinct Task labels were found. The majority of these distinct Task labels (74.6 %), which were detected in the diagrams, follow this *Verb Object Style*, where the object is a noun and the direct object of the verb (e.g., "specify vacancy", "ship item", "review results"). In some cases, an article is added (e.g., „select a pizza"). Only in 2.3 % of all cases, a single verb or a verb together with an adverb is the only label for a Task (e.g., "publish", "rate negatively"). 12.9 % of the Task labels extend the suggested *Verb Object Style* a little bit. In these labels, the object is a noun phrase (e.g., "nomination form" in "send nomination form"). Also, cases were found, where the object is an indirect object (e.g. "communicate to customer") or there are two objects (direct and indirect object) following the verb (e.g., "deliver books to customer"). In 10.2 % of the Task labels, the model designers used other label styles for Tasks. For instance, they used nominalization of a verb (e.g., "delivery"), they used full sentences (e.g., "why have you bought so many sticks of sausage?"), they concatenated verbs (e.g., "add paperwork and move package to pick area") or they used a condition phrase ("check if extra insurance is necessary"). It seems that model designers also like to specify many verbs for the label of a Task. To summarize, the *Verb Object Style* preferred in literature is also used in the majority of cases on the Web (Figure 1).

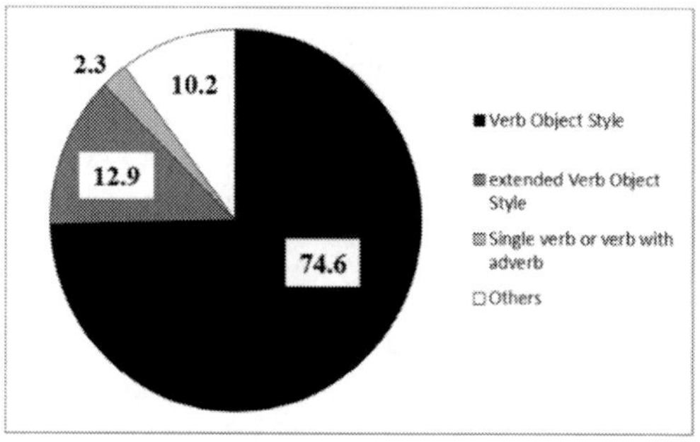

Figure 1. Percentage of Task label styles.

For Sub Processes, the situation is as follows: From the 85 distinct labels of normal Sub Processes, 42.4 % have a nominalization of the verb (e.g., "ordering", "creation") as their label (i.e., *Action Noun Style*). In 55.3 % of the cases, Sub Processes follow the *Verb Object style*. The rest either does not have a label or it is a complex expression (e.g., "send out application forms & reminders"). Hence, no definite labeling preference can be found in these examples from the Web.

There are not enough Event Sub Processes and Transactions in the sample. Therefore, here it is hard to make a good proposition. In these few examples, the labels follow the *Verb Object Style*. There are also not so many Call Activities in order to make a proposition. It could only be observed here that the model designers of the Web examples much more often used a nominalization of a verb rather than the *Verb Object Style*.

B. Relationships between Labels and Specific Task Types

Since about a fifth of all modeled Tasks are modeled as User Tasks, it is interesting what is modeled as a User Task. Especially, it is interesting what is modeled as a User Task in comparison to what is modeled as a Manual Task. Therefore, the labels of the two Tasks are analyzed.

From the point of view of the BPMN specification [1], there is a clear distinction between a User Task and a Manual Task. A User Tasks is performed by a human, but assisted by a business process runtime. A Manual Task is also performed by a human, but without assistance of a business process runtime.

It could be expected that a task that is supported by a system uses other verbs in the label, than a task that is purely done by a human. However, according to the labels it is not always possible to differentiate between a User Task and a Manual Task. Of course, labels with a verb were found that fit with the purpose of a User Task (e.g., "edit 1st level ticket", "fill in purchase form", "book flight", "find student's position"). On the other hand also labels were found, which do not perfectly fit with the purpose of a User Task (e.g., "hire staff", "plan interview", "read book", "rent office", "ship book", "train new employee on job specifics", "discuss nominations", "announce Nobel prices laureate", etc.). The labels for User Tasks and Manual Tasks are set arbitrarily. One interpretation could be that it is the modelers decision to see something as a Manual Task (without process engine support) or a User Task (with process engine support) and it depends on the purpose of the model (i.e., whether it is a workflow model or not). Particularly, a User Task can be more than a simple user interaction with the Information System. Thus, if a workflow for a workflow engine is specified with BPMN then it seems that every Manual Task can also become a User Task. A second interpretation could be that modelers of these introductory learning examples do not really want to distinguish between User Tasks and Manual Tasks at all. Therefore, they prefer to model a User Task even in a situation where a Manual Task would be the right choice.

The frequency of other Task types is very low and, except for Send Tasks, no relationship between labels and these Task types were found. For the 38 distinct labels of Send Tasks, in this sample it turned out that 52.6 % of the distinct Send Task labels start with the verb "send". Further, 26.3 % have a verb like "email", "inform", "notify", "distribute", "post", "submit", "order". All these other label examples can be seen as variants of sending. Thus, it could be concluded that labels of a Send Task are in accordance with the purpose of this Task type.

C. Labels of Events

When talking about labels on Events, firstly, it has to be examined if Events have labels. While BPMN modelers always give labels for Tasks, they are not so systematic if they have to specify labels for Events. From all the Start Events found in the diagrams of the sample, 45.6 % do not have a label. From these, most of the Events (85.7 %) are untyped Events (i.e., Events that are not further classified to be specific types of Events). However, a few cases were also found with Link Events, Message Events and Signal Events that have no label.

For Intermediate Events, fewer cases with no labels exist. Only in 13.7 % of all Intermediate Events no labels were detected. Particularly, the Intermediate Timer Event and Message Event are those types with no labels. These two Event types also had a high frequency within the Intermediate Events types. 37.6 % of all Boundary Events do not have a label. 55.6 % of all End Events do not have a label. From these End Events with no label, 80.8 % are untyped.

To summarize this, for the examples provided on the Web, the modelers responsible for these examples especially do not see the necessity to label Start and End Events. Particularly, this happened if these Start and End Events are untyped Events. Unlabeled model elements, however, cannot be understood well. If novice process modelers see such unlabeled model element examples on the Web, they might take it as a standard although it should be avoided.

After the examination of Events with no labels, it is interesting to see what kind of labels Events have. It is expected that specific Event types have specific types of labels. For example, Message Events and Timer Events are labelled in different ways. For this analysis, six Event types were further examined, since these six Event types cover 87.2 % of all Event types in the sample. These Event types are: Timer Event, Message Event, Signal Event, Compensation Event, Terminate End Event and the untyped Event.

All labels of the Timer Event have, of course, in common that they specify time. However, this is done in various ways. Table I presents a list of representative Timer Event labels. In this list, the grouping of the individual labels, suggests label patterns of similar structure.

TABLE I. TYPICAL LABELS OF TIMER EVENTS

• wait until next business day • 24h; 10 min; 60 minutes; one week; 2 weeks; 24 hours; 14 days; 48-hours • september year n-1 • wait 6 days; wait some time; wait until thursday, 9am • 1st day of month; 20th of each month • 3 business days • friday at 6 pm pacific time; friday, 6 pm pacific time	• timeout; time out (1 week); order timed out • content expired (5 days) • delay 6 days; delay 6 days from announcement • < 60 min; > 60 min • expires at set deadline • auction over • 10 min wait • 12 o'clock • start time; finish time • on next Wednesday • start on Friday • every 10 minuts; every 24 hours

From the examples, it can be seen that they are not in accordance with the Event labeling style recommended in literature (*Verb in Past Participle Style*). Nevertheless in the context of a Timer Event, many of these labels make sense.

For a Message Event, it has to be distinguished between a throwing Message Event and a catching Message Event. Usually, it could be expected that a catching Message Event follows the *Verb in Past Participle Style*. However, the found catching Message Events have a greater variety. Beside the typical *Verb in Past Participle Style* also catching Message Events were found that consists of

- a noun (compound noun) or noun phrase only - i.e., the message (e.g., "payment", "complaints to customer service")
- a complete sentence (e.g., "where is my pizza")
- a verb in past participle only (e.g., "paid").
- a noun with an adjective (e.g., "assignment complete")

Unfortunately, not so much throwing Message Events were found. Most of these throwing Message Events had no label at all. On the basis of the remaining throwing Message Events with labels, it can be said that throwing Message Events use the *Verb Object Style* as it is usual in Task labels. Since a throwing Message Event can be used as an alternative for a Send Task, this label pattern makes sense, although literature recommends the *Verb in Past Participle Style* without considering the specific type of Event.

The found Signal Events (catching or throwing) follow the *Verb in Past Participle Style* to a large extent. Beside this, the following interesting label examples were also found: "on alert", "undeliverable". According to literature, these examples would be out of the scope of the recommendations.

Many of the Compensation Events do not have a label. Those that have a label mainly follow the *Verb Object Style* (e.g., "cancel reservation", "undo book travel"). Many of these labelled Compensation Events are throwing Events. Once again, this is out of scope of the recommendation in the literature, which in general prefers the *Verb in Past Participle Style* for Events. But, in this special case of throwing Events, which rather express an active action than a passive reaction, the *Verb Object Style* makes sense.

Most of the Terminate End Events do not have a label. The few remaining Terminate End Events with labels follow the *Verb in Past Participle Style* or just have the label "terminate" or "end", respectively.

The analysis of untyped Events is split into the analysis of Intermediate Events, Start Events and End Events. No untyped Boundary Events with labels appeared in the sample. This analysis provides the following results. Untyped Intermediate Events follow the *Verb in Past Participle Style*. The labels of untyped Start Events do not only follow this style. Instead, some of them only have

- a noun, compound noun or noun phrase - i.e., the object only (e.g., "application", "existing process"),
- an adjective (e.g., "hungry") or phrases starting with an adjective (e.g., "hungry for pizza"),
- a simple sentence (e.g., "the store opens").

The labels of untyped End Events follow the *Verb in Past Participle Style* to a large extent.

D. *Labels of Gateways*

The labels of Exclusive and Inclusive Gateways vary. The style *Question with Noun and Verb in Past Participle* is not the only one. Again, additional patterns exist: Objects only (i.e., nouns, compound nouns and noun phrases), verb in past participle only, state of an object (i.e., where the state is represented by an adjective or by the word "ok"), comparison with operators (e.g., ">", "<") or with words (e.g., "above"). What is common to many labels is the character "?" at the end of the label. Many Exclusive Gateways and Inclusive Gateways even do not have a label although they branch the process path. Such cases once again can be seen as a contradiction to the recommendations in literature.

Beside the label of the Gateway itself, it is also important to analyze the labels on the Sequence Flows, which leave the Gateways. About a fifth of all these labels have either the value "yes" or "no". The rest varies (e.g., "1";" >=20"; "40 %" "yes"; "2nd level issue"; "50 % education training"; "all items available"; "allow extension"; "bicycle costs >= 500 usd"; "capacity & parts available"; "capacity not available"; "capacity ok"; "employee is ready for work"; "fix in release"; "in stock"; "is junk mail"; "no more responses"; "not accepted"; "payment received == false"; "purchase 1"; "put on hold"; "ready with request"; "simple"). Process Diagrams intended for workflows also have Gateway labels like "${order.price <= 250}" or "${!approved}".

V. Conclusion and Future Work

This paper described how BPMN model examples are presented on the Web. Particularly, three categories of model elements (Activity, Event, and Gateway) and their labels were examined.

In the Web examples, for the labels of atomic Activities called Tasks, there is common consensus to follow the recommended *Verb Object Style,* since the majority of the label examples for model elements on the Web follow this style. For non-atomic Activities (i.e., normal Sub processes), two ways of labeling are preferred: Nominalization of a verb (*Action Noun Style*) and the recommended *Verb Object style*.

In the case of Event types, it turned out that the labeling styles vary depending on the Event type used. Additionally, within the same Event type, variations of labeling styles exist. For some of these labeling strategies, existing literature would even state that these labels have deficiencies. Therefore, it would be good that both providers of such examples and readers of these examples have a more critical look on them. However, it also must be said that some of the label examples for Events (e.g., Timer Event) make sense with respect to the certain type of Event.

If Gateways have a label, then it is quite well understood that a question mark ("?") should close the label, as it is suggested in literature. But, this is the only accordance with literature. Since many of the Gateways do not even have any label, this could be also interpreted that labeling of Gateways for a better understanding of the process paths is not yet understood as an important feature by the community who posts process model examples on the Web. In future, the label quality in other BPMN diagrams, which are provided on the Web, will be examined too.

References

[1] Business Process Model and Notation (BPMN), Version 2.0, OMG Document Number formal/2011-01-03, http://www.omg.org/spec/BPMN/2.0 [retrieved: January 2020].

[2] BPMN 2.0 by Example, Version 1.0 (non-normative), OMG Document Number: dtc/2010-06-02, https://www.omg.org/cgi-bin/doc?dtc/10-06-02.pdf [retrieved: January 2020].

[3] B. Silver, "BPMN method and style," 2nd edition, Aptos: Cody-Cassidy Press, 2009.

[4] https://www.ariscommunity.com/users/roland-woldt/2011-01-28-learning-bpmn-2-which-models-are-available-bpmn [retrieved: January 2020].

[5] I. Moreno-Montes de Oca, M. Snoeck, and H. A. Reijers, "A. Rodriguez-Morffi, A systematic literature review of studies on business process modeling quality," Journal of Information and Software Technology, vol. 58, pp. 187-205, 2015.

[6] J. Mendling, H. A. Reijers, and W. M. P. van der Aalst, "Seven process modeling guidelines (7PMG)," Journal of Information and Software Technology, vol. 52, pp. 127–136, 2010.

[7] A. Koschmider, M. Ullrich, A. Heine, and A. Oberweis, "Revising the Vocabulary of Business Process Element Labels," International Conference on Advanced Information Systems Engineering (CAiSE 2015), Springer LNCS 9097, pp. 69–83, 2015.

[8] H. Leopold, J. Mendling, and H. A. Reijers, "On the automatic labeling of process models," Proceedings of the 23rd International Conference on Advanced Information Systesm Engineering (CAiSE 2011), Springer LNCS 6741, pp. 512–520, 2011.

[9] K. Figl, J. Mendling, and M. Strembeck, "The Influence of Notational Deficiencies on Process Model Comprehension," Journal of the Association for Information Systems, vol. 14 (6), pp. 312–338, 2013.

[10] A. Koschmider, K. Figl, and A. Schoknecht, "A Comprehensive Overview of Visual Design of Process Model Element Labels," Business Process Management Workshops (BPM 2015, 13th International Workshops), Springer LNBIP 256, pp. 571–582, 2015.

[11] H. Leopold, R. H. Eid-Sabbagh, J. Mendling, L. Guerreiro Azevodo, and F. Araujo Baiao, "Detection of naming convention violations in process models for different languages," Decision Support Systems, vol. 56, pp. 310-325, 2013.

[12] H. Leopold, J. Mendling, and O. Günther, "Learning from Quality Issues of BPMN Models from Industry," IEEE Software, July/August 2016, pp. 26–33, 2016.

[13] H. Leopold, H., F. Pittke, and J. Mendling, "Ensuring the Canonicity of process models," Data & Knowledge Engineering, 111, pp. 22–38, 2017.

[14] J. Becker, "Opportunities and Constraints: The Current Struggle with BPMN," Business Process Management Journal, vol. 16 (1), pp. 181–201, 2010.

[15] J. Becker, M. Rosemann, P. Green, and M. Indulska, "Do Ontological Deficiencies in Modeling Grammars Matter?" MIS Quaterly, vol. 35 (1), pp. 57–79, 2011.

[16] BPMN 2.0 Poster available Online: http://www.bpmb.de/images/BPMN2_0_Poster_EN.pdf [retrieved: January 2020].

Swarm Intelligence for Solving a Traveling Salesman Problem

Isabel Kuehner

German Aerospace Center (DLR) Oberpfaffenhofen
Institute of Communications and Navigation
Wessling, Germany
Baden-Wuerttemberg Cooperative State University
Mannheim, Germany
Email: isabel.kuehner@dlr.de

***Abstract*—Learning from the social behavior of animals, like bees or ants, opens the field for Swarm Intelligence (SI) algorithms. They can be applied to solve optimization problems, like the Traveling Salesman Problem (TSP). For SI algorithms, each member of the swarm benefits from the whole swarm and the whole swarm benefits from each individual member. The members communicate either directly or indirectly with each other in order to find an optimal solution. This paper presents an overview of three state-of-the-art SI algorithms, namely, the Ant Colony Optimization (ACO), the Particle Swarm Optimization (PSO), and the Bee Colony Optimization (BCO) for solving a TSP. All three algorithms have been implemented and tested. They have been evaluated with respect to the balance between exploration and exploitation.**

Keywords*—*Swarm Intelligence; Traveling Salesman Problem; Ant Colony Optimization; Particle Swarm Optimization; Bee Colony Optimization.

I. Introduction

Many animal species work and live together in swarms. Insects find their optimal way to a food source by communicating with each other and working together. This observed behavior can be applied to optimization problems, e.g., the Traveling Salesman Problem (TSP). Algorithms have been developed, which simulate the swarm behavior of animals. Such algorithms are categorized as Swarm Intelligence (SI) algorithms.

All SI algorithms have in common that they have to create a balance between exploration and exploitation [1]. Exploration means finding new solutions for a problem. For the TSP, this is realized by creating new paths. Exploitation means the use of currently good solutions, i.e., the use of the best path known at the moment. If the swarm focuses on exploitation, it converges quickly towards a non-optimal solution. Therefore, both aspects, exploration and exploitation need to be balanced [1].

Insects in particular, such as ants, have a great influence on the development of SI algorithms. Their social interactions are a role model for an algorithm called Ant Colony Optimization (ACO) [2]. This algorithm is based on the food searching process of ants by leaving a pheromone trail on their path. Another widespread algorithm in the field of SI is the Particle Swarm Optimization (PSO). It is based on observations of bird flocks and the social interaction between each member of the flock [3]. The third algorithm presented throughout the paper, the Bee Colony Optimization (BCO) algorithm [4], has its origin in the foraging behavior of bees. Honeybees fan out searching for food and communicate their discoveries to the other bees after returning to the hive by means of dancing. All three algorithms have in common that each member of the swarm calculates a solution for the problem. This solution is then compared to the whole swarm or to the direct neighbors of the member. The comparison is either done directly or with indirect communication. The bees' waggle dance is an example for direct communication, whereas ants communicate indirectly by leaving pheromone trails.

The aim of this paper is to introduce the topic of SI, to present the three aforementioned techniques, and to evaluate if they are applicable to solve discrete optimization problems, e.g., the TSP. Furthermore, the importance of exploration and exploitation is highlighted and evaluated. The TSP describes a salesman who wants to visit a specific number of cities and tries to find the shortest way to connect those cities. He wants to visit every city only once. The city where he starts is, moreover, his destination. Throughout this paper, cities are called nodes and the connections between cities are referred to as edges. The edges have different lengths.

All three algorithms have been implemented and tested for the TSP. The experimental results only give an idea how the problem can be solved by the SI algorithms. Those examples are not optimized and better solutions may be possible. In contrast to [5], the experiments focus on the balance between exploration and exploitation. For the evaluation of performance and time efficiency, see [5].

The paper is structured as follows. The ACO algorithm is explained in Section II. Section III focuses on the PSO algorithm. In Section IV, the BCO is presented. The results obtained when applying each of the presented algorithms to a TSP are shown in Section V. The work is concluded in Section VI.

II. Ant Colony Optimization (ACO)

The ACO algorithm is based on the food searching process of ants. While moving, each ant leaves a pheromone trail on its path [6]. Ants communicate indirectly with the other members of the swarm, as information is mediated by the environment. This form of communications is known as stigmergy communication [7]. In the beginning, each individual ant chooses its way randomly. When there are, for instance, two possible ways to a potential food source, one shorter than the other, both paths have the same probability to be chosen. The ants selecting the short path reach the food source earlier than the others. The ants leave pheromones on their path to the food source. They take pieces of the food and bring them back to the nest. If there is much food to gather at the food source and it is good food, the ants leave a trail with more pheromones on their way back [6]. The ants, which chose the long path in the beginning reach the food source later. When returning to the nest, they prefer the path with more pheromones, which is the shorter path. The pheromones on the paths evaporate partly to avoid a convergence of the swarm towards local minima [8]. Nevertheless, the pheromone value on the shorter path is higher than on the longer one. As a result, all ants decide to take the short way in the end [6].

This simplified food searching process is simulated by the ACO algorithm. In the following, this algorithm is explained for an TSP application. For this application, the path is represented by a sequence of nodes, which are connected by edges. The symbols used in the equations are listed in Table I.

TABLE I. Symbols used in the formulas explained in Section II

symbol used	meaning
s	next node
r	current node
u	next possible node
k	ant
$J_{k(r)}$	all nodes that have not been visited yet by ant k
$\tau(r,u)$	pheromone value of an edge between r and u
$\eta(r,u)$	inverse of distance between r and u
β	parameter to manipulate the proportion between distance and pheromone value ($\beta > 0$)
q	random number between [0...1]
q_0	proportion between exploration and exploitation ($0 \leq q_0 \leq 1$)
S	random variable connected to the random-proportional rule
$p_k(r,s)$	probability to choose node s as next node
ρ	pheromone decay parameter for local update ($0 < \rho < 1$)
τ_0	initial pheromone value
α	pheromone decay parameter for global update ($0 < \alpha < 1$)

In the beginning, all edges have the same pheromone value, and each ant chooses its first tour randomly [9].
The ACO is divided into four steps:

1) all ants are planning their tour according to the pheromone value on the path,
2) ants leave pheromones on the path,
3) the pheromone value of the global-best path is updated,
4) the pheromone values on all edges partly evaporate.

Those steps are explained in the following and are visualized in Figure 1.

1) Path Planning: Each ant of the swarm plans its path according to the State Transition Rule

$$s = \begin{cases} \arg\max_{u \in J_{k(r)}} \{[\tau(r,u)] \cdot [\eta(r,u)]^{\beta}\}, \\ \quad \text{if } q \leq q_0 \text{ (exploitation)} \\ S, \quad \text{otherwise (biased exploration)} \end{cases}, \tag{1}$$

where r is the current node of the ant k, s is the next node, and q is calculated randomly [9]. Is q smaller than or equal to q_0, the ant chooses exploitation. Otherwise exploration is chosen. In the case of exploitation, the ant chooses the best path according to the value of pheromones on the edge $\tau(r,u)$ and the length of the distance between the current node r and a possible node u ($\eta(r,u)$). The balance between distance and pheromone value is regulated by β. For all $u \in J_{k(r)}$, i.e., all remaining nodes that have not been visited yet, $\tau(r,u) \cdot \eta(r,u)^{\beta}$ is calculated and the maximum is chosen [9].

If biased exploration is chosen, the next node is selected with the random-proportional rule

$$p_k(r,s) = \begin{cases} \frac{\tau(r,s)\cdot\eta(r,s)^{\beta}}{\sum_{u \in J_{k(r)}} \tau(r,u)\cdot\eta(r,u)^{\beta}} & \text{if } u \in J_{k(r)} \\ 0, & \text{otherwise} \end{cases}, \tag{2}$$

where S represents the result of this random-proportional rule [9]. Equation (2) calculates the probability for each node to be chosen based on the pheromone values on the edges and their length. Short edges with high pheromone values are preferred. For exploration, $\tau(r,s) \cdot \eta(r,s)^{\beta}$ is calculated as well [9]. This results in a weighted value, which includes the pheromone value on the path as well as the length of the path. For this reason, the exploration is referred to as biased exploration [2]. The term is divided by the sum of all $\tau(r,u) \cdot \eta(r,u)^{\beta}$, where u is a possible node that has not been visited yet [9].

After all ants have chosen their tour and have returned to the initial node, the pheromone values are updated.

2) Local Update Rule: While the ants take their tour, they leave pheromones on the path. In analogy to real ants, the values depend on the quality and quantity of the food they encountered. The more and the better the food, the more pheromones they leave [6]. The pheromone value of each edge, which is part of an ant's tour, is updated according to

$$\tau(r,s) = \rho \cdot \Delta\tau(r,s)\,, \tag{3}$$

with $0 \leq \rho \leq 1$ [9]. The value of $\Delta\tau(r,s)$ depends on the implementation [9]. One option is to set it to a const

$$\Delta\tau(r,s) = \tau_0\,. \tag{4}$$

There are other approaches, e.g., using Reinforcement Learning to determine $\Delta\tau(r,s)$ [9]. For the sake of simplicity, the initial pheromone value in (4) is used to update the pheromone values on the ant's path.

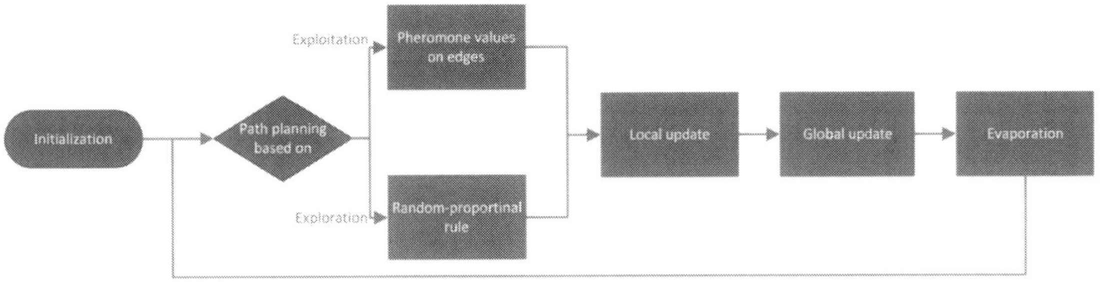

Figure 1. Steps of the ACO algorithm

3) Global Update Rule: After each ant of the swarm has completed its path and updated the pheromone values on the edges it has visited, the global update is performed. Extra pheromones are spread on the globally best tour, i.e., the shortest tour found so far. The shortest tour is identified and the pheromone values of each edge belonging to the globally best path is updated by

$$\tau(r,s) = \alpha \cdot \Delta\tau(r,s)\,, \tag{5}$$

where α is a predefined parameter between 0 and 1 [9].

4) Evaporation: To avoid rapid convergence, parts of the pheromone values evaporate in each iteration. Moreover, this offers the possibility to explore new areas [6]. For each edge, which is updated, the updating rules are modified, so parts of the pheromones evaporate [9]. The global update rule is modified and results in

$$\tau(r,s) = (1-\alpha)\cdot\tau(r,s) + \alpha\cdot\Delta\tau(r,s)\,. \tag{6}$$

An evaporation factor is added to the local update as well,

$$\tau(r,s) = (1-\rho)\cdot\tau(r,s) + \rho\cdot\Delta\tau(r,s)\,. \tag{7}$$

The previously explained steps are iterated for a defined number of iterations.

Besides the TSP application, the ACO has been used in swarm robotics, e.g., for Unmanned Aerial Vehicles (UAVs) [10], or path planning on mobile robots in [11] and [12]. Additionally, the ACO has been applied to load balancing for peer-to-peer networks [13] or fuzzy logic controller [14]. Some variants published over the past few years are summarized in Table II.

TABLE II. ACO VARIANTS

Variant	Summary	Ref.
Inverted ACO (IACO)	inverts effect of pheromones	[13]
ACO Variants Subset Evaluation (AVSE)	finds best solution by comparing solutions of different ACO variants	[14]
Improved ACO (ICMPACO)	divides problem into sub-problems and introduces roles for the ants	[15]
Voronoi-based ACO (V-ACO) (V-ACO)	ACO combined with Voronoi partition with tournament selection method	[16]
Adaptive Continuous Ant Colony Optimization ($AACO_{\mathbb{R}}$)	adaption of evaporation rate based on relative diversity	[17]
Improved Continuous Ant Colony Optimization ($IACO\mathbb{R}$)	success-based random-walk selection (Brownian motion and Lévy flight)	[18]

TABLE III. SYMBOLS USED IN THE FORMULAS EXPLAINED IN SECTION III

symbol used	meaning
$\mathbf{v}_i$	velocity of particle i
c_1, c_2	acceleration coefficients
$\mathbf{R}_1, \mathbf{R}_2$	vector containing random values between $[0...1]$
$\mathbf{p}_i$	personal best position of particle i
$\mathbf{x}_i$	position of particle i
$\mathbf{p}_g$	best position of particles in neighborhood

III. PARTICLE SWARM OPTIMIZATION (PSO)

In contrast to the ACO, which is based on the social behavior of ants, the PSO has its origin in the observation of bird flocks. Imagine a bird flock or a fish school that is moving. Although, there can be hundreds of individuals, the movement of the whole swarm seems as they are one. To achieve this behavior, the individual elements of the swarm interact with their direct neighbors to reach a collective movement. To imitate the aforementioned behavior, the PSO algorithm was developed. The symbols used in equations throughout this section are explained in Table III.

To reach a swarm-like behavior, each individual of the swarm, in the field of PSO called particle, determines the best position with the best fitness. Therefore, it takes its own experience and its neighbors best positions into account. Fitness specifies how good a solution is. The PSO was first mentioned in [3] in the field of simulating bird flocks. For the algorithm presented by the authors, the particles change their position by modifying their velocity in each iteration. The PSO is based on an Adaptive Culture Model mentioned in [19]. It consists of three principles:

- evaluate: the ability to determine if something is good or bad.
- compare: the ability to compare own results with neighbors.
- imitate: the ability to imitate the behavior of superior neighbors .

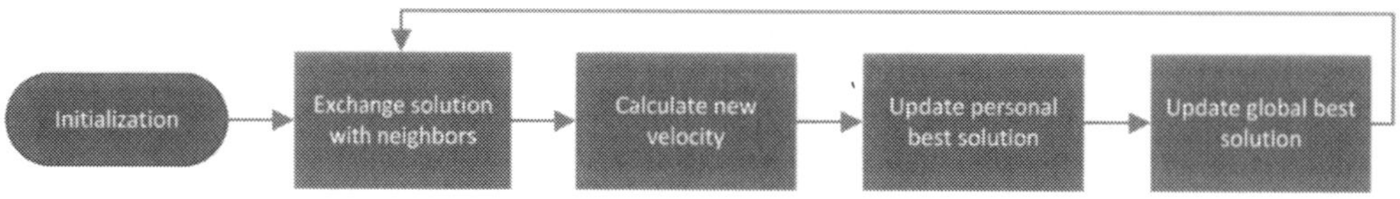

Figure 2. Steps of the PSO algorithm

The steps of the PSO algorithm follow the principles of the Adaptive Culture Model (Figure 2).

In each iteration, all particles of the swarm evaluate their own position. They have a "memory" to store all positions and are able to compare the current position to those stored in the past. The individual particle wants to return to a position that used to be better than the current position [3]. Each particle exchanges its position and their corresponding fitness with its neighbors. The neighborhood can either be the whole swarm, or is limited to a predefined number of nearest members of the swarm [19]. The particle's velocity is then updated according to its own results and its neighbors best positions. The velocity update is calculated by

$$\mathbf{v}_i(t+1) = \mathbf{v}_i(t)+c_1\cdot R_1\otimes(\mathbf{p}_i-\mathbf{x}_i(t))+c_2\cdot R_2\otimes(\mathbf{p}_g-\mathbf{x}_i(t))\,, \tag{8}$$

where $\otimes$ indicates a point-wise vector multiplication. The velocity update can be divided into three parts [6]:

- momentum part
- cognitive part
- social part

The momentum part $\mathbf{v}_i(t)$ specifies the velocity of the particle i of the last iteration. Consequently, the particle stays on track. The cognitive part $c_1\cdot R_1\otimes(\mathbf{p}_i-\mathbf{x}_i(t))$ represents the particle's memory, where $\mathbf{p}_i$ refers to the best position of particle i, $\mathbf{x}_i(t)$ is the current position of i, c_1 is a acceleration coefficient, and $\mathbf{R}_1$ a vector containing random numbers between 0 and 1. The particle tends to go back to better positions it visited in the past. The social part is added by $c_2\cdot\mathbf{R}_2\otimes(\mathbf{p}_g-\mathbf{x}_i(t))$. Here, c_2 is a acceleration coefficient, $\mathbf{R}_2$ refers to vector with a random numbers in the interval $[0..1]$, and $\mathbf{p}_g$ is the best position of a particle in the neighborhood. The social part integrates the neighbors best positions and determines how much the particle is influenced by its neighbors' [6].

Equation (8) is designed for continuous problems, which needs to be adapted to discrete problems, e.g., the TSP. Therefore, the PSO uses permutations. Swap Sequences (SSs) are introduced, which replace velocities. One SS consists of multiple Swap Operators (SOs). A SO contains the information on which nodes are swapped [20]. As an example, a path (a, c, d, e, b) is defined that has been chosen by a particle and an SS $((1,3),(5,2))$. The swaps of all SOs (e.g., $(1,3)$) are performed from left to right. The SO defines the indexes of the elements in the list which are swapped. So, after processing the first SO, the path changes to (d, c, a, e, b). Then, the second swap is performed and the path results in (d, b, a, e, c) [20].

For the TSP, the SS of each particle is updated every iteration according to (8). The difference between the current path of a particle and its personal best path is calculated by an SS. The algorithm searches for all swaps that are needed to transform the current path into the personal best path. The same procedure is followed for the current path and the global best solution. The terms $c_1\cdot\mathbf{R}_1$ and $c_2\cdot\mathbf{R}_2$, respectively, can be replaced by c_1 and c_2. Both variables are random values between 0 and 1 which determine the probability and the tendency to take the personal or global best solution [20].

After updating the velocity, i.e., the SS, the new path $\mathbf{x}_i(t+1)$ is calculated by

$$\mathbf{x}_i(t+1) = \mathbf{x}_i(t) + \mathbf{v}_i(t+1)\,, \tag{9}$$

where $\mathbf{x}_i(t)$ is the path and $\mathbf{v}_i(t+1)$ the velocity [21]. When SSs are utilized, the old path is permuted to compute the new path. Having the new path, the local update is conducted. If the distance of the new path is shorter than the distance of the personal best solution, the personal best path is updated. Furthermore, the new path is compared to the best path on a global level and the global best path is updated if $\mathbf{x}_i(t+1)$ is a better solution. The steps of the PSO are iterated multiple times, so the swarm is able to converge towards a collective solution.

The PSO has a wide range of applications, e.g., tuning of a Proportional-Integral-Derivative (PID) controller [22], or cloud computing [23]. Some variants, which have been published during the last years, are presented in Table IV.

TABLE IV. PSO VARIANTS

Variant	Summary	Reference
Adaptive Learning PSO (ALPSO)	employ Adaptive Learning strategy	[24]
Repository and Mutation based PSO (RMPSO)	introduces repositories for global best and personal best solutions	[25]
Decomposition Cooperative PSO (DCPSO); Merging Cooperative PSO (MCPSO)	assigns sub-swarms to sub-problems (divide-and-conquer)	[26]

IV. BEE COLONY OPTIMIZATION (BCO)

Another algorithm mentioned in the field of SI is the BCO. This algorithm is based on foraging behavior like the ACO [27]. In contrast to ants, honeybees communicate directly with the other members of the swarm. They transmit information without any physical interaction [7]. After the bees have been searching for food, they return to their hive. They dance in order to communicate the location of a food source. With the honeybee's dance, they try to convince the other bees to choose the food source they are advertising [27]. Out of this behavior, an algorithm was designed to solve optimization problems like the TSP. This section focuses on the presentation of the BCO, following the steps of the algorithm visualized in Figure 3.

Each iteration of the algorithm is divided into multiple stages. During each stage, the bees build a partial solution and the following steps are conducted:

1) forward pass,
2) backward pass.

For the TSP application, the number of stages depends on the number of nodes m added to the partial solution during each iteration.

1) Forward Pass: During the forward pass, all bees go out of the hive and each bee builds its own partial solution. For the TSP application, a part of the path is created by adding m nodes [4]. In this implementation, the partial solutions are calculated randomly. After building their partial solution, the bees return to the hive. Then, the backward pass is performed.

2) Backward Pass: For the backward pass, the bees have two options [27]. They can either

- abandon their partial solution (exploitation) or
- dance and advertise their solution to the others (exploration).

If a bee decides to abandon its solution, it exploits the solution of another bee. The shorter the distance of the other bee's partial solution, the more likely the bee chooses this partial solution. After it has made a decision for a partial path, this part is added to the bee's own path [4]. For the TSP, every bee is allowed to visit every city only once. Consequently, it is crucial to check whether the chosen partial solution includes cities that have already been visited. If this is the case, for the implementation presented in this paper, the honeybee returns to its own partial solution.

After conducting forward and backward pass for all stages, a full path has been created. As a next step, the global best path is updated [27]. Therefore, the lengths of the paths of all bees are compared. The global best path is taken into account for the following backward passes and partial solutions of the global best path can also be chosen by the bees. After the global best path has been updated, one iteration is finished. To reach a convergence of the swarm, the steps of the BCO algorithms are iterated for a predefined number of iterations.

Variants of the BCO, e.g., have been employed for a swarm of autonomous drones [28] or path planning [29]. Especially, variants of the Artificial Bee Colony (ABC), which was first introduced in [30], have been published during the past few years. Some of those variants are summarized in Table V. In contrast to the BCO algorithm, the ABC divides the member of the swarm into different groups which perform different tasks.

All three algorithms have been implemented for the TSP and the following section presents the results obtained in experiments for all three algorithms.

TABLE V. BCO VARIANTS

Variant	Summary	Reference
Arrhenius Arrhenius aABC (aABC) (aABC)	position update equation combined with Arrhenius equation	[31]
Lévy Flight ABC (LFABC)	search strategy inspired by Lévy flight search	[32]
ABC with Reinforcement Learning (R-ABC)	reinforcement vector for solution update	[33]
Lbest Gbest ABC (LGABC)	take local best and global best solutions into account	[34]

V. EXPERIMENTAL RESULTS OF THE SI ALGORITHMS FOR THE TSP

The experiments conducted for the three algorithms presented above have a similar setup. Ten nodes are placed randomly on a grid. Those nodes represent the cities for all three algorithms. The distances between the nodes are different. Each algorithm is supposed to find a path which connects all nodes while traveling a minimum distance. The number of iterations has been limited to 200 for each algorithm. Each algorithm has been tested 100 times.

The algorithms have been implemented in Python. Goal of this paper was to test, if it is possible to solve the TSP with each of the algorithms. Therefore, the algorithms have not been implemented with respect to time efficiency and performance. In contrast to [5], the experiments focus on the importance of exploration and exploitation for each algorithm. For the evaluation of performance, see [5].

Table VI summarizes the parameter configuration used for the experiments.

TABLE VI. PARAMETERS USED FOR EXPERIMENTS

ACO		PSO		BCO	
parameter	**value**	**parameter**	**value**	**parameter**	**value**
iterations	200	iterations	200	iterations	200
population	100	population	50	population	100
β	0.7	c_1	0.6	m	3
q_0	0.8	c_2	0.4		
ρ	0.7				
τ_0	10.0				
α	0.9				

For each algorithm, the average length of the path that has been chosen by the swarm is evaluated. As the experiments were repeated 100 times for each algorithm, the path length is averaged over all repetitions. Figure 4 includes the experimental results of all three algorithms. The ACO is visualized in blue, the BCO in red, the PSO in green and the optimal solution in black.

For the ACO algorithm, the swarm consists of 100 ants. In Figure 5, the ants only focus on exploitation. They always choose the path with the highest pheromone value. This leads to a fast convergence of the swarm, but it converges to a local minimum. The swarm agrees on a non-optimal path.

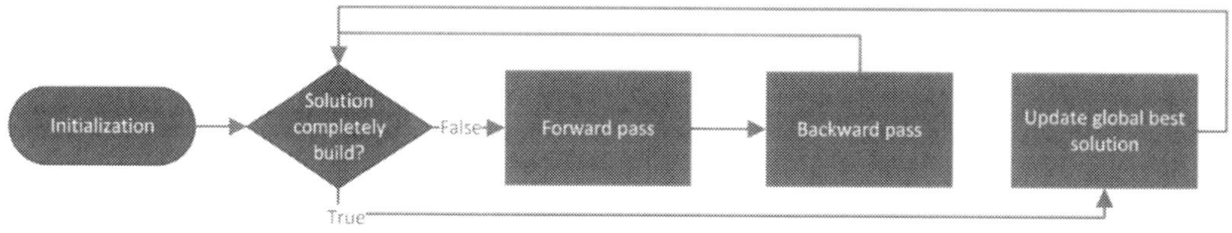

Figure 3. Steps of the BCO algorithm

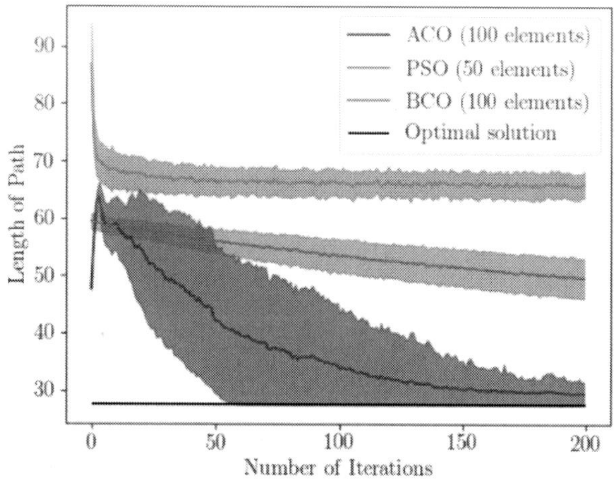

Figure 4. Average length of path by solving the TSP with the ACO (blue), the BCO (red) and the PSO (green)

Figure 4 (blue) shows that better results are obtained if a balance between exploration and exploitation is created. It takes more time until the swarm converges to a solution. However, the swarm's solution is better than the one found by focusing only on exploitation. This experiment shows that the balance between exploration and exploitation is important for SI algorithms.

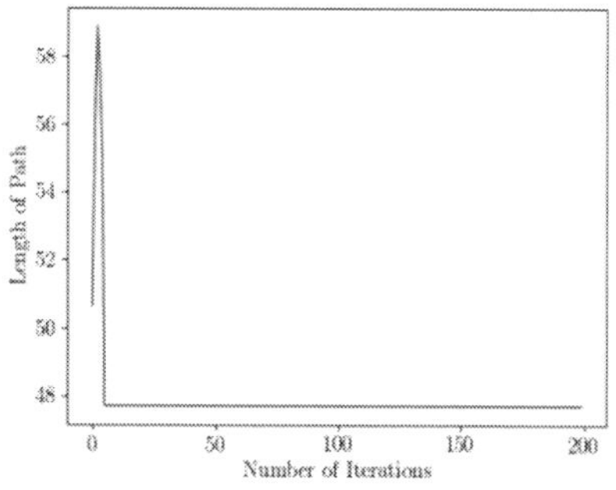

Figure 5. Proportion between exploration and exploitation is $q_0 = 1.0$. The ants choose exploitation with a probability of 100%

The results of the PSO algorithm in Figure 4 (green) are obtained with a swarm of 50 particles. The path length decreases with the number of iterations. The number of total iterations was limited, so the algorithm may have performed better if more iterations would have been allowed. The average path length is decreasing constantly due to an effective balance between exploration and exploitation. The experiments have shown that a large number of particles in the swarm leads to worse results when solving a TSP with PSO.

It is the other way around for the BCO. The more honeybees form the swarm, the better are the experimental results. In Figure 4, the swarm consists of 100 bees and is visualized in red. The advantage of this algorithm is the number of parameters. The user only has to define the size of the partial solutions. The disadvantage, as seen in the graph, is the convergence of the swarm. In contrast to the other algorithms, the length of the paths found decreases rapidly, but in comparison to the other algorithms, towards a non-optimal solution. This means exploitation predominates over exploration.

The experiments have shown that the TSP can be solved by all of the three algorithms. The balance between exploration and exploitation is important. Each algorithm has its advantages and disadvantages. To make a decision which algorithm is used, the number of elements in the swarm plays a role. Moreover, the number of parameters can be an advantage and a disadvantage. On the one hand, tuning takes a lot of time, on the other hand parameters make it possible to apply the algorithm for specific problems. For the TSP application presented in the paper, the ACO algorithm performs best. It includes a weighting of the solutions created by all ants for all iterations. The PSO and the BCO, in contrast, only remember the best solution found. According to the no-free-lunch theorem, it is not possible to favor one of the algorithms over the others for all problems [35]. It is necessary to evaluate each technique for the given application and make the decision which technique to use, based on the problem.

VI. Conclusion and Future Work

All three state-of-the-art SI algorithms are capable to solve a TSP. As PSO was designed for continuous problems, it takes more effort to implement it for discrete problems and the initial algorithm needs to be modified. The other algorithms can be implemented in a straight-forward way for the TSP. For the TSP, ACO performs best, but it depends on the problem, if the algorithms are suitable. Furthermore, exploration and exploitation need to be balanced.

This paper serves as an introduction to SI algorithms. Future work will focus on other applications for SI algorithms. SI algorithms will be implemented and evaluated for board games, in particular for Halma (Chinese Checkers). In this game, each player has 10 or 15 game characters, depending on the number of players. The game characters represent the swarm. For each move, only one game character is allowed to move and the size of the swarm is relatively small. As a result, a combination of the ACO and a modified BCO algorithm is thinkable. The local path of each game character is planned by applying the ACO algorithm. When it is a player's turn, only one game character is allowed to move. The decision which character is chosen is made by the BCO algorithm.

The presented algorithms can also be applied to robotic swarms. For this application, the algorithms can be combined to assign different routes to drones for a disaster management mission.

Acknowledgement

This paper has been written during a cooperative study program at the Baden-Wuerttemberg Cooperative State University Mannheim and the German Aerospace Center (DLR) Oberpfaffenhofen at the Institute of Communications and Navigation.

References

[1] M. Beekman, G. A. Sword, and S. J. Simpson, "Biological foundations of swarm intelligence," in *Swarm Intelligence: Introduction and Applications*, C. Blum and D. Merkle, Eds. Berlin, Heidelberg: Springer Berlin Heidelberg, 2008, pp. 3–41. [Online]. Available: https://doi.org/10.1007/978-3-540-74089-6_1

[2] M. Dorigo, G. D. Caro, and L. M. Gambardella, "Ant algorithms for discrete optimization," *Artificial life*, vol. 5, no. 2, pp. 137–172, 1999.

[3] J. Kennedy and R. Eberhart, "Particle swarm optimization," in *Proceedings of ICNN'95 - International Conference on Neural Networks*, vol. 4, 11 1995, pp. 1942–1948.

[4] D. Teodorović, "Bee colony optimization (bco)," in *Innovations in Swarm Intelligence*, C. P. Lim, L. C. Jain, and S. Dehuri, Eds. Berlin, Heidelberg: Springer Berlin Heidelberg, 2009, pp. 39–60. [Online]. Available: https://doi.org/10.1007/978-3-642-04225-6_3

[5] J. Odili, M. N. M. Kahar, A. Noraziah, and S. F. Kamarulzaman, "A comparative evaluation of swarm intelligence techniques for solving combinatorial optimization problems," *International Journal of Advanced Robotic Systems*, vol. 14, no. 3, p. 1729881417705969, 2017.

[6] C. Blum and X. Li, "Swarm intelligence in optimization," in *Swarm Intelligence: Introduction and Applications*, C. Blum and D. Merkle, Eds. Berlin, Heidelberg: Springer Berlin Heidelberg, 2008, pp. 43–85. [Online]. Available: https://doi.org/10.1007/978-3-540-74089-6_2

[7] V. Trianni, *Evolutionary swarm robotics: evolving self-organising behaviours in groups of autonomous robots*. Springer, 2008, vol. 108.

[8] M. Dorigo and T. Stützle, *Ant Colony Optimization*. Cambridge : MIT Press, 2004.

[9] M. Dorigo and L. M. Gambardella, "Ant colony system: a cooperative learning approach to the traveling salesman problem," *IEEE Transactions on evolutionary computation*, vol. 1, no. 1, pp. 53–66, 1997.

[10] Z. Ziyang, Z. Ping, X. Yixuan, and J. Yuxuan, "Distributed intelligent self-organized mission planning of multi-uav for dynamic targets cooperative search-attack," *Chinese Journal of Aeronautics*, vol. 32, no. 12, pp. 2706–2716, 2019.

[11] Y. Liu, J. Ma, S. Zang, and Y. Min, "Dynamic path planning of mobile robot based on improved ant colony optimization algorithm," in *Proceedings of the 2019 8th International Conference on Networks, Communication and Computing*, 2019, pp. 248–252.

[12] R. Uriol and A. Moran, "Mobile robot path planning in complex environments using ant colony optimization algorithm," in *2017 3rd international conference on control, automation and robotics (ICCAR)*. IEEE, 2017, pp. 15–21.

[13] S. Asghari and N. J. Navimipour, "Resource discovery in the peer to peer networks using an inverted ant colony optimization algorithm," *Peer-to-Peer Networking and Applications*, vol. 12, no. 1, pp. 129–142, 2019.

[14] O. Castillo, E. Lizárraga, J. Soria, P. Melin, and F. Valdez, "New approach using ant colony optimization with ant set partition for fuzzy control design applied to the ball and beam system," *Information Sciences*, vol. 294, pp. 203–215, 2015.

[15] W. Deng, J. Xu, and H. Zhao, "An improved ant colony optimization algorithm based on hybrid strategies for scheduling problem," *IEEE access*, vol. 7, pp. 20 281–20 292, 2019.

[16] C. Xiong, D. Chen, D. Lu, Z. Zeng, and L. Lian, "Path planning of multiple autonomous marine vehicles for adaptive sampling using voronoi-based ant colony optimization," *Robotics and Autonomous Systems*, vol. 115, pp. 90 – 103, 2019. [Online]. Available: http://www.sciencedirect.com/science/article/pii/S0921889018304469

[17] M. Omran and R. Polakova, "A memetic and adaptive continuous ant colony optimization algorithm," in *International Conference on Theory and Application of Soft Computing, Computing with Words and Perceptions*. Springer, 2019, pp. 158–166.

[18] M. G. Omran and S. Al-Sharhan, "Improved continuous ant colony optimization algorithms for real-world engineering optimization problems," *Engineering Applications of Artificial Intelligence*, vol. 85, pp. 818–829, 2019.

[19] J. Kennedy, R. C. Eberhart, and Y. Shi, *Swarm intelligence*, ser. The Morgan Kaufmann series in evolutionary computation. San Francisco [u.a.] Morgan Kaufmann, 2009.

[20] K.-P. Wang, L. Huang, C.-G. Zhou, and W. Pang, "Particle swarm optimization for traveling salesman problem," in *Proceedings of the 2003 International Conference on Machine Learning and Cybernetics (IEEE Cat. No.03EX693)*, vol. 3, 11 2003, pp. 1583–1585.

[21] I. Khan, S. Pal, and M. K. Maiti, "A modified particle swarm optimization algorithm for solving traveling salesman problem with imprecise cost matrix," in *2018 4th International Conference on Recent Advances in Information Technology (RAIT)*. IEEE, 2018, pp. 1–8.

[22] S. Momani, R. El-Khazali, and I. M. Batiha, "Tuning pid and piλdλ controllers using particle swarm optimization algorithm via el-khazali's approach," vol. 2172, no. 1, p. 050003, 2019.

[23] A. Naseri and N. J. Navimipour, "A new agent-based method for qos-aware cloud service composition using particle swarm optimization algorithm," *Journal of Ambient Intelligence and Humanized Computing*, vol. 10, no. 5, pp. 1851–1864, 2019.

[24] F. Wang, H. Zhang, K. Li, Z. Lin, J. Yang, and X.-L. Shen, "A hybrid particle swarm optimization algorithm using adaptive learning strategy," *Information Sciences*, vol. 436-437, pp. 162 – 177, 2018. [Online]. Available: http://www.sciencedirect.com/science/article/pii/S0020025518300380

[25] B. Jana, S. Mitra, and S. Acharyya, "Repository and mutation based particle swarm optimization (rmpso): A new pso variant applied to reconstruction of gene regulatory network," *Applied Soft Computing*, vol. 74, pp. 330–355, 2019.

[26] J. Douglas, A. Engelbrecht, and B. Ombuki-Berman, "Merging and decomposition variants of cooperative particle swarm optimization: New algorithms for large scale optimization problems," in *Proceedings of the 2nd International Conference on Intelligent Systems, Metaheuristics & Swarm Intelligence*, 2018, pp. 70–77.

[27] K. Diwold, M. Beekman, and M. Middendorf, "Honeybee optimisation – an overview and a new bee inspired optimisation scheme," in *Handbook of Swarm Intelligence: Concepts, Principles and Applications*, B. K. Panigrahi, Y. Shi, and M.-H. Lim, Eds. Berlin, Heidelberg: Springer Berlin Heidelberg, 2011, pp. 295–327. [Online]. Available: https://doi.org/10.1007/978-3-642-17390-5_13

[28] A. Viseras, T. Wiedemann, C. Manß, V. Karolj, D. Shutin, and J. M. Gomez, "Beehive inspired information gathering with a swarm of autonomous drones," *Sensors*, October 2019. [Online]. Available: https://elib.dlr.de/129660/

[29] Z. Li, Z. Zhang, H. Liu, and L. Yang, "A new path planning method based on concave polygon convex decomposition and artificial bee colony algorithm," *International Journal of Advanced Robotic Systems*, 2020. [Online]. Available: https://doi.org/10.1177/1729881419894787

[30] D. Karaboga, "An idea based on honey bee swarm for numerical optimization, technical report - tr06," *Technical Report, Erciyes University*, 01 2005.

[31] S. Kumar, A. Nayyar, and R. Kumari, "Arrhenius artificial bee colony algorithm," in *International conference on innovative computing and communications*. Springer, 2019, pp. 187–195.

[32] H. Sharma, J. C. Bansal, K. Arya, and X.-S. Yang, "Lévy flight artificial bee colony algorithm," *International Journal of Systems Science*, vol. 47, no. 11, pp. 2652–2670, 2016.

[33] S. Fairee, S. Prom-On, and B. Sirinaovakul, "Reinforcement learning for solution updating in artificial bee colony," *PloS one*, vol. 13, no. 7, 2018.

[34] H. Sharma, S. Sharma, and S. Kumar, "Lbest gbest artificial bee colony algorithm," in *2016 International conference on advances in computing, communications and informatics (ICACCI)*. IEEE, 2016, pp. 893–898.

[35] D. H. Wolpert and W. G. Macready, "No free lunch theorems for optimization," *IEEE transactions on evolutionary computation*, vol. 1, no. 1, pp. 67–82, 1997.

Extending ASP Based Reasoning to Expressive Constructive Description Logics

Loris Bozzato

Fondazione Bruno Kessler,
Trento, Italy
Email: bozzato@fbk.eu

Abstract—**Constructive description logics provide different interpretations of description logics under constructive semantics. While several constructive semantics for description logics have been proposed, such logics have been mostly studied from the point of view of their formal properties. Practical applications of these logics have been proposed, but there has been no effort in applying them in general in knowledge representation and Semantic Web languages and tools (i.e., the distinctive applications of description logics). In our recent work, we started to address this aspect: we introduced a constructive semantics for the description logic $\mathcal{EL}$ and we established formal results that link this constructive interpretation to answer set semantics. On the base of these results, we presented a datalog translation reasoning on one aspect of such semantics (the generation of information terms of a knowledge base) and an implementation using Semantic Web ontologies and "off the shelf" tools. In this paper, we want to highlight this line of research and its possibilities and the challenges in extending this work to more expressive description logics.**

Keywords–Constructive description logics; Information terms semantics; Answer Set Programming.

I. Introduction

Constructive description logics are interpretations of Description Logics (DLs) under different constructive semantics: the definition of such non-classical semantics for description logics is motivated by the interest in applying their formal properties to solve problems in representation of knowledge or reasoning. Starting from different constructive semantics, several constructive description logics have been proposed, e.g., [1]–[3]. Constructive description logics have been mostly studied from the point of view of their formal properties. However, there have been not many studies for their practical application to knowledge representation and Semantic Web languages and tools. On the other hand, different "real world" uses of constructive description logics in applications and systems have been proposed, for example in managing conflicts over legal ontologies [4], reasoning over incomplete data streams [5], and a framework for the composition of semantic services in heterogeneous domains [6] (based on [7]).

In our recent work [8], we proposed a direction for reducing the gap across the formal and practical aspects of constructive description logics. From the theoretical point of view, we introduced a minimal constructive description logic based on $\mathcal{EL}$ and we extended to its semantics formal results linking it to *Answer Set Programming (ASP)*. On the practical side, by taking advantage of such relation, we presented a datalog encoding managing one task over the constructive semantics (namely, the generation of valid "states" of a knowledge base) and we provided a prototype based on the standard *OWL EL (Web Ontology Language, EL profile)* and "off the shelf" tools.

In [8], we chose to concentrate on $\mathcal{EL}$, since it is one of the simplest description logics over which semantics enjoying constructive properties can be defined (cfr. *explicit definability* property [2]). Moreover, $\mathcal{EL}$ is recognized in applications as one of the reference languages for (low complexity) description logics (e.g., it is at the base of the OWL-EL profile).

We considered the task of the generation of valid *Information Terms (IT)* for a given knowledge base. Intuitively, in *information terms semantics* [2][9] the information terms are syntactical objects that provide a constructive justification for the classical truth of a formula. Information terms have been used to represent the *state* or *answer* of a formula: thus, generating information terms for a knowledge base corresponds to *validate* its contents by generating a set of its possible "snapshots" representing valid states. In particular, the solution in [8] follows the direction studied in [10], where the relation across information terms and answer set semantics has been first studied over propositional theories. In fact, we remark that [8] extends for the first time the study of these relations also in the context of constructive description logics.

Thus, from the formal point of view, the work in [8] can be seen as a starting point for the study of the connection across constructive semantics and answer set semantics on the very simple description logic $\mathcal{EL}$, positioning it as a base for extending the results over more expressive description logics by "pushing the envelope" towards more expressive languages.

In this position paper, we want to highlight this line of research and report the challenges in extending the current proposal to more expressive description logics. Indeed, while this would further move this approach closer to KR applications, the extension to expressive description logics constructs requires non-trivial formal work for the formulation of the relation between constructive semantics and ASP. Moreover, for the practical applicability of the approach, it is required to study efficient extensions of the ASP encoding.

In the following (in Section II), we summarize the most important aspects of the current work in this research direction. In Section III we discuss the challenges for future work.

II. Summary of Current Work

In [8], we introduced the logic $\mathcal{EL}c$, a constructive interpretation of $\mathcal{EL}$ under an information terms semantics. $\mathcal{EL}c$ is a restriction to the syntax of $\mathcal{EL}$ of the basic constructive description logic $\mathcal{BCDL}$ [2][9]. With respect to the language, in order to simplify the definition of the semantics, in [8] we use a restricted form of subsumption $G \sqsubseteq A$ (denoted $\forall_G A$) where G is a *generator* (i.e., a fixed set of individuals). Moreover, the $\top$ operator is also limited to a fixed set $\mathcal{N}$ of objects. In the IT semantics, an information term η for a formula K is a syntactical object that provides a constructive *justification* for the truth of K in a classical model $\mathcal{M}$. For example, in a knowledge base of food and wines, the validity of a formula $\exists hasColor.Color(barolo)$ in a classical model $\mathcal{M}$ can be explained by an information term $(red, \texttt{tt})$, where red is a valid role filler such that $hasColor(barolo, red)$ holds in $\mathcal{M}$ and $\texttt{tt}$ is a (constant) information term inductively justifying the atomic formula $Color(red)$. This semantics is particularly interesting since, as studied in [2], the resulting *realizability relation* $\mathcal{M} \rhd \langle\eta\rangle K$ provides a constructive consequence that can be related to the *proofs-as-programs* paradigm.

Following the direction of [10], in our work we then provide formal results establishing a relation between answer sets for formulas in $\mathcal{EL}$ and for their information terms. In particular, we can show that (minimal) information terms for a set Γ of $\mathcal{EL}$ formulas can be obtained by computing the answer sets of input formulas in Γ. The relation can be established by recognizing that answer sets for a formula K correspond to $\texttt{ans}(\langle\eta\rangle K)$, the "answers" of the *piece of information* $\langle\eta\rangle K$, composed by the minimal set of facts needed to justify $\langle\eta\rangle K$.

Using this correspondence, in [8] we provide two different datalog rewritings for the generation of the sets of information terms of an input $\mathcal{EL}$ knowledge base. The first is limited to the case in which the set of role assertions is "complete", while the second provides a way of generating existential fillers. The encodings have been implemented in Asp-it [11], a prototype for an information terms generator for OWL EL ontologies: Asp-it applies the presented rewritings to the input ontology by interacting with the DLV solver and the resulting information terms are returned as annotations to the OWL axioms.

III. Discussion

For continuing this line of study, we can identify several parallel challenges that need to be considered:

Extension to unrestricted subsumption and $\top$. The first possible extension stands in the adoption in $\mathcal{EL}c$ of all standard elements of the $\mathcal{EL}$ language, which have been restricted to facilitate the definition of the constructive semantics. As discussed in [2], the limited form of subsumption $\forall_G A$ in $\mathcal{EL}c$ can be extended to consider general inclusions in the constructive semantics. However, it still need to be formally verified if the relation with ASP semantics can be extended to such general definition of subsumption. Similarly, allowing an unrestricted use of the $\top$ operator is non-trivial, due to the need to identify individuals in the definition of the IT semantics.

Semantic extension to expressive DL operators. A first step towards extending the approach to more expressive DLs is to introduce negation and falsum. Following [10], negative information can be represented similarly to default negation in logic programming: negative formulas are used as constraints and answer sets are formulated over a suitable positive *reduction* of the input formulas. This leads to a partition of answers for a piece of information $\texttt{ans}(\langle\eta\rangle K)$ in the *positive* and *negative answers*, corresponding to positive and negative literals in the set: if the former correspond to "answers" of the piece of information, the latter represent the "constraints" that such positive answers must respect. Thus, the extension to $\mathcal{ALC}$ (corresponding to the $\mathcal{BCDL}$ logic [2]) is already challenging in establishing the correspondence results across answers sets of formulas and answers of pieces of information by considering the negative constraints. Following the approach of [10], we need to provide a definition of reduction to positive formulas in presence of negation and, on the other side, extend this notion to answers of pieces of information. Moreover, extending our semantics to expressive DL operators (e.g., to all operators of OWL, i.e., to $\mathcal{SROIQ}$) poses the question of providing a faithful IT interpretation for such operators.

ASP translation extension to expressive DLs. Clearly, the extension of the correspondence results to more expressive DLs can provide the base for extending the proposed ASP encoding. On the other hand, as already noted in [8], further study is already needed in the $\mathcal{EL}$ encoding to limit "combinatorial explosion" of the number of the models due to the generation of all admitted combinations of fillers for existential formulas. A possible direction in this regard is to study connections with existential extensions of datalog adding further constraints to limit the generation only to meaningful models.

Further reasoning tasks: manipulation of ITs. While the generation of information terms is a basic task for IT semantics, it only represents a first step towards the use of constructive description logics in practical applications. One fundamental direction (which is also related to the interesting relation of such semantics to the *proofs-as-programs* paradigm) would be to develop and integrate procedures that are able to manipulate the computed information terms. In this regard, a possibility is to study the applicability of this work in conjunction to the Semantic Web service composition calculus based on $\mathcal{BCDL}$ presented in [7].

Implementation and application to real use cases. Finally, another direction stands in the implementation of reasoning tasks and datalog encodings in available tools and languages in order to provide new tools for reasoning over constructive DLs. In this regard, it will be interesting to identify real use cases where the reasoning tasks can be applied and test the procedures over KBs based on well-known ontologies.

References

[1] L. Bozzato, M. Ferrari, C. Fiorentini, and G. Fiorino, "A decidable constructive description logic," in JELIA 2010, ser. LNCS, vol. 6341. Springer, 2010, pp. 51–63.

[2] M. Ferrari, C. Fiorentini, and G. Fiorino, "$\mathcal{BCDL}$: basic constructive description logic," JAR, vol. 44, no. 4, 2010, pp. 371–399.

[3] M. Mendler and S. Scheele, "Towards Constructive DL for Abstraction and Refinement," JAR, vol. 44, no. 3, 2010, pp. 207–243.

[4] E. H. Haeusler, V. de Paiva, and A. Rademaker, "Intuitionistic description logic and legal reasoning," in DEXA 2011 Workshops. IEEE Computer Society, 2011, pp. 345–349.

[5] M. Mendler and S. Scheele, "Towards a type system for semantic streams," in SR2009 - Stream Reasoning Workshop (ESWC 2009), ser. CEUR-WP, vol. 466. CEUR-WS.org, 2009.

[6] M. Hilia, A. Chibani, K. Djouani, and Y. Amirat, "Semantic service composition framework for multidomain ubiquitous computing applications," in ICSOC 2012, ser. LNCS, vol. 7636. Springer, 2012, pp. 450–467.

[7] L. Bozzato and M. Ferrari, "Composition of semantic web services in a constructive description logic," in RR2010, ser. LNCS, vol. 6333. Springer, 2010, pp. 223–226.

[8] L. Bozzato, "ASP based generation of information terms for constructive $\mathcal{EL}$," Fundam. Inform., vol. 161, no. 1-2, 2018, pp. 29–51.

[9] L. Bozzato, M. Ferrari, C. Fiorentini, and G. Fiorino, "A constructive semantics for $\mathcal{ALC}$," in DL2007, ser. CEUR-WP, vol. 250. CEUR-WS.org, 2007, pp. 219–226.

[10] C. Fiorentini and M. Ornaghi, "Answer set semantics vs. information term semantics," in ASP2007: Answer Set Programming, Advances in Theory and Implementation, 2007.

[11] "Asp-it: ASP based information terms generator," 2016, URL: https://github.com/dkmfbk/asp-it [accessed: 2020-01-31].

Acceleration Technique of Two-Phase Quasi-Newton Method with Momentum for Optimization Problems

Mastiyage Don Sudeera Hasaranga Gunathilaka, Shahrzad Mahboubi and Hiroshi Ninomiya
Shonan Institute of Technology
1-1-25 Tsujido-nishikaigan, Fujisawa, Kanagawa, 251-8511 Japan
Email: fujisanjp@live.com, 18T2012@shonan-it.ac.jp and ninomiya@info.shonan-it.ac.jp

Abstract—**This paper describes a novel acceleration technique of the Two-Phase Quasi-Newton method using momentum terms for optimization problems. The performance of the proposed algorithm is evaluated on an unconstrained optimization problem in neural network training. The results show that the proposed algorithm has a much faster convergence than the conventional Two-Phase Quasi-Newton method.**

Keywords–neural networks; training algorithm; Two-Phase Quasi-Newton method; Nesterov's accelerated gradient; momentum terms.

I. INTRODUCTION

From the past to the recent years, much research has been conducted to improve the accuracy and speed of optimization for various problems. Neural Network (NN) training has a high performance when it comes to an unconstrained optimization problem. However, this ability highly depends on the training algorithm used in NNs. In this research, we aimed at constructing a training algorithm with higher performance and higher speed. Many algorithms have been proposed for this research task. In this paper, we consider the optimization problem of

$$\min_{\mathbf{w}\in R^n} E(\mathbf{w}), \tag{1}$$

where $\mathbf{w}$ and $E(\mathbf{w})$ denote the parameter and the objective function, respectively. Optimization problems have been solved with high precision by algorithms based on quadratic convergence characteristics, such as Newton or Quasi-Newton (QN) methods. This is because a solution can be obtained fast and with higher accuracy than algorithms with first-order convergence characteristics [1].

In recent years, for further acceleration and accurate optimization, the Two-Phase Newton method, which is based on third-order approximation, has been proposed [2]. However, this method requires a Hessian of (1) and matrix solutions for each iteration. Therefore, the Two-Phase Newton method takes time to derive a solution. To deal with this problem, the Two-Phase Quasi-Newton (Two-Phase QN) method has been proposed, in which the inverse Hessian is approximated by the gradient of (1) using an iterative formula [3]. This method is more effective for the unconstrained optimization problems, such as (1), than conventional algorithms. On the other hand, the acceleration of the standard QN with momentum terms was proposed as Nesterov's Accelerated Quasi-Newton (NAQ) method [4]. NAQ succeeded in drastically reducing the number of iterations and computational time compared to QN.

In this research, a new Quasi-Newton algorithm based on the third-order approximation is proposed for the acceleration of Two-Phase QN incorporating the momentum terms in the same way as NAQ. This method is referred to as Two-Phase Nesterov's Accelerated Quasi-Newton (Two-Phase NAQ) method. In this paper, the performance of the proposed algorithm is demonstrated through computer simulations using NN training for a simple unconstrained optimization problem and compared with the conventional method.

The contents of this paper are structured as follows: Section II introduces the conventional algorithms, such as Two-Phase Newton and Two-Phase QN. Section III proposes the novel algorithm, Two-Phase NAQ, which is the acceleration method of Two-Phase QN by introducing the momentum term. Section IV provides simulation results to demonstrate the validity of the proposed Two-Phase NAQ. Section V concludes this paper and describes future works.

II. TWO-PHASE QUASI-NEWTON METHOD

The Two-Phase Newton method for optimization utilizes the gradient and Hessian of the objective function to result in the third-order approximation [2]. The iterative formulae of Two-Phase Newton are defined using the two-phase update scheme of the parameters (2) and (3).

$$\mathbf{z}_k = \mathbf{w}_k - \overline{\alpha}_k\left[\mathscr{H}(\mathbf{w}_k)\right]^{-1}\nabla E(\mathbf{w}_k), \tag{2}$$

$$\mathbf{w}_{k+1} = \mathbf{w}_k - \alpha_k\left[(1/2)\left(\mathscr{H}(\mathbf{w}_k) + \mathscr{H}(\mathbf{z}_k)\right)\right]^{-1}\nabla E(\mathbf{w}_k). \tag{3}$$

where $\nabla E(\mathbf{w}_k)$ and $\mathscr{H}(\mathbf{w}_k)$ are the gradient and the Hessian of (1). α_k and $\overline{\alpha}_k$ are the stepsizes at $\mathbf{w}_k$ and $\mathbf{z}_k$ along the directions $[\mathscr{H}(\mathbf{w}_k)]^{-1}\nabla E(\mathbf{w}_k)$ and $[(1/2)(\mathscr{H}(\mathbf{w}_k) + \mathscr{H}(\mathbf{z}_k))]^{-1}\nabla E(\mathbf{w}_k)$, respectively. Two-Phase Newton needs to calculate the Hessian and its inverse. Therefore, Two-Phase QN was proposed to reduce these computational costs by the approximation of the inverse Hessian using Broyden-Fletcher-Goldfarb-Shanno (BFGS) formulae [3] of QN. Actually, $\mathbf{H}(\mathbf{z}_k)$ which is the approximated inverse Hessian of $\mathscr{H}(\mathbf{z}_k)^{-1}$, is obtained by

$$\mathbf{H}(\mathbf{z}_k) = \left(\mathbf{I} - \frac{\mathbf{s}_k\mathbf{y}_k^{\mathrm{T}}}{\mathbf{y}_k^{\mathrm{T}}\mathbf{s}_k}\right)\mathbf{H}_k\left(\mathbf{I} - \frac{\mathbf{y}_k\mathbf{s}_k^{\mathrm{T}}}{\mathbf{y}_k^{\mathrm{T}}\mathbf{s}_k}\right) + \frac{\mathbf{s}_k\mathbf{s}_k^{\mathrm{T}}}{\mathbf{y}_k^{\mathrm{T}}\mathbf{s}_k}, \tag{4}$$

where $\mathbf{s}_k = \mathbf{z}_k - \mathbf{w}_k$ and $\mathbf{y}_k = \nabla E(\mathbf{z}_k) - \nabla E(\mathbf{w}_k)$. As a result, the iteration formulae of Two-Phase QN is shown as (5) and (6) based on [3].

$$\mathbf{z}_k = \mathbf{w}_k - \overline{\alpha}_k\mathbf{H}_k\nabla E(\mathbf{w}_k), \tag{5}$$

$$\mathbf{w}_{k+1} = \mathbf{w}_k - \alpha_k\mathbf{H}_{k+1}\nabla E(\mathbf{w}_k), \tag{6}$$

where $\mathbf{H}_{k+1}$ is calculated by

$$\mathbf{H}_{k+1} = \lambda\mathbf{H}_k + (1-\lambda)\mathbf{H}(\mathbf{z}_k). \tag{7}$$

III. Proposed Algorithm - Two-Phase Nesterov's Accelerated Quasi-Newton Method

In this section, the Two-Phase NAQ is proposed. Two-Phase QN is accelerated by using the momentum acceleration technique in the same way as NAQ. Specifically, Two-Phase NAQ is derived by the third-order approximation of (1) around $\mathbf{w}_k+\mu_k\mathbf{v}_k$, whereas (1) was approximated around $\mathbf{w}_k$ in Two-Phase QN [3]. The proposed method drastically improves the convergence speed of Two-Phase QN using the gradient vector at $\mathbf{w}_k+\mu_k\mathbf{v}_k$ of $\nabla E(\mathbf{w}_k+\mu_k\mathbf{v}_k)$ called Nesterov's accelerated gradient vector [4]. The iterative formulae of the proposed Two-Phase NAQ are defined as

$$\hat{\mathbf{z}}_k = \mathbf{w}_k + \mu_k\mathbf{v}_k - \overline{\alpha}_k\hat{\mathbf{H}}_k\nabla E(\mathbf{w}_k + \mu_k\mathbf{v}_k), \quad (8)$$

$$\mathbf{w}_{k+1} = \mathbf{w}_k + \mu_k\mathbf{v}_k - \alpha_k\hat{\mathbf{H}}_{k+1}\nabla E(\mathbf{w}_k + \mu_k\mathbf{v}_k), \quad (9)$$

where, $\mu_k\mathbf{v}_k$ is the momentum term, in which $\mathbf{v}_k = \mathbf{w}_k - \mathbf{w}_{k-1}$ and μ_k is the momentum coefficient. In (8), $\hat{\mathbf{z}}_k$ denotes the middle-step suggested by the two-phase technique, in order to accelerate using the third-order approximation. (9) is considered as Two-Phase Newton method with the momentum term. The $\hat{\mathbf{H}}_k$ matrix is iteratively updated by

$$\hat{\mathbf{H}}_{k+1} = \lambda\hat{\mathbf{H}}_k + (1-\lambda)\hat{\mathbf{H}}(\hat{\mathbf{z}}_k), \quad (10)$$

Here, $\hat{\mathbf{H}}(\hat{\mathbf{z}}_k)$ is iteratively approximated by (11).

$$\hat{\mathbf{H}}(\hat{\mathbf{z}}_k) = \left(\mathbf{I} - \frac{\mathbf{p}_k\mathbf{q}_k^{\mathrm{T}}}{\mathbf{q}_k^{\mathrm{T}}\mathbf{p}_k}\right)\hat{\mathbf{H}}_k\left(\mathbf{I} - \frac{\mathbf{q}_k\mathbf{p}_k^{\mathrm{T}}}{\mathbf{q}_k^{\mathrm{T}}\mathbf{p}_k}\right) + \frac{\mathbf{p}_k\mathbf{p}_k^{\mathrm{T}}}{\mathbf{q}_k^{\mathrm{T}}\mathbf{p}_k}. \quad (11)$$

where, $\mathbf{p}_k = \hat{\mathbf{z}}_k - (\mathbf{w}_k+\mu_k\mathbf{v}_k)$ and $\mathbf{q}_k = \nabla E(\hat{\mathbf{z}}_k) - \nabla E(\mathbf{w}_k+\mu_k\mathbf{v}_k)$. In this paper, the momentum coefficient μ_k is set to the adaptive scheme suggested in [4]. The algorithm of Two-Phase NAQ is illustrated in Figure 1. In this research, λ is set to 0.5.

1. $k = 1$;
2. Initialize $\mathbf{w}_k$= random$[-0.5, 0.5]$, $\hat{\mathbf{H}}_k$ and $\hat{\mathbf{H}}(\hat{\mathbf{z}}_k) = \mathbf{I}$ (unit matrix) and $\mathbf{v}_k = \mathbf{0}$;
3. **While**($||\nabla E(\mathbf{w}_k)|| > \epsilon$ and $k < k_{max}$)
   (a) Update μ_k;
   (b) Calculate $\nabla E(\mathbf{w}_k + \mu_k\mathbf{v}_k)$;
   (c) Update $\hat{\mathbf{z}}_k$ using (8);
   (d) Calculate $\nabla E(\hat{\mathbf{z}}_k)$;
   (e) Update $\hat{\mathbf{H}}_{k+1}$ using (10) and (11);
   (f) Update $\mathbf{w}_{k+1}$ using (9);
   (i) $k = k + 1$;
4. **return** $\mathbf{w}_k$;

Figure 1. Algorithm of the proposed Two-Phase NAQ.

IV. Simulation Results

Computer simulations are conducted to demonstrate the validity of the proposed Two-Phase NAQ for optimization problems. In this simulation, NN training is considered as an example for optimization problems. The function (12) is approximated using a feedforward NN with one hidden layer [4][5].

$$f(x) = 1 + (x + 2x^2)\sin(-x^2). \quad (12)$$

The input and output are x and $f(x)$, respectively. The sample dataset includes 400 training and 10,000 test points. The training and the test datasets are generated with 0.02 intervals and the random sampling in $x \in [-4, 4)$, respectively. The trained network has a hidden layer with 7 neurons. Therefore, the structure of the NN is 1-7-1. Each hidden neuron has a sigmoid function as the activation. In this research, the Mean Squared Error (MSE) is considered as the objective function of (1) for the training of the NN. 10 independent runs with $\mathbf{w}$ initialized by uniform random numbers in the range $[-0.5, 0.5]$ are conducted. The trained NN is estimated by the average, best and worst of $E_{train}(\mathbf{w})$ and $E_{test}(\mathbf{w})$, with the average of computational time (s) and the average of iteration count (k). The termination conditions are set to $\epsilon = 1.0\times10^{-6}$ and $k_{max} = 30,000$. The performance of Two-Phase NAQ is compared with the conventional Two-Phase QN [3]. The stepsizes α_k and $\overline{\alpha}_k$ for each algorithm are determined according to Armijo's conditions [4]. The simulation results of (12) are summarized in Table I. The table shows that the proposed Two-Phase NAQ converges faster than Two-Phase QN without loss of optimization properties. That is, the iteration counts and time of Two-Phase NAQ are much smaller than Two-Phase QN. At the same time, both algorithms here have comparable results for $E_{train}(\mathbf{w})$ and $E_{test}(\mathbf{w})$. The effect of increasing speed by Two-Phase NAQ is shown in Figure 2. Figure 2 shows the best training errors $E(\mathbf{w})$ for the iteration count (k) of Two-Phase QN and Two-Phase NAQ, which are $E_{train}(\mathbf{w}) = 0.67\times10^{-3}$ and $E_{train}(\mathbf{w}) = 0.31\times10^{-3}$, respectively. From this figure, it is shown that the errors of Two-Phase NAQ drastically decrease in the early stages of the training compared to Two-Phase QN. Furthermore, the calculation times per iteration of Two-Phase QN and Two-Phase NAQ are 0.25×10^{-3} and 0.27×10^{-3} (s), respectively. As a result, it is confirmed that the total simulation time of Two-Phase NAQ is faster than Two-Phase QN. This result is obvious from the following consideration. The summary of the computational cost is illustrated in Table II. The cost of function and gradient evaluations can be considered to be *nd*, where n is the number of training samples involved and d is the number of parameters. The Two-Phase NAQ and Two-

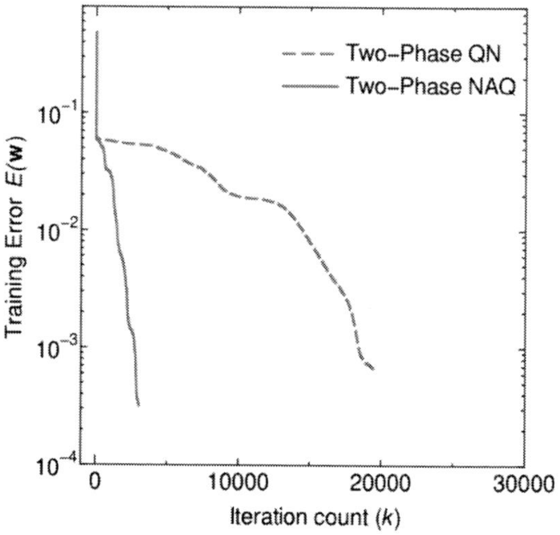

Figure 2. Plot of training error vs iteration count.

TABLE I. SUMMARY OF SIMULATION RESULTS OF (12).

Algorithm	$E_{train}(\mathbf{w})(\times 10^{-3})$ Ave / Best / Worst	Time (sec)	Iteration counts	$E_{test}(\mathbf{w})(\times 10^{-3})$ Ave / Best / Worst
Two-Phase QN	6.85 / 0.67 / 18.64	4.49	17,200	6.66 / 0.66 / 18.12
Two-PhaseNAQ	5.67 / 0.31 / 18.61	**0.80**	**2,854**	5.56 / 0.31 / 18.08

TABLE II. SUMMARY OF THE COMPUTATIONAL COST.

Algorithm	Computational Cost
Two-Phase QN	$2nd + 2d^2 + 2\zeta nd$
Two-PhaseNAQ	$2nd + 2d^2 + 2\zeta nd$

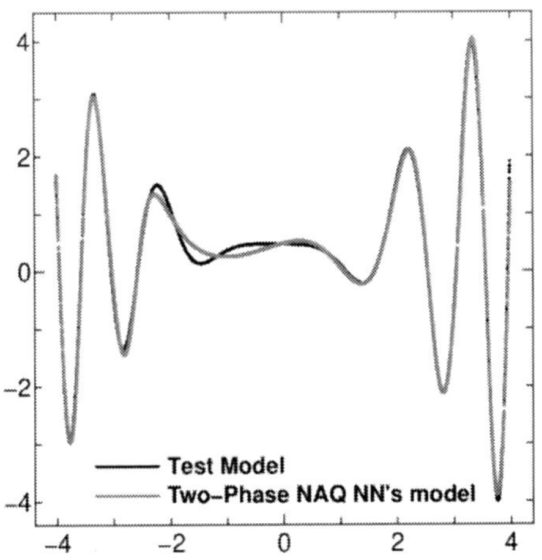

Figure 3. Plot of comparison between the test and the Two-Phase NAQ NN's model.

Phase QN compute the gradient twice per iteration. In both algorithms, the step length is determined by the line search method which involves ζ function evaluations until the search conditions are satisfied. As a result, it can be considered that the Two-Phase QN and the proposed Two-Phase NAQ require the same computational cost. For measuring the accuracy of modeling, the output of the neural model trained by Two-Phase NAQ with $E_{test}(\mathbf{w}) = 0.31 \times 10^{-3}$ is compared with the test data in Figure 3. Figure 3 shows a good match between the neural model and the test data.

V. CONCLUSION

In this research, we proposed a novel optimization algorithm, which was referred to as Two-Phase Nesterov's Accelerated Quasi-Newton (Two-Phase NAQ) method. The proposed algorithm was developed based on the third-order approximation method incorporating a momentum acceleration technique. The effectiveness of the proposed Two-Phase NAQ was demonstrated through computer simulations compared with the conventional Two-Phase QN for the training of NNs. From the simulation results, it can be concluded that the proposed method succeeded in surpassing the acceleration of Two-Phase QN without increasing the computational cost.

In the future, the convergence properties and further improvements of the proposed algorithm will be studied. Also, the validity of the proposed algorithm for large-scale and complicated real-world optimization problems, such as microwave circuit modeling [4], will be demonstrated.

REFERENCES

[1] J. Nocedal and S.J. Wright, *"Numerical Optimization Second Edition"*, Springer, 2006.

[2] D. K. R. Babajee and M. Z. Dauhoo, "An Analysis of The properties of the Variants of Newton's method with Third Order Convergence", *Applied Mathematics and Computations Journal*, Vol.1, No.1, 2006, pp. 659-684.

[3] S. K. Chakraborty and G. Panda, "A Two-Phase Quasi-Newton Method for Optimization Problem", Jul. 2018, arXiv preprint arXiv: 1807.11001.

[4] S. Mahboubi and H. Ninomiya, "A Novel quasi-Newton with Momentum Training for Microwave Circuit Models using Neural Networks", *Proc. ICECS'18*, Dec. 2018, pp. 629-632.

[5] N. Benoudjit, C. Archambeau, A. Lendasse, J. Lee and M. Verleysen, "Width optimization of the Gaussian kernels in radial basis function networks", *Proc. Eur. Symp. Artif. Neural Netw*, 2002, pp. 425-432.

Efficient Parameters for Rotation Processing of Data Augmentation

Naoki Nakamura
School of Information and
Telecommunication Engineering
Tokai University
Tokyo, Japan
e-mail: nakamura.naoki@star.tokai-u.jp

Duke Maeda
School of Information and
Telecommunication Engineering
Tokai University
Tokyo, Japan
e-mail: maedaduke@gmail.com

Kenta Morita
Graduate School of Engineering
Mie University
Mie, Japan
e-mail: k-morita@ip.elec.mie-u.ac.jp

Naoki Morita
School of Information and
Telecommunication Engineering
Tokai University
Tokyo, Japan
e-mail: morita@tokai.ac.jp

Abstract— **Deep learning typically requires a large amount of training data. However, in some cases, it is not possible to prepare enough data to achieve the desired recognition accuracy. A number of approaches to training models with a limited amount of data are available, such as data augmentation and fine-tuning. In the present study, we focus on rotation processing, which has the capacity to augment image data more easily than other augmentation methods. With this method, for example, we could produce 360 images from a single image by rotating the image a full 360° by 1° increments. However, if the rotation angle is not chosen appropriately, essential features of the rotated object may be lost. No clear standards have been previously determined for setting appropriate rotation parameters. This study presents an approach to efficient rotary processing for cases in which the key features of the object either does or does not distort, depending on the angle of rotation. The approach should make it easier for general users to set proper parameters when using rotation processing for data augmentation.**

Keywords- Convolutional neural network; Training data augmentation; Rotation angle; Augmentation rate.

I. INTRODUCTION

A Convolutional Neural Network (CNN) [1] is a machine learning algorithm frequently used for image recognition. For training, a CNN requires a dataset consisting of many pairs of images and labels. Training conducted with insufficient data impairs the ability of the CNN to accurately recognize objects.

Large labeled datasets, such as CIFAR-10 [2] and MNIST [3], are available for training. However, such published datasets cover limited categories, so it is not uncommon for practitioners to create their own datasets. Unfortunately, creating an original dataset normally requires a substantial investment in time and human resources, since more than 1,000 images per object are typically needed. In such cases, data augmentation [4] offers an attractive solution. Data augmentation is a technique that enables practitioners to significantly increase the diversity of the data available for training without actually collecting new data. Data augmentation takes various forms, including rotation, horizontal flipping, and color jittering. In this study, we focus on rotation.

The paper is structured as follows: Section II defines a rotation operation; Section III describes the purpose of the study; Section IV describes the experiments conducted, presents results and considerations; and Section V provides a summary and offers conclusions.

II. ROTATION

For the purposes of data augmentation, a rotation has two parameters: Rotation Angle (RA) and Augmentation Rate (AR). Augmentation Rate is defined as the number of augmented images produced from a single image. For example, if an image is rotated 360° in 1° increments, 360 images will be created. The corresponding values of the RA and the AR would be 1° and 360, respectively.

One notable disadvantage of rotation processing is that key features of the training object can be lost or distorted depending on the angle of rotation, leading to incorrect object recognition. Letters and numbers are one such example. For instance, when the number "6" is rotated by 180°, it becomes "9". As shown in Figure 1, as the rotation angle increases, recognition accuracy decreases.

Kitakaze et al. found rotation to be an effective data augmentation approach for recognizing harmful birds. In their study, each image was rotated over a range of -15° to +15° in 5° increments, resulting in an AR of 7 [5]. In a binary classification test, they reported a recognition accuracy rate of 85% using 536 images per object (for a total of 2 x 536 = 1,072 images). When the dataset was augmented with the rotated images, the accuracy rate increased to 90%. In another study, L. Taylor et al. used Caltech101 to show that the recognition accuracy could be improved by using images that were rotated over a range of -30° to +30° [6]. Hu et al. rotated CIFAR-10 and MNIST images to determine the effects of rotation. They reported that, when the RA was between -30° and +30°, an AR of two or three times was sufficient for training [7].

In this paper, we call an object whose core appearance is unchanged by the angle of rotation an "unaffected object." For such an object, RA × AR = 360°, as the essential meaning of the object is not altered even if rotated by any possible angle.

Kawasaki et al. used a leaf dataset consisting of 800 images composed of three objects to identify plant diseases. The AR was 36 and RA was 10°. They reported that recognition accuracy improved from 77.0% to 92.5% after the rotated images were included [8].

Object	0° 5° 45° 90° 180°
Alphabet (6)	

Figure 1. Rotation processing (Example)

III. PURPOSE

The present study has two purposes. First, we attempt to determine a method for efficiently rotating objects in a dataset consisting of images that are not affected by the rotation processing. Finding the optimal RA and AR values in such cases would clearly be desirable. As described above, Kawasaki et al. reported that recognition accuracy increased from 77% to 92.5%. when the RA was set to 10° and the resulting AR was 36. It is possible that the recognition rate may be further improved by setting the rotation angle to 5° and AR to 72.

One might assume that there is a straightforward relationship between recognition accuracy and the augmentation rate, and that recognition accuracy will continue to improve as the number of images increases. However, it seems at least as plausible that at some point the recognition rate will no longer improve, since smaller angular increments will produce many similar images. If a CNN can accurately recognize objects that are rotated with a lower AR, then increasing the AR becomes unnecessary. We need to be able to determine at what point the accuracy stops increasing as RA is reduced.

The second objective is to identify the effective way to apply rotation processing to images that are affected by rotation. Images that are affected by rotation may be distorted depending on the angle of rotation, so care must be taken when performing rotation processing.

Our overall intent is to identify a simple way to set proper RA and AR parameters to ensure a high degree of recognition accuracy for any object.

IV. EXPERIMENT I: EFFECTIVE PARAMETERS FOR UNAFFECTED OBJECTS

Experiment 1 was conducted in order to determine the most efficient value for AR for cases in which the images are not affected by the rotation. The datasets, experimental method, and results are described below.

A. Dataset

In this experiment, we used three datasets which consist of unaffected objects: a HEp-2 cell dataset, a Malaria-infected cell dataset [9], and a Branches dataset, as shown in Table I. The HEp-2 cell dataset was provided by the 22nd International Conference on Pattern Recognition (ICPR 2014). We rotated the objects to augment the three datasets with an AR of 2 to 10. The RA of the augmented datasets conforms to the equation RA×AR = 360°.

TABLE I. DATASETS OF UNAFFECTED OBJECTS

	For learning	*For validation*
HEp-2 cell (4 classes)	500 images per object (2000 images in total)	100 images per object (400 images in total)
Malaria-infected cell (2 classes)	200 images per object (400 images in total)	50 images per object (100 images in total)
Branches (4 classes)	300 images per object (1200 images in total)	200 images per object (800 images in total)

B. Experimental methods

We used 100 epochs for training with the HEp-2 and Branches datasets and 300 epochs for the Malaria-infected cell dataset. The experimental conditions are shown in Table II.

TABLE II. EXPERIMENT CONDITIONS

OS	Ubuntu 18.04 LTS
CUDA	10.0.130
cuDNN	7.6.4.38
Python	2.7.15+
OpenCV	3.4.0
Framework	Caffe [10]
Network	GoogleNet

For testing, we used 200 test images per object. We evaluated the training models with the F-measure [11], which is the harmonic mean of precision and recall, as defined below.

$$\text{F-measure} = \frac{2 \times Precision \times Recall}{Precision + Recall}$$

The experimental results are shown in the next section. The results represent the average value when the experiment was performed 3 times.

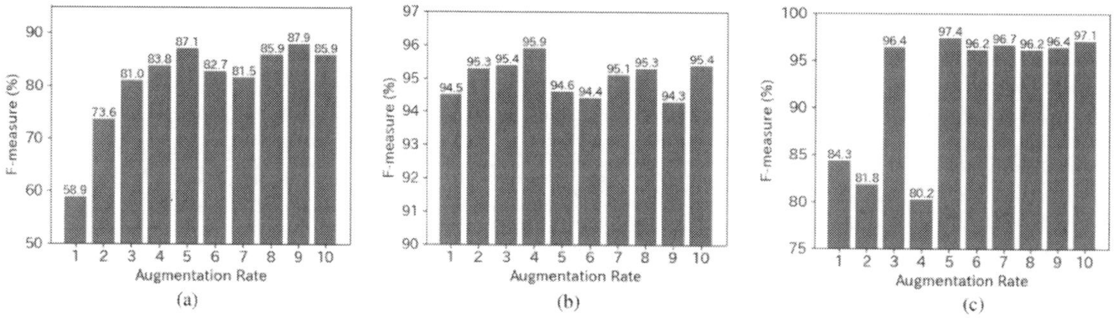

Figure 2. Results for unaffected objects datasets: (a) HEp-2 cell, (b) Malaria-infected cell, (c) Branches

C. *Results and Discussion*

Figure 2 shows the training results for unaffected objects datasets. According to the results for the HEp-2 cell and branch datasets, rotation processing in which the AR values were from 1 to 5 the performance improved. An AR of more than 6 produced no significant improvement.

For the malaria-infected cell dataset, rotation processing in which the AR values were from 1 to 4 the performance improved. For an AR of more than 5, no further improvement occurred.

These results suggest that there are limits to the capacity of rotation processing to improve the performance of CNNs. It is assumed that once the AR exceeds 4 or 5, the training data includes many similar images. Thus, simply increasing the number of similar images has little effect on increasing accuracy, as the features of the object do not increase. The learning time, however, does increase. This suggests that efficient rotation processing for unaffected objects should use an AR of 4 to 5.

It should be noted that for the branches dataset, when AR was set to either 2 or 4, performance decreased. In these two cases, it is assumed that the decrease was related to the object's specific characteristics, as suggested in Figure 3. When AR was 2, for example, the training data consisted exclusively of images rotated by 0° and 180°. These images are very similar, since branches are essentially linear objects. Results also show a decrease in performance for the HEp-2 cell dataset when AR is 6 or 7. Investigation of the reason for this will be conducted in future studies.

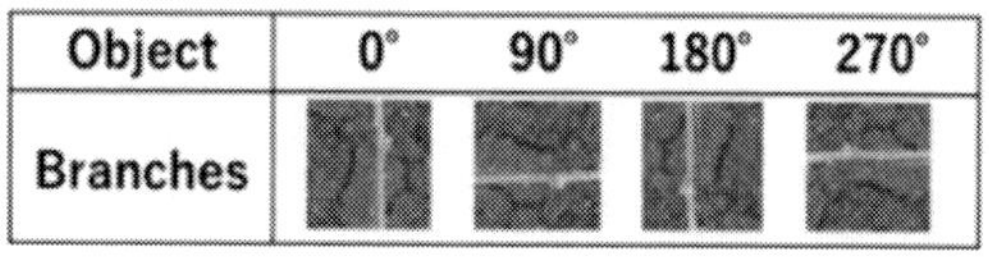

Figure 3. Rotation processing for Branches

V. Experiment II: Effective Parameters For Objects Affected By The Rotation

The purpose of Experiment 2 was to determine the most efficient rotation procedure—that is, the best combination of the parameters AR and RA—for images affected by the rotation.

A. *Datasets*

Two datasets which consist of objects affected by the rotation were used: ImageNet [12] and MNIST (Table III). We augmented the datasets with AR = 2 and AR = 3.

To accomplish the targeted augmentations, we used the following rotation scheme: For an AR of 3, we rotated the original image plus x° and minus x°, where x is set to a specific value. (For example, we could triple the size of the dataset by using the original image plus the image rotated 5° clockwise and 5° counterclockwise, or 10° clockwise and 10° counterclockwise, etc.) For an AR of 2, we simply removed the base dataset from the AR = 3 augmented data. We used seven possible angles for x, from 5° to 35°, in 5° increments.

TABLE III. Datasets of Objects Affected by the Rotation

	For learning	*For validation*
ImageNet (10 classes)	450 images per object (4500 images in total)	50 images per object (500 images in total)
MNIST (10 classes)	180 images per object (1800 images in total)	20 images per object (200 images in total)

B. *Experimental methods*

We trained 100 epochs using the training data described in Table III, with 100 test images per object. The experimental results using the F-measure are shown in the next section. The experimental conditions are the same as in Table II. The results are given as the average value when the experiment was performed 3 times.

C. *Results and Discussion*

Figure 4 shows the results for ImageNet and MNIST when the size of the dataset was doubled and tripled, respectively.

From the experimental results, it seems that the most efficient rotation procedure for objects affected by rotation is defined by RA = 15° or 20° and AR = 3.

The result for ImageNet with AR = 3 showed that the performance improved with the increase in RA. For RA of more than 25°, the performance dropped. For the result of AR = 2, the performance degraded with an increase in RA.

The results for the MNIST dataset showed the same tendency as the results for the ImageNet dataset. For the result of AR = 3, performance improved with the increase in RA. For RA of more than 20°, the performance dropped.

From these results, the performance when the dataset was tripled was better than when the dataset was doubled in most cases from 5° to 35°. From this result, it is reasonable to believe that the tripled dataset contains more information about the objects in the dataset than the doubled dataset. These results suggest that adjusting an RA more than a certain RA value started to distort the key features of the training object.

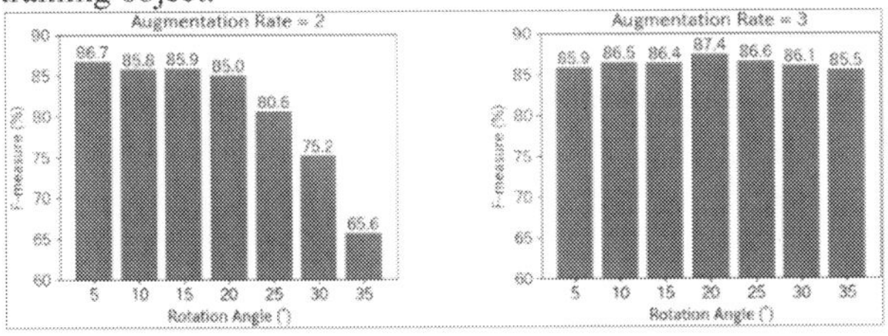

(a)

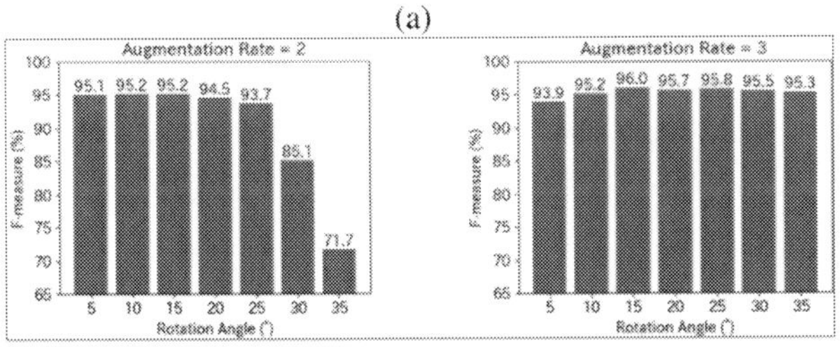

(b)

Figure 4. Results for datasets of objects affected by the rotation: (a) ImageNet, (b) MNIST

VI. CONCLUSION

In the present study, we clarified an efficient rotation processing procedure for augmenting a dataset for training a CNN. Our results provide a reference when performing rotation processing.

When rotating images of objects whose meaning is affected by their rotation, such as those of alphanumeric characters, cars, and dogs, the efficient rotation procedure is to augment the number of images tripled and tilt images to -15°, 0°, 15° or -20°. 0°, 20°. When rotating images of objects whose essential meaning is unchanged when rotated, such as those of cells and branches, the most efficient rotation procedure is to augment the number of images from 4 to 5 times over the full 360° range.

Rotation is only one of many data augmentation techniques. In the future, we plan to clarify optimum parameters for other augmentation approaches.

REFERENCES

[1] Y. LeCun et al., "Handwritten Digit Recognition with a Back-Propagation Network." Advances in Neural Information Processing Systems, pp. 396-404, 1990.

[2] A. Krizhevsky, "Learning Multiple Layers of Features from Tiny Images" Tech. Rep., University of Toronto, 2009.

[3] Y. LeCun and C. Cortes, "The MNIST database of handwritten digits.", http://yann.lecun.com/exdb/mnist/, [retrieved: February 2020]

[4] European Space Agency. ESA: Missions, Earth Observation: ENVISAT. [Online]. Available from. https://bair.berkeley.edu/blog/2019/06/07/data_aug/, [retrieved: February 2020]

[5] H. Kitakaze, S. Okabe, R. Yoshihara, and R. Matsumura, "Recognition Rate-Improvement of Injurious Bird Recognition System by Increasing CNN Learning Image using Data Augmentation" The Japanese Journal of the Institute of Industrial Applications Engineers, Vol. 7. No. 2, pp. 69-76, 2019.

[6] L. Taylor and G. Nitschke, "Improving Deep Learning using Generic Data Augmentation" IEEE Symposium Series on Computational Intelligence, pp. 1542-1547, 2018.

[7] B. Hu, C. Lei, D. Wang, S. Zhang, and Z. Chen, "A Preliminary Study on Data Augmentation of Deep Learning for Image Classification" arXiv:1906.11887v1, 2019.

[8] Y. Kawasaki, H. Uga, S. Kagiwada, and H. Iyatomi, "Basic Study of Automated Diagnosis for Viral Plant Diseases with Convolutional Neural Networks" 31st Fuzzy System Symposium, pp.391-394, 2015.

[9] S. Rajaraman et al., "Pre-trained convolutional neural networks as feature extractors toward improved malaria parasite detection in thin blood smear images" PeerJ, Vol. 6, p. e4568, 2018.

[10] Y. Jia et al., "Caffe: Convolutional Architecture for Fast Feature Embedding" 22nd ACM international conference on Multimedia, pp. 675-678, 2014.

[11] M. Sokolova, N. Japkowicz, and S. Szpakowicz, "Beyond Accuracy, F-Score and ROC: A Family of Discriminant Measures for Performance Evaluation" 19th Australian Joint Conference on Artificial Intelligence, pp. 1015-1021, 2006.

[12] J. Deng et al., "Imagenet: A large-scale hierarchical image database" IEEE Conference on Computer Vision and Pattern Recognition, pp. 248-255, 2009.

Shoot Counting System Based on SegNet

Funa Ito
School of Information and
Telecommunication Engineering
Tokai University
Tokyo, Japan
E-mail: funa.ito@outlook.jp

Duke Maeda
School of Information and
Telecommunication Engineering
Tokai University
Tokyo, Japan
E-mail: maedaduke@gmail.com

Naoki Nakamura
School of Information and
Telecommunication Engineering
Tokai University
Tokyo, Japan
E-mail: nakamura.naoki@star.tokai-u.jp

Kenta Morita
Graduate School of Engineering
Mie University
Mie, Japan
E-mail: k-morita@ip.elec.mie-u.ac.jp

Naoki Morita
School of Information and
Telecommunication Engineering
Tokai University
Tokyo, Japan
E-mail: morita@tokai.ac.jp

***Abstract*—In the present paper, we analyze an aerial photograph of a vineyard to count the number of shoots using SegNet, which is a tool for extracting the area of an object. However, occluded object regions make it difficult to recognize the hidden surface. The area of the object in the background is divided into two areas. It is thus necessary to connect the divided areas to obtain the correct number of shoots. Here, we propose a system that combines adjacent pixels and then connects all parts of the segmented area based on the segmentation output.**

Keywords - SegNet; Segmentation; Shoot; Pruning; Grapes.

I. Introduction

Some vineyards in Japan have adopted shelf cultivation, for which overhead work is required. Farmers can only see a tiny area at a given time when working on the vineyard. There is a project in Japan that helps vineyard farmers [1]. The goal of this project is to develop a system that can count the shoots on a tree from an aerial photograph of the vineyard taken by a drone.

Here, we propose a method that uses image recognition technology based on object area detection. In this study, we use SegNet [2] with the Caffe deep learning library for area detection. SegNet has an encoder, which has a general convolutional neural network structure, and a decoder. The encoder can be changed to ResNet, or other similar networks, to improve recognition accuracy. Figure 1 shows an aerial photograph taken by a drone. Figure 2 shows the result of area detection obtained with the VGG16 encoder for the photograph in Figure 1. Segmented branch pixels are shown in red, segmented shoot pixels are shown in yellow, and other pixels are shown in gray.

However, it is insufficient to count the number of new treetops per branch using only SegNet. As shown in Figure 2, there are two issues, namely shoots occlude branches and misrecognition. Although we use SegNet in the present study, the same issues arise using, for example, U-Net [3], DANet [4], and OCNet [5].

The purpose of this study is to determine the number of new treetops per branch from one aerial photograph.

The remainder of this paper is organized as follows. Section II describes the proposed concept. Section III validates the concept. Section IV gives the conclusions.

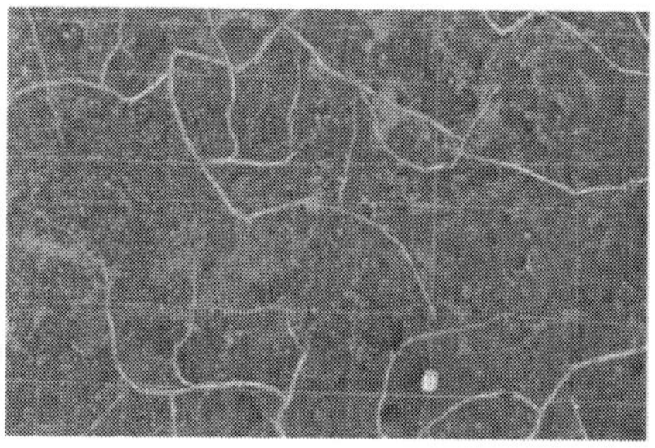

Figure 1. Original photograph.

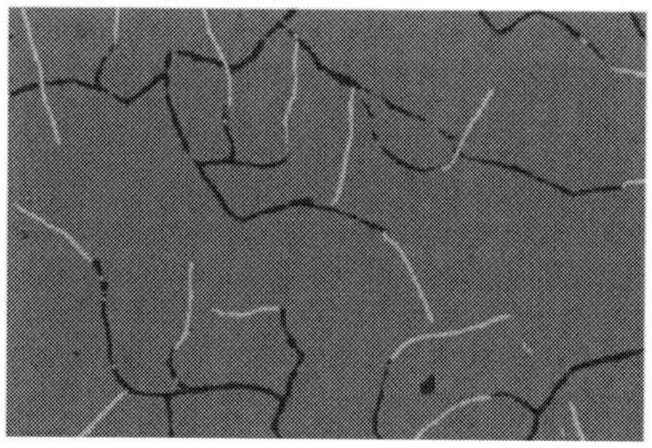

Figure 2. Segmentation result.

II. Proposed Concept

ID numbers are assigned to each red and yellow region and connected part pairs are counted to determine the number of shoots. The same ID number is assigned to parts of a divided area.

In this section, we describe a method for counting all treetops in the segmented image shown in Figure 2 and a method for assigning ID numbers to separate areas. We first describe the proposed processes and then demonstrate them with examples. The proposed process is as follows:

A. Allot ID numbers to all areas based on the segmentation results.

B. Detect divided areas.

C. Reassign ID numbers based on the results of B.

C-(1) Connect divided red areas.

C-(2) Connect separated branch regions using recognized shoot areas.

C-(3) Connect separated branch regions using unrecognized shoot areas.

D. Obtain the number of shoots for each branch.

A. Allot ID Numbers to all Areas Based on Segmentation Results

The aerial photograph of part of the vineyard is first segmented. Then, ID numbers are allotted to branch and shoot regions. A given region is assigned the same ID for adjacent pixels of the same color, and the neighbor list adds the shoot ID numbers adjacent to each branch ID number. The allotted branch ID numbers are given in red and the shoot ID numbers are given in yellow. Yellow areas that have fewer pixels than the threshold are changed to red. Red areas in contact with fewer yellow areas than the threshold are changed to yellow. Red areas not in contact with a yellow area are changed to gray. Figure 4 shows the results of assigning ID numbers to Figure 3.

B. Detect Divided Areas

The red region is enlarged by the thickness of the shoots and target areas are connected. If the pixels of the extended area are yellow, they are changed to orange. If they are gray, they are repainted blue. Figure 5 shows the diagram obtained after adding a connection target area in Figure 4.

C. Reassign ID Numbers Based on Results of B

1) Connect divided red areas: All branches in contact with each other via a blue area are reassigned to have the same ID. However, if a blue area is in contact with an orange area, it will not be a target. If a blue area is in contact with an orange area and also in contact with areas that are not in contact with the orange area, it will be a target. Figure 6 shows the diagram obtained after reassigning the same ID to selected areas relative to Figure 5.

2) Connect separated branch regions using recognized shoot areas: If there is an orange region between two branch ID numbers, the two branches areas are reassigned the same ID. This branch ID is excluded as a new tree adjacent ID.

3) Connect separated branch regions using unrecognized shoot areas: If the orange area is adjacent to more than three branch ID numbers, the user determines which two regions are the separated areas. At this time, the image of the vertical and horizontal threshold pixels is displayed as a pop-up window centered on the orange area, and the same branch area is selected, as shown in Figure 7. Then, the ID of the area determined to be the adjacent area is changed to the same ID. This branch ID is excluded as the newest adjacent ID. Figure 8 shows the diagram obtained after reassigning the same ID to selected areas relative to Figure 6.

D. Obtain Number of Shoots for Each Branch

All shoot ID numbers in contact with branch ID numbers are counted to determine the yellow area. The results are shown in Figure 9.

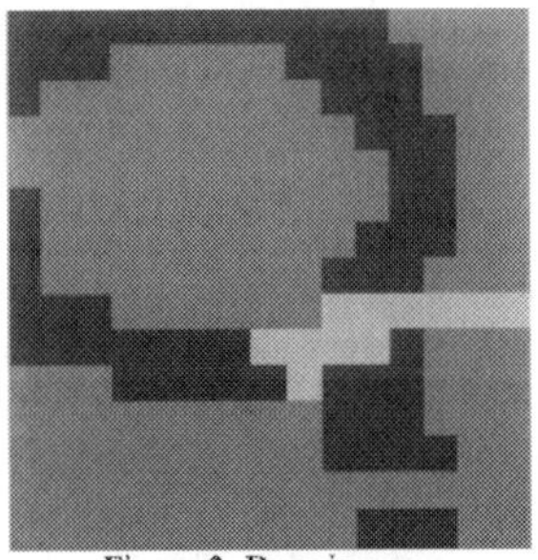

Figure 3. Base image.

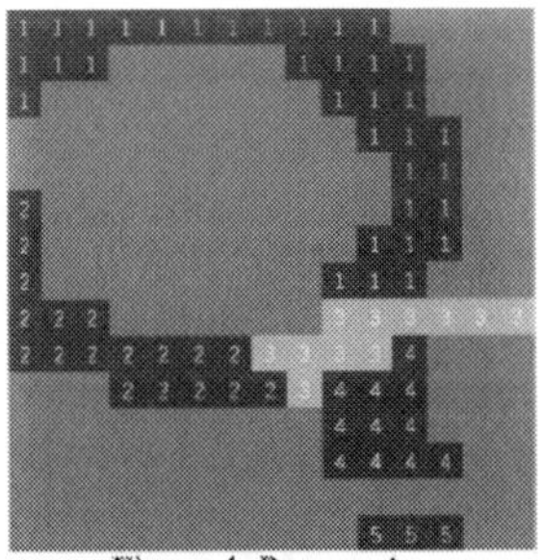

Figure 4. Process A.

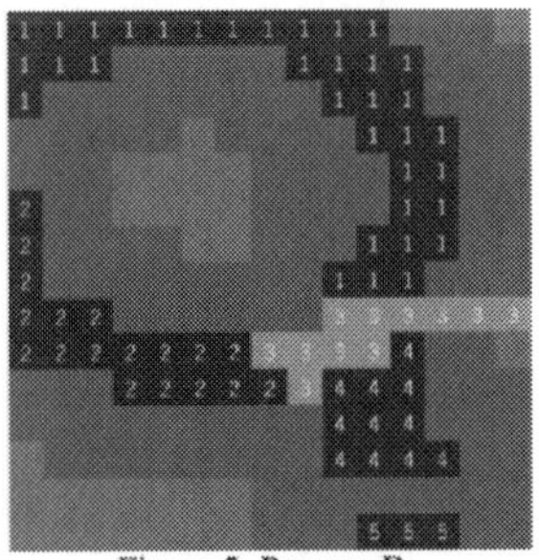

Figure 5. Process B.

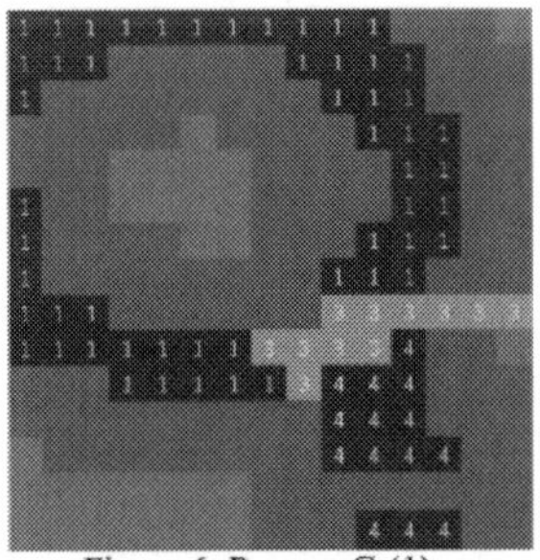

Figure 6. Process C-(1).

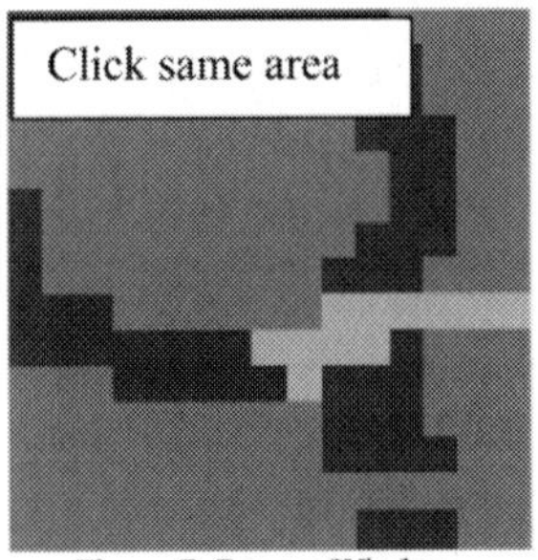

Figure 7. Pop-up Window.

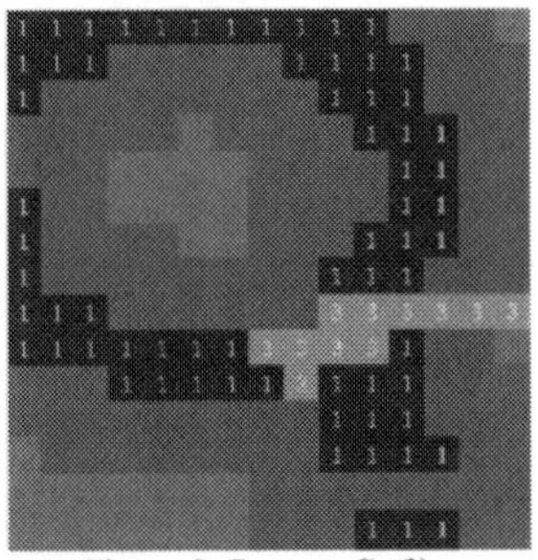

Figure 8. Process C-(3).

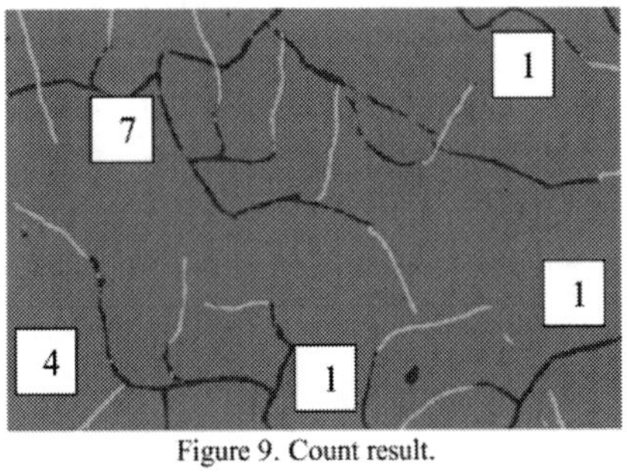

Figure 9. Count result.

III. VALIDATION OF PROPOSED CONCEPT

To implement the system, we confirmed the thresholds used in the proposed processes. We first obtained the size of the branch and shoot areas for repainting misrecognized areas. The results of the verification show that the red and yellow areas had at least around 3000 and 5000 pixels, respectively. The replacement target red and yellow areas had at most 1000 and 2100 pixels, respectively.

We also obtained the maximum width of the segmented shoot area for process B. The results of the verification show that the maximum width was 40 pixels. A threshold of 80 pixels also worked. The threshold thus has a wide range.

IV. CONCLUSION

This study proposed a method for counting the number of shoots on branches based on an aerial photograph taken by a drone. We used SegNet to detect and count shoots on a vine. However, this does not yield the correct number because shoots overlapped branches and thus the branch region was separated into several areas. To overcome this problem, we enlarged branch regions and detected the juncture branches. In future work, we will connect multiple photographs taken by a drone to count all shoots in a vineyard.

REFERENCES

[1] http://www.miraikikin.org/activities/agriculture/rihoku.html [retrieved: Februaty 2020]

[2] V. Badrinarayanan et al., :"SegNet :A Deep Convolutional Encoder- Decoder Architecture for Image Segmentation.", IEEE trans. on PAMI, vol. 39, pp. 2481-2495, 2017. [retrieved: February, 2020]

[3] O. Ronneberger, P. Fischer and T. Brox, U-Net: Convolutional Networks for Biomedical Image Segmentation, arXiv:1505.04597, 2015. [retrieved: February, 2020]

[4] J. Fu et al., Dual Attention Network for Scene Segmentation, arXiv:1809.02983v4, 2019 [retrieved: February, 2020]

[5] Y. Yuan and J. Wang, OCNet: Object Context Network for Scene Parsing, arXiv:1809.00916v3, 2019[retrieved: February, 2020]

The Individual and Collective Outcomes of Decision-Making

Monique Borges, João Marques, Eduardo Castro
GOVCOPP, Dept. of Social, Political and Territorial Sciences
University of Aveiro
Aveiro, Portugal
email: monique@ua.pt, jjmarques@ua.pt, ecastro@ua.pt

Abstract — **Solving decision-making problems often depends on the use of methods for multi-criteria evaluation of alternatives. Generally, the challenge relies on the ability to structure long-term goals, while establishing accurate criteria matrices and weights for assessing alternatives. Complexity increases when preference functions become important to define global utilities or determine final rankings. This topic is of high importance for the policy making process, where decisions result from group-thinking and collective processes. Therefore, high levels of subjectivity are associated with the decision process, typically reflected in preferences and options. The application of different software tools or multi-criteria decision-making methods can lead to non-identical outputs. Collective decisions result from aggregation metrics and weighing procedures. This paper discusses the balances of individual and collective decisions, based on the rational choice theory and the shift to behavioural economics. Subsequently, data from decision-making in real practice supports the debate on the use of multi-criteria methods.**

Keywords - Decision-making; Decision theory; Multi-criteria methods; Preferences; Governance; Policy making.

I. INTRODUCTION

Governance arrangements recall a response to direct and hierarchical models. In addition, they show that, among the forms of governance, it is fundamental to deal with the behaviour of the various actors involved in the decision process, either through cooperation, partnerships or networking. Inevitably, new types of management and coordination tools emerge, and changes occur leading to the adaptation of organizational models, and integration of different logics of public service delivery. Public decisions are no longer considered to be totally dependent on hierarchically organized structures and are defined by the interaction of a diverse set of organizations located at different territorial levels [1]. The theory of institutional logics suggests that decisions and outcomes reflect the interaction between individual behaviour and institutional structures; so, individuals and organizations can look for the power, status and economic advantages, as well as their means and ends to respond to their interests, but both are dependent on the institutional logics [2]. Thus, institutions are expected to meet the demands of collective decision-making in increasingly complex circumstances. In this specific context, the need to articulate the multiplicity of agents and interests in the pursuit of common goals is at the basis of the development of decision support strategies. There is a blind will to provide collective results, neglecting the basis and meaning of individual placement and preferences. Decision theories find theoretical and empirical evidence since the seventeenth century, supporting either a rational perspective to explain complex decision-making contexts, or providing complementary research to understand the behavioural mechanisms of individuals and, therefore, deal with the errors and biases of reasoning [3]–[5].

This paper is structured in four sections, besides the Introduction. First, decision-making is framed within the public policy process, focusing on the challenges deriving from governance arrangements. Group decision-making plays a key role as individual decision heuristics, preferences and expectations meet collective purposes and goals. The rational choice theory and the shift to behavioural economics frames this debate. In real (policy) decision-making contexts multi-criteria methods are used to structure and organize priorities among alternatives; thus, a short review is presented. The paper follows with a comparison of individual and collective outcomes by applying different aggregation metrics and Multi-Criteria Decision-Making (MCDM) methods to a real decision-making problem. Finally, conclusions focus on the main findings and further research recommendations.

II. PUBLIC POLICY AND DECISION-MAKING

Governance does not mean the end of politics, but its practice in a context of broader interaction subject to a game of cooperation and conflict across all institutions and actors of government arrangements. Within these arrangements institutions are required to develop a couple of interrelated steps: i) to establish a consensual and strategic vision based on stakeholders' motivations, preferences and expectations; ii) to structure decision processes towards priorities; and iii) to develop effective coordination mechanisms in the integration and regulation of the process [6]. This complexity discloses the notion that decisions reflect the functioning of various decision heuristics, which include decision rules, logical reasoning structures, and value systems [3][4][7]. Thus, decision-making is often associated with high degrees of uncertainty and complexity, resulting from the limited resources, multiple actors with (conflicting) motivations and preferences. Individual or collective choices are made from a set of alternatives, which can change over time or when subject to different evaluation criteria. Gowda and Fox [8] remind other scholars who strived to understand how people's choices operate under conditions of high uncertainty and risk, and conclude that people do have a systematic way to achieve their decisions and choices. During decision-making, certain heuristics or rules of thumb are followed, moving away from the typical rational decision process advocated and used by economists (see, for e.g., the works [3][7]). Even though preferences are assumed to be determined by different utilities and probabilities, and one can assume that people choose to maximize expected utilities [9][10], individuals do not always have all the information, or the ability to process, manage and evaluate the consequences of their final options [4]. In addition, other cognitive, normative and motivational elements that delimit and characterize the individual and collective behaviour explain behaviour patterns [3][11].

Group decision-making is a topic of major interest. Roy [12] refers to the comprehensive dimension of decision, as the decision results from the interactions among individuals, entities, communities and the conflicts of their preferences. Regardless the individual perspective of a decision, when placed in the policymaking process, it is shaped by specific information systems, behaviours and organizational structures. There is a challenging effort to balance the relations between actors involved in the decision process, ranging from the alternative definition to the combination of preferences. The perception of alternatives and decision-making depends on a set of sociological and psychological factors, often dealt with communication techniques and strategies. Concepts such as agenda setting, framing and priming mirror this complexity, as they describe how different groups, with different degrees of power, interact and define the political debate and, consequently, contribute to the construction of the political agenda. In what concerns decisions, the problem particularly consists in assessing the option's feasibility, risks and consequences, where setting the wrong priorities may imply inefficient use of available resources and opportunity costs [13]. Indeed, the discussion on the decision-making process within the public policy formation can be multifaceted as you concern, for instances, the organization of all related steps of the decision process; the selection and design of decision techniques and models; the knowledge background, potential bias, interactions and system-thinking of individuals during decision-making moments.

The following section intends to capture two basic elements: i) the actors and their relations during decision processes and ii) the need of decision support tools able to deal with the complexity related with the patterns of behaviour, rules or structures.

III. Decision Theory and Methods in Practice

A. Rational choice and behavioural economics

Good policy decisions depend on both recognizing the importance of multilevel governance for pursuing micro level goals, by structuring integrated programs grounded in external strategic frameworks, and considering the possible evolution of exogenous factors. These decisions require policy coordination and territorial governance strategies, often using decision support tools. The concept of decision support systems has accommodated multiple perspectives, suggesting the combination of generic and technical principals to respond to the decision design of governance arrangements involving a diversity of social actors and sectorial perspectives. Empirical and theoretical findings are set on the readings of the research of [14]–[19]. As these studies show, decision problems are context-dependent and there is no universal choice pattern to apply. Besides subjective and asymmetric information issues, choices and preferences are subject to great uncertainty and inaccuracy, for which the cognitive characteristics of individuals and the social, institutional and economic structures play a key role.

Moreover, to explain such diversity and complexity, since the 17th century, decision theory has covered rigorous mathematical and quantitative assumptions, defending its rational foundation, and supported other approaches focused on the cognitive basis of human behaviour, analysing the meaning of heuristics and bias [4][7][14][20]–[23]. We believe that the complex equilibrium between individual and group decisions requires both descriptive assumptions and rationalist components. The standard view of traditional microeconomic theory explains human behaviour by using rational choice, therefore, following principles such as unbounded rationality and self-interest. At the basis is the assumption of an optimization approach, subject to consistent criterion assessment. Individual preferences and choices, however, seem to be much more complex. Understanding how and why individuals decide in one way or another underpins psychological and socio-cognitive insights. These questions seem to be captured by behavioural economics studies. This balance of socio-cognitive and rational aspects are somehow present in the work of Mathis et al [24], who present individual and social decisions based on key assumptions and theoretical foundations of rational choice and behavioural economics, for which preferences and restrictions are placed in a debate of maximization of individual and social utility. A variety of studies evidence the characteristics of decision makers and encounter several modelling choice mechanisms to deal with heuristic decision rules, (un)predictable behaviour patterns, typical decision routines, preferences (stated and revealed) and self-oriented motivations [3][4][7][25][26]. Research has evolved providing insights on linking cognitive and social psychology to shed light on how individuals and groups deal in decision contexts (interesting reading on this matter are [3][11][27]). Cognitive and behavioural biases are extremely important to understand decision outputs. However, there is no unified approach regarding the link between socio-cognitive aspects and decision-making; though, efforts towards modelling frameworks grounded on multiple economic, behavioural and cognitive theories are identified, as well as attempts on applying theories of situated cognition and social cognition (see [26][28]–[32]).

In this paper, the rational and socio-cognitive decision-making assumptions are narrowly presented, as these require the combination of multiple preferences, choices and decisions and encounter technical challenges for the design of decision strategies and tools (Table I).

A set of key assumptions and analytic dimensions are put through the above-mentioned aspects. This paper discusses the preference formation process while dealing with the individual-collective shift. This analysis is complex due to multiple drivers, as shown in Table II. Empirically, is assumed the challenge of applying this background to real context decision-making processes where multi-criteria techniques where used.

TABLE I. THEORETICAL GUIDELINES

Analytic dimensions	**Rational choice**	**Behavioural economics**
External incentives	... assumed to be unalterable in the short term and incapable of explaining changes	... reaction to external incentives account for changes in preference patterns
Preferences	... result from assessing benefits and costs, accounting for highest gains among alternatives	... thinking structure has its own benefits and drawbacks; so, they are difficult to predict, but can be indirectly determined through individuals' order of preference via observing both behaviour and restriction
Restrictions	... are relatively easy to identify	... are context dependent
Complexity	... reduced, as people are confined to a few individual characteristics ... available information is believed to lead to an efficient result	... high, as the assumption of rationality is relativized ... acknowledges that information deficit is unable to account for all deviations
Individual or collective explanation capacity	... there is no attempt to understand the individual, but the behaviour of large groups of individuals ("aggregates")	... there is an effort to provide a more realistic perspective on behaviour based on the analysis of the psychological foundations of economics
Social decisions	... efficiency is generally defined as Pareto efficiency or Kaldor-Hicks efficiency	... social, economic and legal conditions influence the a reciprocal conduct; thus, most people do not always act according to their best self-interest

Source: Based on Mathis and Steffen [24].

TABLE II. KEY ASSUMPTIONS AND ANALYTICAL DIMENSIONS

Rational choice	Completeness Transitivity Continuity Substitutability Choice rules Utility functions Arrow's axioms & impossibility theorem
Behavioural economics	Availability Bias Hindsight Bias Anchoring Effect Confirmation Bias Egocentric Bias Loss Aversion Status Quo Preference Endowment Effect Framing Effect
Additional assumptions	Perfect information Choice under uncertainty Limited cognitive ability Type of preferences (stated or revealed) Consistency assumption

B. Multi-criteria methods

The following considerations lie on multi-criteria analysis, based on the assumption that it allows preference relations by combining different assessment on quantitative and qualitative criteria. With rational and/or behavioural guidelines, the decision problem focuses on choosing (most appropriate alternative), ranking (differentiating worst and best options) and sorting (from a list of plausible possibilities) [33]. Some methods enable defining admissible decisions while encountering uncertainties about current or future impacts [34]. A common characteristic of multi-criteria decision-making methods is the evaluation of options by comparing several alternatives, based on individual or collective assessments on several, and perhaps conflicting, criteria. The best alternative derives from the aggregation of all evaluations and comparisons. As Sabaei et al. [35] advise, different types of problems suggest the design and application of adequate methods, whose selection should result on expert's judgments or any other technical restraints.

Amongst the most well-cited and common methods used in publications are the AHP (Analytic Hierarchy Process), the ELECTRE (elimination ET choix traduisant la realite), TOPSIS (Technique for Order of Preference by Similarity to Ideal Solution), SAW (Simple Additive Weighting), and PROMETHEE (Preference Ranking Organization METHod for Enrichment of Evaluations) [35]–[39]. Generally, these methods include different outranking methods, possibility of combining qualitative and quantitative data, and ability to deal with uncertainty.

IV. ANALYSING INDIVIDUAL AND COLLECTIVE PREFERENCES DURING PUBLIC POLICY FORMULATION

A. Decision-making in real practice

This section presents how AHP was used to structure group decision-making during a strategic municipal plan. The AHP, in comparison with other methods, was considered the more prevalent rank order weighting method due to both its theoretical and application simplicity. This method was developed by Saaty [40], which decomposition principle requires the comparison of pairs of various elements that structure the decision process, allowing ranking the various elements, evaluating the relative importance of alternatives and clarifying prioritization.

To derive and synthesize priorities, the criteria followed a hierarchical structure, further evaluated based on pairwise comparisons with a relative scale. Once individual priorities were obtained, the responses of the various participants were combined to build a collective choice pattern. In practical problems, given people's different positions on the same options (criteria, alternatives, etc.), from which strong convictions and contrasting valuations may arise, reciprocal assumption plays an important role for the collective outcome. As theoretically described by Saaty [41], the decisions must be combined so that the reciprocal of the aggregate responses is equal to the inverse synthesis of these responses. In other words, if $a/b = c/d$, then $b/c=d/c$. Thus, no category or answer prevails over the set of options. A key debate issue regards to the consistency of the individual answers. During pairwise comparison, inconsistent answers might appear. In extreme cases this inconsistency may lead to rejection of the answers. This happens in situations where if A> B and B> C, then C≤A; If the answer is A> B, B> C and C> A, then the answer set is inconsistent. In order to solve problems of logical inconsistency, a control value (R^2) was defined, sensitive to random responses, to the mismatches resulting from the scale used and to the subjectivity that this type of exercise involves. The control value was tested and adjusted to real-context circumstances, as the application of the original recommended by Saaty, did not conform to human reasoning and its capacity for information processing. Wolf et al. [42] and Nogueira et al. [43] further explain this application of AHP (which was applied to four strategic plans: 3 municipalities and 1 regional tourism development association). Generally following AHP assumptions', the alternative classification resulted from the combination of scores (detailed matching of alternatives within criteria) and weights (resulting from public processes) – the output is shown in Tables III and IV.

TABLE III. WEIGHTS ASSIGNED TO THE TWO-LEVEL CRITERIA TREE, USING THE AHP

Criteria - Level 1	Weight index	Criteria - Level 2	Weight index
Economy	100	Economy of the future	100
		Infrastructure	97
		Services and other	78
		Labour / workforce	76
Quality of life	100	Basic services (health, education ...)	100
		Vulnerable social groups	77
		Employability	76
Social Inclusion	97	Civic participation	100
		Culture	89
		Sport and leisure	80
Natural heritage	92	Environment (protection)	100
		Risks (prevention and mitigation)	99
		Tourism	88
		Local amenities	83
Urban space	82	Accessibility and mobility	100
		Built heritage	75
		Territorial identity	74
		Urban areas	71

TABLE IV. ORIGINAL RANKING AND RELATIVE IMPORTANCE OF ALTERNATIVES

Case-A_Alternatives	Order	Rank
Case-A_A1	90	9
Case-A_A2	92	6
Case-A_A3	96	3
Case-A_A4	94	5
Case-A_A5	89	10
Case-A_A6	95	4
Case-A_A7	92	7
Case-A_A8	100	1
Case-A_A9	97	2
Case-A_A10	90	8

B. *Methods and possible non-identical outcomes*

1) *Preference aggregation*

As reminded by Wang et. al. [44], multi-criteria methods rely on criteria selection, weighting, evaluation, and final aggregation. They suggest three categories of weighting methods i) subjective weighting, ii) objective weighting and iii) combination weighting methods and point several methods based on weighted sum, priority setting, outranking, fuzzy set methodology. Such statement supports the multiple perspectives leading to different outputs, which change what was initially considered a collective decision. Thus, the following are discussed 1. the collective outcomes by assessing to what extent individual weights when using different aggregation metrics deviate from the results; and 2. the priorities when using other multi-criteria methods.

The use of arithmetic or geometric means, for example, changes the results. The interest in this comparison results from the application of the geometric mean in contexts where it is necessary to obtain an aggregation of items classified with different scales. Although it is not an issue of different scales, criteria vary in number of sub-criteria. Additionally, the scores matrix, which classifies the alternatives in each criterion, has different numerical ranges. It is, therefore, debatable an overestimation of an alternative or criterion deriving from the application of the arithmetic mean. Another discussion around the aggregation of preferences refers to the way in which these are initially evaluated: ordinal, pairwise or cardinal choice. Although the data collected (pairwise) was adjusted to transform the final (and normalized) weights into an ordinal choice matrix, such was not conducted. It would remain unjustified whether potential divergences resulted from the method or from the way judgment is structured in one case or another (such validation would be impossible). Instead, the results were compared with those that would occur with the application of the cardinal choice method. Since the most voted can also be the most rejected, how divergent can the results be?

For decision support purposes, a combined reflection of the information that results from the comparison of real results when subjected to calculations of arithmetic and geometric means, as well as cardinal classification, is relevant. The results show that in more general criteria (therefore, more subjective) extreme values seem more accurate, while in-between values require greater attention. In general, sub-criteria concern to specific issues, where preference matrices evidence greater disparity among options. For analytical and decision support purposes considering other coefficients and dispersion indexes are suggested to consolidate the analysis (e.g. Herfindahl-Hirschman index, Theil index localization and specialization coefficients).

2) *Scores, weights and multi-criteria decision methods*

In general, a multi-criteria problem is performed by defining criteria, alternatives and the link between both. The criteria are valued to prioritize alternatives. As previously mentioned, there is a wide range of methods, whose assumptions of normalization and ordering differ. This work contributes to this debate by demonstrating how these methods can influence decisions made in a real context. Despite the need to shape the input data to run the MCDM methods, its homogenization was ensured, reducing possible bias in the conclusions drawn. The selection of SAW, TOPSIS and ELECTRE is due to their similarity regarding the use of matrices of scores and weights, without having to tamper the actual data. Some scale correction procedures were, however, necessary. PROMETHEE rankings were not calculated due to the inability to match real data to preferences, indifferences and incomparability.

The comparable ranking results (Table V) are consistent with the most and least relevant alternatives. The AHP, SAW and TOPSIS allow to infer relative importance, under different analytical perspectives. The AHP is via the scale used for comparisons; SAW is due to the additive weighting algorithm and TOPSIS for its performance indicator, comparing each alternative with best and worst ideal ones. The ELECTRE does not allow this differentiation and, in this case, it presented transitivity problems (Table VI).

TABLE V. RANKING COMPARISON WITH APPLICATION OF MCDM METHODS

Case-A_Alternatives	Original	AHP	SAW	TOPIS	ELECTRE
Case-A_A1	9	10	10	10	9
Case-A_A2	6	3	6	8	3
Case-A_A3	3	5	8	4	3
Case-A_A4	5	6	3	9	5
Case-A_A5	10	4	5	6	6
Case-A_A6	4	9	2	5	6
Case-A_A7	7	8	1	3	6
Case-A_A8	1	2	4	7	2
Case-A_A9	2	1	9	2	1
Case-A_A10	8	7	7	1	9

TABLE VI. RELATION BETWEEN ALTERNATIVES: INTRANSITIVE CASES

A2 > A5	A2 > A6	A2 > A7				
A3 > A2	A3 > A6	A3 > A7				
A4 > A5	A4 > A7					
A5 > A6						
A6 > A4						
A7 > A6						
A8 > A1	A8 > A2	A8 > A4	A8 > A7			
A9 > A1	A9 > A2	A9 > A4	A9 > A5	A9 > A6	A9 > A7	A9 > A8

V. CONCLUSION

Typically, the conceptual and mathematical background of multi-criteria decision methods is based on examples describing alternatives with objective criteria (e.g. choosing printers or selecting candidates for a job). It is frequently used in the entrepreneurial context, where the type of problems dealt with allows greater objectivity of the input data. The focus is often on maximizing utility functions, reducing costs, optimizing production or processes. Operational research has contributed to the development of decision support systems that fulfil these purposes. Although dealing with and articulating multiple criteria are a concern in these approaches, the policy-making context opens other debates. Groups are put together to define action plans, based on priorities fulfilling strategic development paths. Understanding individual and collective positioning is a key aspect to support and toughen the decisions. The study on MCDM evidences solid knowledge on structuring priorities, but a lack of coverage on the aggregation of responses. As well, the weight assignment process is described in AHP, but in the other MCDM methods it is assumed as an input data (not deriving from the methods' procedures). While focusing on alternatives, few is said about the combination of scores and weights. Thus, efforts were made to comply with the methods' requirements. The simplicity of MCDM methods is an advantage for its application; however, the difficulty of adjusting them to real decision contexts limits their potential. As explained, the complexity of decision in real practice motivated the adjustment of AHP original assumptions.

To conclude, in addition to those presented, testing aggregate differences based on other ways of collecting preferences is not possible, as the original pairwise data is not prepared for this purpose. This work does not emphasis all assumptions and key analytical dimensions theoretically discussed. It focuses on some of the identified problems, such as transitivity and the use of decision support instruments to overcome the rational limited capacity. Moreover, it opens path to discuss the need to adjust the parameters of the models and methods used, as verified in the real context of application of the AHP.

This work provides an analytic framework, extensible to other cases, allowing to compare and assess the sensitivity and robustness of the results and methods. The apparent consistency at the extremes of the priorities (most and less valued alternatives) suggests the need to consider other decision approaches to tune how intermediate values are calculated. Additional testing by reducing alternatives or the number of criteria can change these conclusions. Further research topics go for explaining how decision makers deal with uncertainty and how groups influence individual decisions. The use of foresight techniques supports the discussion about the methods that allow dealing with uncertainty, in a more or less objective manner (projections, estimates or scenario analysis, as suggested by Borges et al. [45] and Marques et al. [46][47]). Finally, research on group-thinking brings an additional layer to the decision theory. The preferences of decision maker's ex-ante and ex-post collective debate can derive. Explaining this shift based on (socio) cognitive indicators is, as well, useful for supporting decision processes.

ACKNOWLEDGMENT

This work is based on a PhD thesis in progress (funding reference SFRH/BD/118478/2016, from FCT-Fundação para a Ciência e a Tecnologia) and COMPETE 2020-POCI. It is as well a contribution for the research project: DRIVIT-UP – DRIVIng forces of urban Transformation: assessing pUblic Policies (POCI-01-0145-FEDER-031905) funded by national funds through FCT.

REFERENCES

[1] P. John, Local Governance in Western Europe. SAGE Publications, 2001.

[2] P. H. Thornton and W. Ocasio, "Institutional Logics," in The sage handbook of organizational institutionalism, R. Greenwood, C. Oliver, R. Suddaby, and K. Sahlin-Andersson, Eds. SAGE Publications, 2008, pp. 99–129.

[3] A. Kruglanski and I. Ajzen, "Bias and error in human judgment," Eur. J. Soc. Phsycologysycology, vol. 13, pp. 1–44, 1983.

[4] H. A. Simon and A. Newell, "Human problem solving: the state of the theory in 1970," Am. Psychol., vol. 26, no. 2, pp. 145–159, 1971.

[5] J. Doyle and R. H. Thomason, "Background to Qualitative Decision Theory," AI Mag. Vol., vol. 20, no. 2, pp. 55–68, 1999, doi: 10.1109/11.735906.

[6] J. S. Davies, "Local Governance and the Dialectics of Hierarchy, Market and Network," Policy Stud., vol. 26, no. 3–4, pp. 311–335, Sep. 2005, doi: 10.1080/01442870500198379.

[7] A. Tversky and D. Kahneman, "Judgment under Uncertainty: Heuristics and Biases", Science (80-.)., vol. 185, no. 4157, pp. 1124–31, Sep. 1974, doi: 10.1126/science.185.4157.1124.

[8] R. Gowda and J. Fox, Judgments, Decisions, and Public Policy. Cambridge: Cambridge University Press, 2002.

[9] S. Miguens, "Notas sobre Racionalidade. Trabalho preparatório para projeto de investigação: Meaning and rationality," / *"Notes on Rationality. Preparatory work for research project: Meaning and rationality,"* 2000.

[10] J. Pligt, "Decision making," in The Blackwell encyclopedia of social psychology, A. Manstead and M. Hewstone, Eds. Oxford: Blackwell, 1999.

[11] Y. Surel, "The role of cognitive and normative frames in policy-making," J. Eur. Public Policy, vol. 7, no. 4, pp. 495–512, Jan. 2000, doi: 10.1080/13501760050165334.

[12] B. Roy, Multicriteria Methodology for Decision Aiding. Springer Science+Business Media Dordrecht, 1996.

[13] G. Majone, "Agenda setting," in The oxford handbook of public policy, M. Moran, M. Rein, and R. Goodin, Eds. Oxford University Press, 2006, pp. 228–250.

[14] D. Arnott and S. Gao, "Behavioral economics for decision support systems researchers," Decis. Support Syst., vol. 122, no. February, p. 113063, 2019, doi: 10.1016/j.dss.2019.05.003.

[15] D. Arnott and G. Pervan, "A Critical Analysis of Decision Support Systems Research," J. Inf. Technol., vol. 20, no. 2, pp. 67–87, Jun. 2005, doi: 10.1057/palgrave.jit.2000035.

[16] H. B. Eom and S. M. Lee, "A Survey of Decision Support System Applications (1971–April 1988)," Interfaces (Providence), vol. 20, no. 3, pp. 65–79, Jun. 1990, doi: 10.1287/inte.20.3.65.

[17] J. Levin and P. Milgrom, "Introduction to Choice Theory," 2004.

[18] J. Marques, M. Borges, P. Batista, C. Gonçalves, and J. Wolf, "Drivers and models to support policies of territorial transformation," in Conference Proceedings on the 4th International Conference on Changing cities: Spatial, Design, Landscape & Socio-economic Dimensions, 2019.

[19] A. M. McCosh and B. A. Correa-Perez, "The optimization of what? Intelligent decision-making support systems." London: Springer, 2006.

[20] S. J. Hoch, H. C. Kunreuther, and R. E. Gunther, Eds., Wharton on making decision. John Wiley & Sons, Inc., 2001.

[21] A. Tversky and D. Kahneman, "The Psychology of Preferences tend to follow regular patterns that can be described mathematically," Sci. Am., vol. 246, pp. 160–173, 1981.

[22] S. Moscovici, "Notes towards a description of Social Representations," 1988.

[23] D. Jodelet, "Social representations: The beautiful invention," J. Theory Soc. Behav., vol. 38, no. 4, pp. 411–430, 2008, doi: 10.1111/j.1468-5914.2008.00383.x.

[24] K. Mathis and A. D. Steffen, "From Rational Choice to Behavioural Economics," in European perspectives on behavioural law and economics, K. Mathis, Ed. Springer, 2016, p. 276.

[25] T. Betsch and S. Haberstroh, The routines of decision making. Lawrence Erlbaum Associates, 2005.

[26] T. Dohmen, A. Falk, D. Huffman, and U. Sunde, "On the relationship between cognitive ability and risk preference," J. Econ. Perspect., vol. 32, no. 2, pp. 115–134, 2018, doi: 10.1257/jep.32.2.115.

[27] R. Ranyard, R. Crozier, and O. Svenson, Decision making. Cognitive models and explanations. Taylor & Francis, 1997.

[28] R. D. Gorbunov, M. Rauterberg, and E. I. Barakova, "A cognitive model of social preferences in group interactions," Integr. Comput. Aided. Eng., vol. 26, no. 2, pp. 185–196, 2019, doi: 10.3233/ICA-180590.

[29] B. Alexandre, J. Navarro, E. Reynaud, and F. Osiurak, "Which cognitive tools do we prefer to use, and is that preference rational?," Cognition, vol. 186, no. February, pp. 108–114, 2019, doi: 10.1016/j.cognition.2019.02.005.

[30] A. Chatzidakis, M. Kastanakis, and A. Stathopoulou, "Socio-Cognitive Determinants of Consumers' Support for the Fair Trade Movement," J. Bus. Ethics, vol. 133, no. 1, pp. 95–109, 2014, doi: 10.1007/s10551-014-2347-9.

[31] C. R. Kuehnhanss, "The challenges of behavioural insights for effective policy design," Policy Soc., vol. 38, no. 1, pp. 14–40, 2019, doi: 10.1080/14494035.2018.1511188.

[32] P. Cairney and C. M. Weible, "The new policy sciences: combining the cognitive science of choice, multiple theories of context, and basic and applied analysis," Policy Sci., vol. 50, no. 4, pp. 619–627, 2017, doi: 10.1007/s11077-017-9304-2.

[33] R. Ewa, "Multi-Criteria Decision Making Models By Applying the Topsis Method To Crisp and Interval Data," Mult. Criteria Decis. Making/University Econ. Katowice, vol. 6, no. MCDM, pp. 200–230, 2011.

[34] C. D. Gamper and C. Turcanu, "On the governmental use of multi-criteria analysis," Ecol. Econ., vol. 62, no. 2, pp. 298–307, Apr. 2007, doi: 10.1016/j.ecolecon.2007.01.010.

[35] D. Sabaei, J. Erkoyuncu, and R. Roy, "A review of multi-criteria decision making methods for enhanced maintenance delivery," Procedia CIRP, vol. 37, pp. 30–35, 2015, doi: 10.1016/j.procir.2015.08.086.

[36] R. Ewa, "Multi-Criteria Decision Making Models By Applying the Topsis Method To Crisp and Interval Data," Mult. Criteria Decis. Making/University Econ. Katowice, vol. 6, no. MCDM, pp. 200–230, 2011.

[37] J. Rezaei, "Best-worst multi-criteria decision-making method," Omega (United Kingdom), vol. 53, pp. 49–57, 2015, doi: 10.1016/j.omega.2014.11.009.

[38] M. D. L. Siahaan, Elviwani, A. B. Surbakti, A. H. Lubis, and A. P. U. Siahaan, "Implementation of Simple Additive Weighting Algorithm in Particular Instance," Int. J. Sci. Res. Sci. Technol., vol. 3, no. 6, pp. 442–447, 2017.

[39] M. Patel, M. P. Vashi, and B. V. Bhatt, "SMART- Multi-criteria decision-making technique for use in planning activities," in NHCE, 2017.

[40] T. L. Saaty, "A scaling method for priorities in hierarchical structures," J. Math. Psychol., vol. 281, pp. 234–281, 1977.

[41] T. L. Saaty, "Decision making with the analytic hierarchy process," iIternational J. Serv. Sci., vol. 1, no. 1, p. 83, 2008, doi: 10.1504/IJSSCI.2008.017590.

[42] J. Wolf, M. Borges, J. L. Marques, and E. Castro, "Smarter Decisions for Smarter Cities: Lessons Learned from Strategic Plans," in New Paths of Entrepreneurship Development: The Role of Education, Smart Cities and Social Factors, C. Rego and M. I. Sánchez-hernández, Eds. Springer, 2019, pp. 7–30.

[43] F. Nogueira, M. Borges, and J. H. Wolf, "Collaborative Decision-Making in Non-formal Planning Settings," Gr. Decis. Negot., pp. 1–16, 2017, doi: 10.1007/s10726-016-9518-2.

[44] J.-J. Wang, Y.-Y. Jing, C.-F. Zhang, and J.-H. Zhao, "Review on multi-criteria decision analysis aid in sustainable energy decision-making," Renew. Sustain. Energy Rev., vol. 13, no. 9, pp. 2263–2278, Dec. 2009, doi: 10.1016/j.rser.2009.06.021.

[45] M. Borges, "Análise prospetiva. O caso do mercado da habitação" / *"Foresight Analysis. Application to the housing market,"* Universidade de Aveiro, 2012.

[46] J. Marques, M. Viegas, M. Borges, and E. Castro, "Designing the housing market for 2030 – a foresight and econometric approach," in 53rd Congress of the European Regional Science Association; 27-31 August; Palermo-Italy, 2013.

[47] J. Marques, J. Wolf, and M. Borges, "Modelling the urban transformation at local scale," Riv. Urban. Inf. dall'Istituto Naz. di Urban., pp. 80–83, 2018.

The Perceived Usage Scenario's of Continuous Monitoring, Continuous Auditing and Continuous Assurance: an Explorative Study

Martijn Zoet
Zuyd University of Applied Sciences
Sittard, the Netherlands
e-mail: Martijn.zoet@zuyd.nl

Koen Smit
HU University of Applied Sciences Utrecht
Utrecht, the Netherlands
e-mail: Koen.smit@hu.nl

Eric Mantelaers
Zuyd University of Applied Sciences
Sittard, the Netherlands
e-mail: Eric.mantelaers@zuyd.nl

Abstract—**Continuous monitoring, continuous auditing and continuous assurance are three methods that utilize a high degree of business intelligence and analytics. The increased interest in the three methods has led to multiple studies that analyze each method or a combination of methods from a micro-level. However, limited studies have focused on the perceived usage scenarios of the three methods from a macro level through the eyes of the end-user. In this study, we bridge the gap by identifying the different usage scenarios for each of the methods according to the end-users, the accountants. Data has been collected through a survey, which is analyzed by applying a nominal analysis and a process mining algorithm. Results show that respondents indicated 13 unique usage scenarios, while not one of the three methods is included in all of the 13 scenarios, which illustrates the diversity of opinions in accountancy practice in the Netherlands.**

Keywords-usage scenarios; continuous monitoring; continuous auditing; continuous assurance.

I. INTRODUCTION

The growth of business intelligence and analytics technology has increased in the last decades. It has helped organizations to get better insights into their operations, make better decisions and allow for evidence-based management. Still, it has been estimated that more than 50% of business intelligence and analytics implementations do not deliver the intended value [1]. Reasons for value dilution are not attributed to the technical perspective, but to the organizational alignment of business intelligence. For example, Hackathorn [2] identified the following three failures: 1) lack of relevance, 2) lack of actionable decision support technologies and 3) lack of alignment with the business. In a literature study by Trieu [3], a decade later, five themes emerged, also focusing on organizational alignment, namely 1) context/environmental factors, 2) business intelligence-conversion processes, 3) business intelligence-use processes, 4) business intelligence competitive process, and 5) latency effects. In this work, Trieu concludes that gaps are existing concerning how to focus on business intelligence development from an operational and competitive advantage and how do configurations and organizational routines impact business intelligence operational effectiveness [4].

A sector that depends highly on business intelligence and analytics technology is the accountancy sector. However, in current research, accountants hardly apply these specific terms. Accountants rather use the term Computer Assisted Audit Techniques (CAATs) [5]. CAATs is an umbrella term for software such as generalized audit software, utility software, test data, application software tracking and mapping, and audit expert systems, that help internal auditors directly test controls built into computerized information systems and data contained in computer files [4]. From a business intelligence and analytics perspective, the previously mentioned CAATs techniques can be seen as narrow business intelligence tools, which is because these tools have predefined data analysis that is defined and built in to support the accountants' tasks. Since recent years, the need for ongoing time assurance has increased [4], so has the need for real-time business intelligence and analytics. Accountants have formulated three different methods of real-time business intelligence namely, 1) continuous monitoring, 2) continuous auditing, and 3) continuous assurance (which will be further detailed in the following section). Research on continuous monitoring, continuous auditing and continuous assurance focuses mainly on technology usage in general [6], the application of business intelligence in specific environments [7], and taxonomy of technology and maturity models [8]. Despite the accumulation of literature, there is a surprisingly scarce amount of research that examines the manner in which the technology is applied, and in addition, whether accountants think that continuous monitoring, continuous auditing and continuous assurance are practically feasible. This presents a gap in current research since accountants are the actual end-users of the methods and underlying information technology. Taking previous statements into account, the following research question arose, which will be tackled in this paper: "*What are the usage scenarios of continuous monitoring, continuous auditing and continuous assurance according to accountants?"*

The current study extends previous research by researching from a macro level the usage scenarios of the three methods applied by accounting. It thereby adds to previous studies that have taken a micro-analysis approach.

The remainder of the paper is organized as follows. In Section 2, a discussion on the theoretical foundations of the background and related work is provided, being foundations on CAATs and accounting. This is followed by the elaboration of the research method in Section 3. In Section 4, the data collection and analysis is presented. Then, in Section 5, the results are presented. This is followed by the conclusions that can be drawn from our data collection and analysis in Section 6, the discussion with a critical view on this study and its results in Section 7, and lastly, a definition of future research directions in Section 8.

II. BACKGROUND AND RELATED WORK

Information technology is applied in most, if not all, occupations to support the execution of tasks. From an activity theory viewpoint, see Figure 1, three elements are applied to reason about this task [9]. These three elements are: 1) the tool applied, 2) the subject that performs the tasks, 3) and the object on which the task is performed. Each of the activities must be seen within the context that they are performed. From an auditing perspective, the subject that performs the activity are accountants.

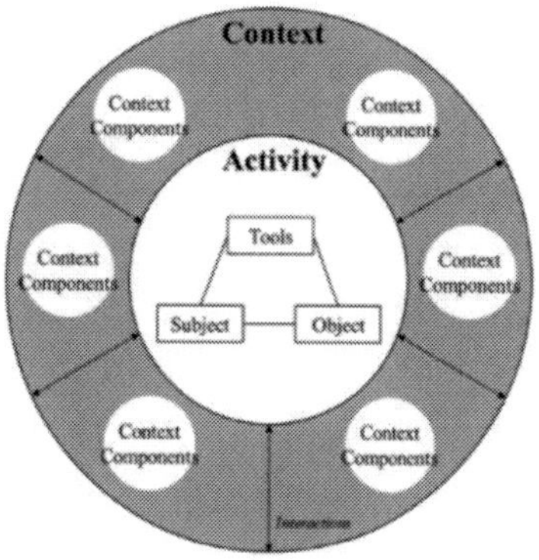

Figure 1. Human activity and context: activity theory and activity-centric view [9].

Accountants perform their tasks on various objects, for example, balance sheet items (e.g., inventory, cash, accounts payable, and accounts receivable), as well as all items from the income statement (e.g., cost of goods sold and sales). If an accountant is responsible for capitals other than purely financial capitals, CO_2 statements are also examined. The goal of performing these tasks on various objects is to provide reasonable assurance that all items are both accurate and complete. To provide reasonable assurance, multiple tools are applied by accountants. Examples of such tools are comprehensive relationship tests. An example of a relationship test is: *"Beginning Accounts Payables + Acquisition (Inventory) - Disbursements = Ending Accounts Payables"* [10]. In addition to generic tools, different information technology is applied by accountants. For example, generalized audit software, spreadsheet software, scripts developed using audit-specific software, specialized audit utilities, CAATs, commercially packaged solutions, and custom-developed production systems. Although information technology is applied, each of the activities executed by the accountant is done retrospectively [11]. From an information systems perspective, many of the tasks performed by accountants can be translated into three steps: 1) collect input data, 2) analyze input data, and 3) report results.

However, as stated in the previous section, accountants still rely heavily on spreadsheet software and only sparsely apply additional techniques. This is because the context variables in which an accountant performs his tasks allowed him or her to do so. Two trends have realized that the accountant has been looking to change from a retrospective to a more proactive approach. On the one hand, the pace of change of organizations and the fact that they have to respond more rapidly to change and emerging risk [12]. On the other hand, the advancements in information technology have made it possible to perform ongoing risk and control assessments [12].

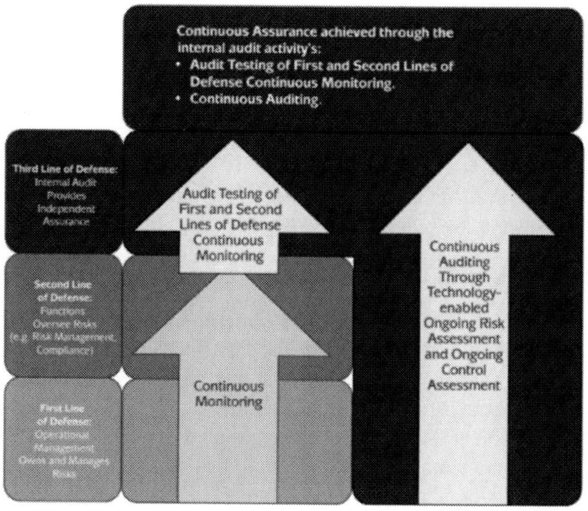

Figure 2. Three lines of defense [13].

From an information technology/data science perspective, this change can be categorized as a change from stand-alone analytics to infused analytics [14]. Standalone analytics is defined as analytics that is performed outside the production system on the data extracted from the production system, the current way of working within accountancy practice. Infused analytics are performed ongoing and real-time. This is where multiple forms of data analyses are applied, such as process mining and decision mining. Within the audit community, three forms of ongoing assessment are recognized, namely: 1) continuous monitoring, 2) continuous auditing and 3) continuous assurance.

Continuous Monitoring (CM) is a method that monitors, on an ongoing basis, whether internal controls are operating effectively [13]. During this monitoring, they assess business risks, financial and operational results and to re-prioritize and rank audit trigger events and risks to control intervals (daily, weekly, monthly, quarterly). Responsible for CM are the operational management, risk management and compliance business functions. When continuous monitoring has been realized the next phase is continuous auditing [13]. Continuous Auditing (CA) is a method that combines technology-enabled ongoing risk assessment and ongoing control assessments. CA enhances the ability of accountants to identify risk indicators, evaluate risk parameters by analyzing systems for changes, security incidents, outliers, and transactions. The goal of CA is issuing audit reports simultaneously with, or a short period after, the data that is entered into the information system or evaluation of the current system. To realize continuous auditing, multi-information systems are applied, for example, generalized audit software, spreadsheet software or scripts developed using audit-specific software, specialized audit utilities, CAATs, commercially packaged solutions, and custom-developed production systems. CA has been broadly researched by multiple researchers [10][15][16]. For example, Kogan et al. [17] researched the continuous monitoring of transactions with a hospital supply chain, utilizing patterns within the business processes to supply information to internal auditing. In addition to research, multiple guidance reports by regulatory bodies also have been published, for example, GTAG 3 Continuous Auditing: Implications for Assurance [13], Monitoring, and Risk Assessment [13] and Information Systems Audit and Control Association (ISACA) its IT Audit and Assurance Guidelines [18]. In 2010, the Australian Institute of Chartered Accountants also published its Continuous Assurance for the Now Economy [19]. Still, multiple studies show that the adoption has been lacking [17][20][21]. Continuous Auditing is the responsibility of both internal auditing and external auditing business functions. When an organization has realized CM and CA, the next phase is Continuous Assurance (CAS). CAS is performed by internal or external audit and is a combination of CA and testing of first and second lines of defense CM. It does so, using technology, by processing information immediately to produce audit results simultaneously or within a short period after the occurrence of relevant events [12]. The CM, CA, and CAS processes are integrally visualized in Figure 2.

III. RESEARCH METHOD

The goal of this study is twofold: firstly, to identify the perceived use of different methods by accountants and secondly to study if accountants are able to make a distinction between different methods. As stated in the introduction of this paper, the utilization of continuous monitoring, continuous auditing, and continuous assurance is mostly studied from the perspective of various data engineering-related roles, lacking the view of the end-user, the accountant. Because the context of the subject under research is widely researched, a quantitative approach is appropriate, which allows us to, on a relatively large scale, research the accountants' perspective with regards to the three techniques. To do so, a survey is selected as a modus operandi for this study. The survey enables, in an empirical manner, to translate the views of accountants into the analysis and development of narrative scenarios [22], [23].

The survey will be conducted among members of the Dutch national accountant's association, spread over several accountancy agencies in the Netherlands. To increase the validity of the results a combination of two accountant-types were included in this study. The first type of accountant included concerns the accounting consultants/auditors (AA in Dutch), which are responsible for, e.g., compilation engagements, advisory regarding tax consultancy, and bookkeeping. The second type of accountant included concerns the chartered auditor (RA in Dutch), which are responsible for, e.g., statutory audits and other assurance engagements.

In total, the survey comprises seven elements, represented by one question each. The first question focuses on deriving the workplace and is used to ensure a proper spread of respondents is achieved amongst our total sample. The second question focuses on the responsibilities of the accountant, concretely, whether the accountant has decision rights (e.g., by mandate) or is a member of the board of directors of the workplace in question. Then, the following three questions focus on the utilization of the three methods, being continuous monitoring, continuous auditing, and continuous assurance. Additionally, the respondents were asked to elaborate on the timeframe they think the methods, for each method, are used or will be used. For this question, the following four answers were possible; 1) I don't know, 2) currently applying the method, 3) will apply the method in one to five years, or 4) it will take more than five years to apply the method. Lastly, two questions were posed that focus on the respondents view of the application of the methods in the accountant's practice in general as well as how the respondent rank themselves against the application of the methods by the accountant's practice in general.

IV. DATA COLLECTION AND ANALYSIS

The survey was distributed to a sample of 8,393 respondents in total, of which 727 responded, which is a response rate of 8.66%. The respondents could return the survey starting from July 11, 2019, until October 16, 2019.

To establish the narrative scenarios from the data collected, a process mining algorithm is applied in Microsoft Power BI. To do so, three input variables were utilized; 1) the case ID, represented by the respondent ID, e.g., 004, 452, 2) the activity ID, represented by the application of the method, i.e., continuous monitoring, continuous auditing, continuous assurance, and 3) the timestamp, represented by the timeframe the respondent thinks the method will be applied, e.g., currently applying the method and one to five years.

V. RESULTS

Regarding the data analysed in an overall sense, thirteen scenarios were discovered, see Figure 4. The majority of respondents (n=466, 64%) indicated that either continuous monitoring, continuous auditing and/or continuous assurance is going to be applied within the accountancy practice. The remainder of the respondents (n=261, 36%) indicate that they either do not know if one of the techniques is going to be implemented or state it is not relevant. Looking at the distribution of the scenarios amongst the respondents, 86.1% indicated their preference for either scenario one, two or three. We argue that the collection of the first three scenarios significantly represent our sample. Therefore, only the first three scenarios are reported in this section.

A. *Board of directors vs. non-board of directors*

As described earlier in this paper, one of the questions in the survey focused on the decision rights of the respondents. In Figure 3, the largest scenarios are depicted, further drilled down to the number of respondents that have decision rights versus respondents that do not have decision rights.

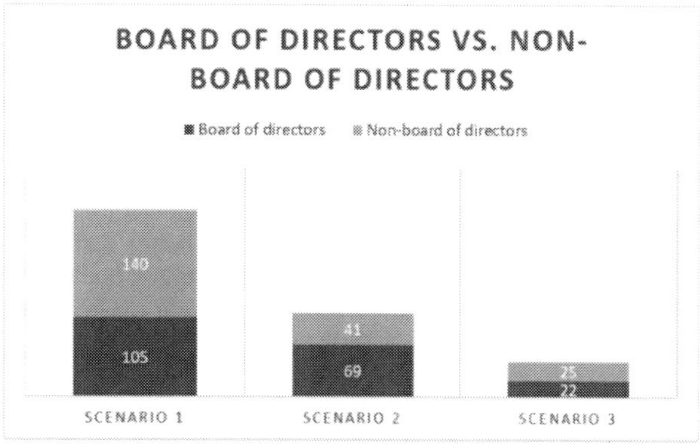

Figure 3. Board of directors versus non-board of directors.

Although the number of respondents with both roles entered all three scenarios similarly, 35 respondents without decision rights more than respondents with decision rights entered the first scenario. The differences between both groups are smaller for the second and third scenario.

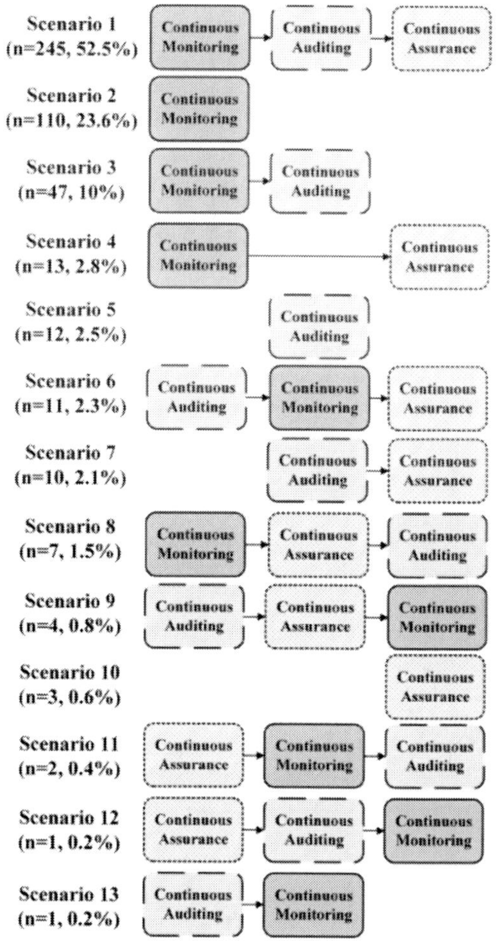

Figure 4. Overview of the discovered usage scenarios.

B. *Type of accountancy practice*

As it can be observed from Figure 5, a large portion of the sample operates either from the public practice or commercial practice.

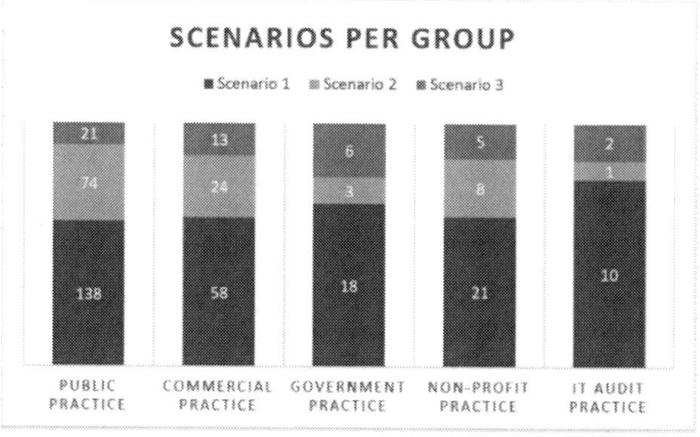

Figure 5. Scenarios per type of accountancy practice.

Across all groups, most indicated the first scenario. Furthermore, although the IT audit practice type of accountants are represented by a relatively small amount of respondents in this study, the distribution of the scenarios seems more skewed towards the first scenario compared to the other types of accountants.

C. *Perceived usage of IT by accountancy practice in general*

The survey also considered the view of respondents with regards to accountancy practice in general. As described earlier in this paper, this was operationalized by a question that focuses on the perceived usage of IT in accountancy practice.

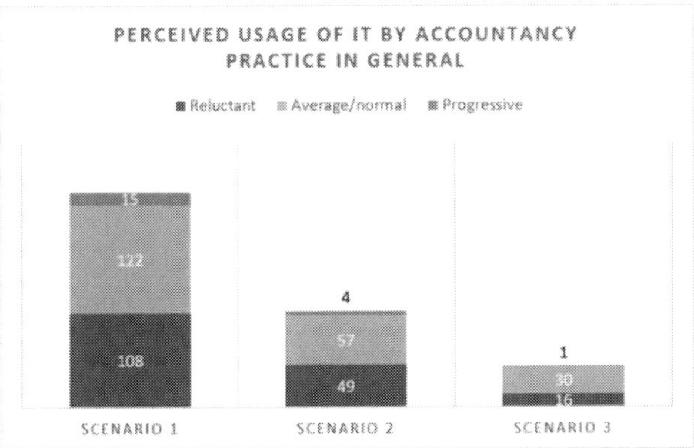

Figure 6. Perceived usage if IT by accountancy practice in general.

As it can be observed from Figure 6, a relatively small number of respondents indicate that the accountancy practice, in general, are not progressive in their IT usage. A similar number of respondents indicated both reluctant and average/normal IT usage.

VI. Discussion

Like all research studies, this study has several limitations that should be considered when interpreting the results and conclusions. The first limitation concerns the percentage of respondents that filled in the survey. Out of the 8.393 surveys sent, 727 respondents completed the survey, which results in a response rate of 8.66%. Considering the fact that a third party database with email-addresses was used to send out the questionnaire, we consider 8.66% percent as a respectable return rate [26]. In addition to the number of respondents, another limitation is the population to which the survey was distributed. This population exists out of registered accountants, of both types described, in the Netherlands. Previous research has shown that accountants in the western world have a likewise adoption of information technology. However, this research can therefore only be generalized towards the Dutch population of accountants. Lastly, one could argue that the results presented in this paper offer a view into what accountants 'think about' the use of CM, CA and CAS in combination with technology, therefore producing a possible difference between 'empirical' experience, opinions and perception. This does not compromise the findings of this preliminary empirical research that should be utilized to further research the actual usage (hard figures) of technology to perform CM, CA and CAS by accountants.

VII. Conclusion

In this paper, an answer is provided to the following research question: *'What are the usage scenarios of continuous monitoring, continuous auditing, and continuous assurance according to accountants?'* To answer this question, a survey is distributed amongst a large sample of Dutch accountants. In this study, because of the nascent nature of the perspective of the accountant in a mature research domain, no inferential analysis was utilized. To ground the conclusions, it is important to note that, from a literature point of view, the scenario of 1) continuous monitoring, 2) continuous auditing, and 3) continuous assurance is the most fundamentally researched and proven approach, e.g., see [13][24][25]. The same holds for the practical application of IT in accountancy, where it is, from a technical point-of-view, impossible to first establish continuous assurance before continuous monitoring is implemented. This also validates the decision to only include the first three scenarios in the analysis as some combinations of scenarios four to thirteen are impossible to implement in practice. An explanation for combinations that seem impossible to implement in practice could lie in the fact that respondents believe that only part of the methods of 1) continuous monitoring, 2) continuous auditing, and 3) continuous assurance lies within their responsibility. For example, an accountant might think that continuous monitoring and continuous auditing should be conducted by a client so that the accountant him or herself can provide continuous assurance. Although this explanation validates scenarios in which only one or two of the three methods are indicated, it does not explain practically impossible scenarios in which the sequence is scrambled.

Based on the descriptive statistics of the board of directors versus the non-board of directors, differences are observed between the number of respondents that indicated the first scenario, although they do not insinuate significance. The same holds for the scenarios indicated per type of accountancy practice. Taking a closer look at the differences in scenarios indicated by types of accountancy practice, the IT audit practice seems to suggest a stronger preference for scenario one compared to the other types of accountancy practice. This is interesting as it could suggest that more technology-savvy accountants understand the sequence and dependencies between the three methods. Lastly, the results regarding the perceived usage of IT by accountancy practice, in general, seems to depict a negative attitude towards IT adoption by accountancy practice in general. This could be part of the explanation for the impossible scenarios because many accountants could lack awareness of the possibilities that technology brings for them to support the methods of continuous monitoring, continuous auditing and continuous assurance.

VIII. Future Research

The first direction for future research concerns the addition of accountants registered in other countries, whereby western as non-western countries should be included in the sample, as practices can differ. The second direction for further research is triggered by the scenario's that only apply continuous auditing and/or continuous assurance. One possible explanation for these scenarios can be that the accountants believe that continuous monitoring and/or continuous auditing should be implemented by their clients. To investigate this possible explanation further, future research should include the expected usage of the previously mentioned methods by audit clients. Since this research is characterized as explorative, additional research should be performed. Future research should focus on an analysis of the situational factors to assess the minimal number of situational factors necessary to classify the continuous auditing, continuous monitoring and continuous assurance problem space, which in term can be used to define specific implementation scenarios. Lastly, the relationship between combined assurance (see e.g., [27]) and the results of this study could be further investigated in future research.

References

[1] I. S. Ko and S. R. Abdullaev, "A Study on the Aspects of Successful Business Intelligence System Development," in *Proceedings of the Int. Conf. on Computational Science*, 2007, pp. 729–732.

[2] R. Hackathorn, "Making business intelligence actionable," *DM Rev.*, p. 32, 2002.

[3] V. H. Trieu, "Getting value from Business Intelligence systems: A review and research agenda," *Decis. Support Syst.*, vol. 93, pp. 111–124, 2017.

[4] M. A. Vasarhelyi, M. Alles, S. Kuenkaikaew, and J. Littley, "The acceptance and adoption of continuous auditing by internal auditors: A micro analysis," *Int. J. Account. Inf. Syst.*, vol. 13, no. 3, pp. 267–281, 2012.

[5] S. A. Sayana and C. CISA, "Using CAATs to support IS audit," *Inf. Syst. Control J.*, vol. 1, pp. 21–23, 2003.

[6] H. Abou-El-Sood, A. Kotb, and A. Allam, "Exploring auditors' perceptions of the usage and importance of audit information technology," *Int. J. Audit.*, vol. 19, no. 3, pp. 252–266, 2015.

[7] J. R. Kuhn Jr and S. G. Sutton, "Continuous auditing in ERP system environments: The current state and future directions," *J. Inf. Syst.*, vol. 24, no. 1, pp. 91–112, 2010.

[8] E. Mantelaers and M. Zoet, "Continuous Auditing: A Practical Maturity Model," in *MCIS 2018 Proceedings*, 2018, pp. 1–12.

[9] J. Kim, Y. Chang, A. Y. L. Chong, and M.-C. Park, "Do perceived use contexts influence usage behavior? An instrument development of perceived use context," *Inf. Manag.*, vol. 56, no. 7, pp. 103–155, Nov. 2019.

[10] E. Mantelaers, M. Zoet, and K. Smit, "The Impact of Blockchain on the Auditor's Audit Approach," *J. Adv. Manag. Sci.*, vol. 8, no. 1, p. IN PRESS, 2020.

[11] Z. Rezaee, R. Elam, and A. Sharbatoghlie, "Continuous auditing: the audit of the future," *Manag. Audit. J.*, vol. 16, no. 3, pp. 150–158, 2001.

[12] R. A. Teeter and M. A. Vasarhelyi, *Audit Analytics and Continuous Audit: Looking Toward the Future*. New York, USA: AICPA, 2015.

[13] B. Ames, R. D'Cunha, P. Geugelin-Dannegger, P. B. Millar, S. Rai, and A. Robertson, "Global Technology Audit Guide (GTAG) 3: Continuous Auditing: Cordinate Continuous Auditing and Monitoring to Provide Continuous Assurance," 2015.

[14] M. Goul, T. S. Raghu, and R. D. St Louis, "Governing the Wild West of Predictive Analytics and Business Intelligence," *MIS Q. Exec.*, vol. 17, no. 2, 2018.

[15] A. Kogan, M. G. Alles, M. A. Vasarhelyi, and J. Wu, "Design and evaluation of a continuous data level auditing system," *Audit. A J. Pract. Theory*, vol. 33, no. 4, pp. 221–245, 2014.

[16] S. Flowerday, A. W. Blundell, and R. Von Solms, "Continuous auditing technologies and models: A discussion," *Comput. Secur.*, vol. 25, no. 5, pp. 325–331, 2006.

[17] A. Kogan, E. F. Sudit, and M. A. Vasarhelyi, "Continuous online auditing: A program of research," *J. Inf. Syst.*, vol. 13, no. 2, pp. 87–103, 1999.

[18] ISACA, "G42 Continuous Assurance," 2010.

[19] M. A. Vasarhelyi, M. Alles, and K. T. Williams, "Continuous assurance for the now economy," 2010.

[20] M. Alles, G. Brennan, A. Kogan, and M. Vasarhelyi, "Continous monitoring of business process controls: A pilot implementation of a continuous auditing system at Siemens," *J. Account. Inf. Syst.*, pp. 137–161, 2006.

[21] M. G. Alles, A. Kogan, and M. A. Vasarhelyi, "Feasibility and economics of continuous assurance," *Audit. A J. Pract. Theory*, vol. 21, no. 1, pp. 125–138, 2002.

[22] E. G. Mishler, "Models of narrative analysis: A typology," *J. Narrat. life Hist.*, vol. 5, no. 2, pp. 87–123, 1995.

[23] J. Mahoney, "Nominal, ordinal, and narrative appraisal in macrocausal analysis," *Am. J. Sociol.*, vol. 104, no. 4, pp. 1154–1196, 1999.

[24] R. van Hillo and H. Weigand, "Continuous auditing & continuous monitoring: Continuous value?," in *IEEE Tenth International Conference on Research Challenges in Information Science (RCIS)*, 2016, pp. 1–11.

[25] Z. Rezaee, A. Sharbatoghlie, R. Elam, and P. L. McMickle, "Continuous auditing: Building automated auditing capability," *Audit. A J. Pract. Theory*, vol. 21, no. 1, pp. 147–163, 2002.

[26] R. I. Radics, S. Dasmohapatra, and S. S. Kelley, "Public perception of bioenergy in North Carolina and Tennessee," *Energy. Sustain. Soc.*, vol. 6, no. 1, p. paper 17, 2016.

[27] K. Barac and J. Forte, "Combined assurance: a systematic process," *South. African J. Account. Audit. Res.*, vol. 17, no. 2, pp. 71–83, 2015.

A Functional Architecture for the Elicitation, Design and Specification of Business Decisions and Business Logic

Koen Smit
HU University of Applied Sciences Utrecht
Utrecht, the Netherlands
e-mail: koen.smit@hu.nl

Sam Leewis
HU University of Applied Sciences Utrecht
Utrecht, the Netherlands
e-mail: sam.leewis@hu.nl

Martijn Zoet
Zuyd University of Applied Sciences
Sittard, the Netherlands
e-mail: martijn.zoet@zuyd.nl

***Abstract*—Functional architectures are created to be used as a standard by their respective industry. Organizations use reference functional architectures to guide their development or as a means to become compliant. However, a reference functional architecture to manage business decisions and business logic does not yet exist. One research field that focuses on the management of business decisions and business logic is Business Rules Management (BRM). By analyzing the functional requirements of seven Dutch governmental institutions with regards to the elicitation, design and specification of business decisions and business logic, we aim to propose the first version of a reference functional architecture for BRM. To do so, we utilized three thematic coding rounds to analyze 536 functional requirements for BRM solutions, resulting in 18 functional categories and mapped the functional categories to the BRM capabilities. The results form a first basis for the construction of a reference functional architecture for BRM capabilities, also identifying multiple directions for future research.**

Keywords-Business Rules Management; Functional Architecture; Functional Requirements.

I. INTRODUCTION

Decisions are amongst the most important assets of an organization [1], and business decisions and business logic are an important part of an organization's daily activities. Therefore, the performance of an organization depends on the ability to manage its business decisions and business logic [2].

To structure the process of managing business decisions and business logic, Business Rules Management (BRM) could be utilized. BRM comprises a systematic and controlled approach to support the elicitation, design, specification, verification, validation, deployment, execution, governance, and monitoring of business decisions and business logic [3]–[6], see Figure 1.

Considering the BRM research domain, a predominant focus towards technically-oriented research can be identified. For example, Nelson et al. [7] state: "*studies provide beginnings of a business rules research program, but collectively the research often overlooks major steps in BRM and fails to focus on business rules specific challenges and the larger context that rules play in organizations.*" Moreover, Kovacic [8] argues about the current research directions in the BRM research field, stating: "*With so much emphasis towards the technological aspects, we can lose sight of the management of information systems considerations.*"

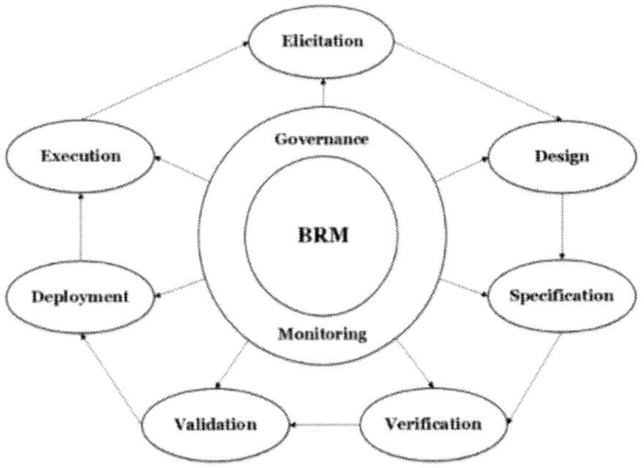

Figure 1. BRM capability overview [3]–[6].

Therefore, we identify that there is an imbalance when comparing technical-oriented research to the management of information systems and BRM artefacts used in BRM processes. In addition, in the work of Arnott and Pervan [9] featuring a thorough literature review, a conclusion is drawn stating that the field has lost its connection with industry some time ago and research input with practical relevance is scarce. Arnott and Pervan revisited the knowledge base in 2014 and concluded that a transition is taking place towards a more practical-oriented approach, whilst a strong connection between theory and practice is still lacking [10], which is also concluded in the work of Zoet [11]. Therefore, research conducted in the area of BRM should also ground practical usability, while taking into account the theory as part of the existing academic knowledge base on BRM.

In this study, we revisit an extended version of our dataset containing functional requirements from seven large Dutch governmental institutions intending to derive a functional architecture that other organizations could utilize to design BRM solutions. In an earlier study [12] we identified that some research has been conducted on BRM-related functional architectures. For example, Schlosser, Baghi, Otto and Oesterle [5] propose three architectural perspectives that could guide organizations designing BRM solutions, however, do so at a high-level of abstraction. Our previous study, in which we analyzed a set of 750 BRM-related functional requirements, resulted in a functional framework in which we identified several themes per BRM capability [12]. This study seeks to extend the understanding of functional requirements, in the context of BRM, by exploring the required functionalities for Business Rules Management Systems. This paper focuses on the first three BRM capabilities, being elicitation, design, and specification. To do so, we aim to answer the following research question: "Which functional requirement categories should be taken into account when designing a BRM functional architecture for the elicitation, design and specification capabilities?"

The remainder of this paper is structured as follows: In Section 2, we provide insights into the elicitation, design and specification BRM capabilities, as well as the value of functional architectures in the domain of BRM. In Section 3, the research method that was utilized to collect and analyze the data required to construct the functional architectures is described. In Section 4, the manner in which the data is collected, as well as analyzed is presented. In Section 5, the functional architectures are presented and elaborated in the results Section. In Section 6, we discuss the conclusions of our research and provide discussion about our research method and results. Section 7 presents possible directions for future results.

II. BACKGROUND AND RELATED WORK

Organizations are increasingly looking for ways to automate products and services. Doing so, organizations need to ensure that these products and services take into account all legal sources that influence the organization doing business, i.e., law, regulations, internal policies or international conventions [13]. To do so, business decisions and underlying business logic are implemented. Business decisions and business logic are an important part of an organization's daily activities. A business decision is defined as: "A conclusion that a business arrives at through business logic and which the business is interested in managing" [14]. Moreover, business logic is defined as: "a collection of business rules, business decision tables, or executable analytic models to make individual business decisions" [15]. In theory and practice, business decisions and business logic comprise several different concepts, such as derivation structures, decision tables, business vocabularies, fact type models and rule requirements [16], [17]. However, as our focus in this paper is not to define these different concepts that are utilized in a variety of ways by organizations, we adhere to these concepts as artifacts in a general sense. Example artefacts (i.e., sources, contexts and business rules) used to define and implement business decisions and business logic are depicted in Figure 2. See, for a detailed description of each of the concepts to design, specify, and execute business decisions and business logic in the work of Smit and Zoet [17]. When individual artefacts are affected in the functional category, the artefact is specified with a label, e.g., '*derivation structure*'. However, when it concerns the collection of all artefacts, the general term 'artefact' is used in this paper.

The previous section already mentioned the specific focus of this study on the elicitation, design and specification BRM capabilities. Based on the definition of [15], a capability is defined as: "*An ability that an organization, person, or system, possesses.*" A detailed explanation of each capability can be found in [6], [17]. However, to ground our research, a summary of the elicitation, design, specification, verification, deployment, execution, governance and monitoring capabilities is provided here.

The purpose of the elicitation capability is twofold. First, the purpose is to determine the knowledge that needs to be captured from various legal sources to realize the value proposition of the business rules [18]. Different types of legal sources from which knowledge can be derived are, for example, laws, regulations, policies, internal documentation, guidance documents, parliament documents, official disclosures, implementation instructions, and experts. Depending on the type of knowledge source(s), for example, documentation versus experts, different methods, processes, techniques and tools to extract the knowledge are applied [19]. The second purpose is to conduct an impact analysis is if a business rule architecture is already in place. When all relevant knowledge is captured, the business decisions need to be designed in the design capability. The purpose of the design capability is to establish a business rules architecture, which contains the business decisions and how the business decisions are derived to deliver the value proposition [16]. After the business rule architecture is designed, the contents of the business decisions need to be specified in the specification capability. The purpose of the specification capability is to write the business logic and create the fact types needed to define or constrain some particular aspect of the business. After the business logic is created, it is verified and validated in the verification and validation capabilities, respectively.

The capabilities described are implemented by organizations in different ways. One common approach is to implement information systems that are tailored to one or a combination of the elicitation, design and specification capabilities. Such information systems are often referred to as Business Rules Management Systems (BRMS) [18][19]. Looking at the architecture of Information systems, decomposition can be achieved by the creation of several different architectural views or perspectives, i.e., technical, functional, information, data, process, components, service or classes [20]. Analysis of the BRM body of knowledge shows that the functional perspective, also referred to as the functional architecture, has received little attention [5][7], [8] compared to the technical perspectives. The functional architecture perspective is equally important compared to the other perspectives as it guides, especially business stakeholders, with the exact functionality an information system offers to execute a capability. Developing a functional architecture for BRM capabilities is therefore also in line with the lack of research in the BRM domain that is practically oriented [9]–[11]. In this paper we adhere to the following definition of a functional architecture: a functional architecture comprises a modular decomposition of the functionality of an information system [21].

Functional Architecture of software products, which comprises: a modular decomposition of the product functionality; a simple notation for easy comprehension by non-specialists; and applicability in any line of business, offering a uniform method for modeling the functionalities of software products [21]. Functional architecture perspectives are, for example, utilized in practice by integrating them in standard operating models [22][23]. Examples of such models are the eTOM business process framework [24], the Insurance Application Architecture (IAA) [25] and the Banking Industry Architecture Network (BIAN) [26]. Functional architectures for BRM can be established using both inductive, as well as deductive reasoning. The current body of knowledge does not contain detailed contributions to help the construction of a functional architecture for the BRM capabilities. Therefore, the approach in this paper follows an inductive approach to construct a BRM functional architecture from the BRM-related requirements that are collected. In this paper, we solely focus on functional requirements with regards to BRM systems as a functional requirement emphasizes what is required, and not how. This is in line with the notion of a capability, which also focuses on what (value) an organization can deliver, but not how the value is delivered. The functional requirements are often created by subject-matter experts, which are also the stakeholders and end-users of the BRMS that is being designed or developed. This strengthens the validity of the resulting functional architecture.

In literature and practice, several methods exist to formulate functional requirements, i.e., personas, wireframing, use cases, mockups, and user stories [27]. User stories are increasingly being adopted and are comprehensible by, i.e., both developers and customers and support participatory design by all stakeholders as they are all able to design the behavior of the system. In addition to user stories, the agile community [28] also utilize epics and themes. An epic is a large user story while a theme is a collection of user stories. Making use of user stories enables empirical-focused design by enabling the designers to make decisions by studying prospective users in typical situations [28]. The organizations analyzed all defined their functional requirements employing user stories. Therefore, in our study, the unit of analysis is a user story.

III. RESEARCH METHOD

This research aims at creating a functional architecture containing the BRM capabilities: Elicitation, Design, and Specification. Therefore, qualitative research is selected as our research methodology. Case study research is chosen as the most suitable strategy for this research.

By selecting case study research, the researchers were able to gather functional requirements for the BRM capabilities Elicitation, Design, and Specification in the Dutch public sector. Our study utilizes a holistic case study approach, more on this in the work of Yin [29]. This case study approach features one context, BRM solutions requirements phase, and four cases containing in this context. The BRM solution-related set of functional requirements of the participating organizations is set as the unit of analysis. The data collection consisted of secondary data, which is a form of third-degree data collection. According to [30], when data, such as requirements are studied, third-degree data collection is the best fit. The coding of the functional architecture consists of three rounds of coding according to Strauss and Corbin's process of open coding, axial coding, and selective coding [31].

IV. DATA COLLECTION AND ANALYSIS

The data collection for this study occurred for eleven months, between November 2016 and September 2017. The selection of the participants is based on the group of individuals, organizations, information technology, or community which best represents the studied phenomenon [31]. Related to this study, the studied phenomenon is represented by organizations, and individuals within these organizations, which deal with the selection of BRM solution-related requirements. Organizations dealing with these BRM solution-related requirements are often financial and government institutions because of the large-transaction, knowledge-intensive, digital products and services they deliver. Therefore, several Dutch executive governmental agencies were invited to provide requirements for this study. Executive governmental agencies are responsible for the execution of a variety of services like the screening of immigrants, handling student loans, tax returns etc. thereby serving approximately 17 million citizens and organizations in the Netherlands. The participating governmental agencies are comparable in terms of business processes. The participating seven governmental agencies requested that their data is handled anonymously. Therefore, from this moment on, the organizations are labelled as A, B, C, D, E, F, and G, as shown in Table I. The participating organizations were invited to gather and send all their BRM solutions-related requirement documentation to the researchers. Each organization defined their BRM solution-related requirements with a team existing of an enterprise architect, business rules architect, business rules analyst, legal or policy expert. Additional support was provided by a procurement officer, BRM project manager, business consultant, IT architect and external advisors.

Based on the data received, the researchers analysed and structured the functional requirements. The data analysis consisted of three rounds of thematic coding, according to Strauss and Corbin's process of 1) open coding, 2) axial coding, and 3) selective coding [31]. During the coding rounds, two researchers coded separately from each other thereby increasing the inter-reliability in the coding [32].
The first round of coding is the open coding round. The open coding round identifies the functional requirements from the secondary data together with the meta-data of the functional requirements. To ensure optimal analysis the researchers numbered each requirement with a unique ID. Additionally, for each requirement the responsible role (i.e., manager or business rule analyst) was added, the feature (what does the owner or role wants with the functionality), the feature outcome (the benefit of the functionality), organization and an organization ID (to ensure the traceability of the functional requirement towards the case organization documents). During this round of coding, two situations occurred: I) The functional requirements could be documented explicitly by registering the organization name and organization ID, as shown in Table I, or II) the functional requirements were stated implicitly as nested requirements or plain text.

The second round of coding is the axial coding round. Axial coding refines and differentiates concepts that are already available and code them into categories [33]. The axial coding round was utilized to structure the functional requirements over the BRM capabilities Elicitation, Design and Specification proposed by [6][17]. Therefore, the coding scheme in this round is as follows: Elicitation, Design, and Specification. For example, the two requirements in Table I are coded into the Elicitation capability.

The third and thereby last round of coding is selective coding. The purpose of the selective coding round is the identification of functional categories [33]. This round of coding is focused on the identification of categories within the set of functional requirements distributed over the BRM capabilities in the axial coding round. Our earlier work on functional requirement themes for BRM capabilities is also taken into account in this coding round, which resulted in eleven functional themes [12]. These were (Elicitation) 1) Import Sources, 2) Annotate Sources, 3) Generate Overviews, 4) Perform Impact-Analysis, (Design) 5) Create Business Decisions, 6) Create Relationships, 7) Create Overviews, 8) Reuse Business Decisions, (Specification) 9) Define Business Logic, 10) Add Meta-Data, and 11) Create Relationships. These themes could influence the functional architecture that is being constructed in this paper.

TABLE I. EXAMPLES OF CODED FUNCTIONAL REQUIREMENTS

ID	Role	Feature	Outcome	Organization	Organization reference	Category
7	Rule Analyst	I want an overview of all relevant sources	So that I can scope the project	A	5.3	Create Overview
13	Rule Analyst	I want to be able to include a source in the analysis environ-ment	So that the source is in the system ready for analysis	B	PR13_UR_A_1	Import Sources

Additionally, the coded categories in the three capabilities are checked for possible overlap. An example of this is the category ''impact analysis'' which exists in the Elicitation, Design, and Specification capability

V. RESULTS

In this section, the results of our data collection and analysis are presented and elaborated. Per coding round, as described in the previous section, descriptive results are provided. This is followed by the presentation of the functional architecture and the elaboration of the functional categories it comprises.

TABLE II. BREAKDOWN OF FUNCTIONAL REQUIREMENTS RECEIVED FROM THE CASE ORGANIZATIONS

Organization	Total number of functional requirements identified
A	130
B	52
C	126
D	67
E	123
F	38
G	0

For the construction of the functional architecture, to the knowledge of the authors, no explicit practices or specific guidelines exist. However, to theoretically ground the construction of the functional architecture, several definitions are analyzed that comprise one or multiple characteristics that compose a functional architecture. This leads us to the following criteria [21][34][35]: 1) a functional architecture represents a high-level view of the major functions from a usage perspective, 2) a functional architecture specifies the interactions of functions internally between each other and externally with other products, 3) the functionalities presented represent arrangements of requirements, 4) the functional architecture should be expressed in easy to understand diagrams, 5) the functional architecture should be constructed with the input of relevant stakeholders, such as product managers, architects, and managers.

The open coding resulted in the registration of 536 functional requirements, originating from seven organizations, see Table II.

TABLE III. BREAKDOWN OF FUNCTIONAL REQUIREMENTS PER BRM CAPABILITY

Organization/ Capability	Elicitation		Design		Specification		Total
A	0	0.0%	8	1.6%	122	22.7%	130
B	1	0.1%	4	0.8%	47	8.7%	52
C	12	2.2%	52	9.7%	62	11.5%	126
D	20	3.7%	25	4.6%	22	4.2%	67
E	42	7.8%	14	2.7%	67	12.5%	123
F	1	0.1%	7	1.4%	30	5.7%	38
G	0	0%	0	0%	0	0%	0

Subsequently, the second round of coding consisted of assigning the functional requirements to either the elicitation, design or specification BRM capability as described in the previous section. The results of this process are presented in Table III. In the second coding round, no differences were identified between both researchers.

The third round of coding resulted in the identification of 18 functional requirement categories, see Figure 3. For each functional requirement category, we report on its number, functionality and possible overlap with functionality categories as part of the other BRM capabilities. In the third coding round, 14 differences were identified in the coding and were resolved by the third researcher. Lastly, to better understand the artefacts described in this section, we refer to Section 2 in this paper, as well as the work of Smit and Zoet [6].

A. *Elicitation*

With regards to the elicitation capability, four functional categories were identified: 1) Import Sources, 2) Annotate Sources, 3) Perform Impact Analysis, and 4) Compare Sources.

1) Import Sources - The knowledge needed to create business decisions and business logic is elicitated from a variety of different sources, i.e., laws, regulations, policies, internal documentation, guidance documents, parliament documents, implementation instructions, and official disclosures [12]. This functionality encompasses the import of a source, which must be supported in both manual and automated style. As these sources come in different formats or type of documents, the functionality should support as many as possible extensions that can be imported, i.e., MS Office document types, PDF, XML, other open-source word processors, or HTML. Also, in some source types, tables and figures or other representations are important to take into account. Therefore, functional support for importing media as part of sources is deemed important.

2) Annotate Sources – Concerns the manual annotation of sources used to create business decisions and business logic, i.e., derivation structures, terms, or roles. As organizations all differ significantly from each other in terms of what concepts to annotate in sources, i.e., fact types, sentences or sections, functional support to ensure organizations can modify the concepts to annotate should be taken into account. This also includes the support for definition and use of templates for analysts to use during the annotation process.

3) Compare Sources – Encompasses the functional support to compare two or more sources. This is required by analysts that are tasked to review the changes to legal sources that affect the already implemented business decisions and business logic. Comparison of sources must be supported in an automated way in which the machine recognizes and labels Create, Update, and Delete modification types. Similar to the import source functionality, functional support for multiple document types is essential as these documents need to be compared exactly as published by their source. Functional support for automatic comparison of sources enables the reduction of human error and could boost efficiency because of the decrease in manual comparison.

4) Perform Impact Analysis – Allows the user to determine the impact of modified sources with regards to already implemented business decisions and business logic. This functionality should enable the selection of artefacts to review its dependencies with other artefacts, which, on the one hand, encompasses the support for manual impact analysis. On the other hand, functional support for an automatic impact assessment that enables a user to input scenario variables to calculate the impact should be present as well. Automatic impact assessment is regarded as it allows for higher efficiency and less human error. The results of an impact analysis are often used for communication with stakeholders and to determine a course of action. Therefore, there must be functional support for exporting (part of) the impact assessment results in the format and with the variables that the organization requires.

B. *Design*

With regards to the design capability, two functional categories were identified: 5) Navigate Artefact Structure and 6) Define templates.

5) Navigate Artefact Structure – The roles responsible for creating or modifying business decisions and business logic need to be able to search and navigate efficiently and effectively to be able to do so. This could be achieved in several ways, depending on the requirements of the organizations, however, the navigation should support the selection of all possible artefacts to view during navigation through business decisions and business logic. While doing so, maintaining a proper level of abstraction is important, modifying the level of abstraction by minimizing or maximizing artefacts is deemed important. Lastly, functional support to navigate by selecting an artefact type or the relationship between artefacts should be taken into account as well.

6) Define templates – To promote consistency when structuring artefacts, organizations must be able to define and manage templates. Utilization of templates ensures that artefacts are structured consistently. Templates can be required by the machine that is responsible for executing the templates, being business decisions and underlying business logic. Organizations must be able to modify templates to match their context, on top of being able to use standard templates (usually included by the vendor of the software).

C. Specification

With regards to the specification capability, three functional categories were identified: 7) Import Artefact, 8) Export Artefact, and 9) Compare Artefacts.

7) Import Artefact – Similar to the import of sources, import of artefacts is useful as it enables roles to efficiently create or modify artefacts without having to manually insert one of many variables required to do so. Because organizations organize their elicitation and design capabilities different, either supported by information systems or by using word processors, this category requires functional support for different formats or type of documents, see also functional category one. Additionally, when importing artefacts, a role must be able to select what artefacts, type of artefacts and relationships to import. According to the data, a translation of annotation and artefacts between the elicitation and specification capabilities may be required. This means that a role must be able to translate annotations automatically into artefacts utilized in the specification capability. Lastly, because more artefacts are shared nowadays, also between colleague government institutions, import of artefacts from external data sources must be supported.

8) Export Artefact – At some point during or after the specification of business decisions and business logic, a user must be able to export artefacts, which can have several reasons. Usually, this is for either the testing/acceptation, communication or documentation of the business decisions and underlying business logic. Each reason requires different file formats, thus the user must be able to select the type of document that must be exported. Additionally, the representation of the contents in the export is an important factor, depending on the reason for the export. A user must be able to select the representational notation in which the contents are presented in the exported document, i.e., decision tables [36], structured English (controlled natural language) [37] or The Decision Model (model-based) [16]. Similar to importing artefacts, a user must be able to modify whether all artefacts within a given scope or a selection of artefacts or artefact types are exported.

9) Compare Artefacts – The comparison of artefacts is different from the comparison of sources as it focuses on artefacts that are internally created, modified or implemented. Comparison of artefacts must be supported in an automated way in which the machine recognizes and labels Create, Update, and Delete modification types. While comparing artefacts, presentation of meta-data of the artefacts is important, as well as it allows for quick identification and reduces human error.

D. Overlapping functional categories

With regards to the overlapping functional categories that show overlap with all three capabilities, six functional categories were identified: 10) Verify Artefact and Relations, 11) Capture Artefact Meta-data, 12) Capture Additional Artefact Information, 13) Create Overviews, 14) Filter Artefacts, and 15) Capture Artefact Relationships.

10) Verify Artefact and Relations – During the execution of processes along with the elicitation, design and specification capabilities, a multitude of artefacts are created, updated or deleted. The capability following the specification capability is verification, which ensures all business decisions and underlying business logic is syntactically and semantically correct. However, there is no fixed sequentially of the processes conducted as part of the specification or verification capabilities, mainly because this is dependent on how verification is executed, as well as the tooling that is used. Verification can be performed using four techniques: 1) manual detection, 2) manual preventions, 3) automatic detection, and 4) automatic prevention [38]. The data shows that a user must be able to request verification or an artefact or a relationship between artefacts while using a system, as well as being supported by a system that interrupts a user when a syntax or semantic error is detected. Therefore, functional support for a combination of automatic detection (initiated by a user) and automatic prevention must be taken into account.

11) Capture Artefact Meta-data – This functional category focuses on all data captured to support the governance capability, which consists of three sub-capabilities: 1) traceability management, 2) version management, and 3) validity management. More meta-data captured in the elicitation, design and specification capabilities result in more efficient and effective governance during the entire lifecycle of a business decision and its underlying business logic. For example, development status is more efficiently determined when all artefacts under a business decision that is being designed and specified are accompanied by a status and/or version number, which is required for proper version management. For validity management, this means that a user must be able to capture and store variables that represent the validity status of the artefact as provided by the source. For traceability management, this means that a user must be able to capture and store variables that focus on coupling artefacts with each other in a specific format. Additionally, the organization must be able to modify the functionality to capture meta-data as the requirements with regards to governance are different for each organization.

12) Capture Additional Artefact Information – Additional to capturing meta-data required for the governance capability, the data shows a demand for functional support for capturing additional artefact information that is not required to be able to execute or govern the business decision and underlying business logic. Additional artefact information is required, mainly, due to two reasons. First, it enables more effective communication among stakeholders that are responsible for (parts of) the artefacts being created or modified. Second, it enables communication with end-users or clients actually using the business decision, i.e., a governmental portal in which citizens apply for child benefits. The variables allowed to be additionally captured with regards to an artefact depends on the organization and its context. Examples of additional artefact information that were identified in the data are: explanations, motivation/rationale, notes, design or specification decisions per person or role, help text or appendices. Also, a user must be able to capture additional artefact information in each of the, usually, several abstraction levels, i.e., fact-level, decision logic-level, and decision requirements-level [6].

13) Create Overviews – In most organizations large amounts of artefacts are utilized to implement business decisions and underlying business logic. These amounts can pose challenges when searching or reporting certain artefacts, artefact relationships or artefact types. A user must, therefore, be able to create overviews (also referred to as reports) per artefact or other units of analysis. One type of overview that is often identified in the data are meta-data overviews (i.e., generating an overview with all version numbers and validity periods of an artefact), which emphasize that there must be functional support to create overviews for meta-data as well. Additionally, similar to exporting artefacts, a user must be able to select the representational notation in which the contents of the overview are presented. Lastly, depending on the type of modification that has to be processed regarding an implemented business decision and its underlying business logic, users must be able to find and replace efficiently within such overviews.

14) Filter Artefacts – Additional to searching certain artefacts, artefact relationships or artefact types, our data shows that filtering and sorting functionality is deemed important. Additionally, filtering or sorting is not only required for certain artefacts, artefact relationships or artefact types, but meta-data as well.

15) Capture Artefact Relationships – Relationships between artefacts are essential to create decompositions, as well as to ground traceability. Therefore, a user must be able to capture relationships between artefacts, on all abstraction levels of business decisions and business logic. Additionally, organizations must be able to modify relationship types to match their context, on top of being able to use standard relationship types (usually included by the vendor of the software).

With regards to the overlapping functional categories that show overlap with the Design and Specification capabilities, two functional categories were identified: 16) Define Artefact and 17) Issue Management.

16) Define Artefact – According to the data, artefacts that comprise a business decision and underlying business logic are created in the design and specification capabilities. All organizations utilize different stakeholders and tooling. Therefore, a user must be able to define artefacts in multiple representational notations, such as mentioned under functional category export artefact. Another measure to improve efficiency when defining artefacts is to re-use existing artefacts, while a user must be able to change all variables of the existing artefact. Because artefacts are often created or modified by more than one role, collaboration could improve when there is functional support for simultaneously working on artefacts. Additionally, transparent presentation to see which stakeholders have the responsibility and who is working on a (part of a) artefact, should be supported.

17) Issue Management – Collaboration between stakeholders during the development of business decisions and business logic poses several communication challenges. To mitigate this, functional support for issue management is required. Issue management should enable the registration of issues to be solved per artefact in each abstraction layer. Furthermore, all stakeholders must be able to maintain a to-do list, also with the goal to effectively balance the work between relevant stakeholders.

With regards to the overlapping functional categories that show overlap with the elicitation and specification capabilities, one functional category was identified: 18) Artefact Change Support.

18) Artefact Change Support – Changes to sources impacting business decisions and underlying business logic are inevitable, as well as errors that force the organization to modify artefacts throughout the elicitation and specification processes. While we argue that Artefact Change Support could be of importance as a functionality for the design capability, our data did not contain requirements aimed towards the need for artefact change support in the design processes.

The required collaboration between stakeholders or individuals sharing role responsibilities to modify business decisions and underlying business logic often includes hierarchy. For example, based on experience level, some roles or individuals are allowed to process a modification but are disallowed to process the actual change. Functional support to approve changes is deemed important and should be taken into account. Similarly, roles or individuals tasked with reviewing changes made should be supported to roll-back these changes, for example, when errors are detected. Meta-data is an important factor to be taken into account when processing changes but requires additional labour to maintain manually for each change. Therefore, a user must be supported by automatically modifying the meta-data of the changed artefact or suggesting changes to the meta-data so that the user can approve them.

VI. CONCLUSIONS

The goal of this research is to derive a functional architecture that other organizations could utilize to design BRM solutions. To be able to do so, the following research question was addressed in this paper: "Which functional requirement categories should be taken into account when designing a BRM functional architecture for the elicitation, design and specification capabilities?" In order to answer this question, we utilized case study research and conducted three rounds of coding, involving 536 functional requirements specified by seven large Dutch governmental agencies. From a theoretical perspective, our study provides a fundament for future research towards (functional) architecture development in the BRM research field. This is needed as the current knowledge base lacks empirically grounded research into the functional application that facilitate the implementation of BRM capabilities at organizations. From a practical perspective, (governmental) organizations, can use the architectural views per BRM capability presented in this paper as guidance. Organizations that are innovating by applying automating products and services with business decisions and business logic are often searching for guardrails to design their BRM solutions. The results in this paper offer an empirically grounded functional view, based on a large collection of functional requirements, which could function as a guardrail.

VII. DISCUSSION AND FUTURE RESEARCH

Like in this study, the conclusions are solely drawn based on data collected from seven Dutch governmental institutions, which limits the generalizability of the results presented. The first limitation is the sampling, which prevents broad generalization towards other industries. However, we argue that the goal of the functional architectures is to represent a guardrail to be used as a best practice, organizations active in industries other than the government, can utilize what fits best with their context. Also, the sample size is limited and a broad generalization of the results can be achieved when larger sample sizes are used to collect and validate the data, as well as validate the functional architecture. Future research should, therefore, focus on incorporating larger amounts of functional requirements, preferably from a mix of different industries to further validate the current set of functional requirement categories, as well as to compare between different industries with the goal to provide situational sets of functional requirements. This enables better contextualization of the functional architectures based on the industry and organization using the functional architectures.

To create a functional architecture covering all BRM capabilities mentioned in the introduction of this paper, more research is needed. This is necessary as business decisions and business logic are processed in and by several other BRM-related processes and stakeholders before being implemented. Furthermore, as can be derived from Table 2, one organization submitted secondary data which comprised no functional requirements according to our coding but contained functional requirements for other BRM capabilities outside the scope of this paper. For transparency, we retained the organization in the data collection.

Another limitation is the lack of a mixed-method approach to construct the functional architectures. While literature analysis, case study research and secondary data analysis is combined during this research, future research should focus to further improve upon the validity and generalizability of the research results by executing a mixed-method approach. Doing so also enables the inclusion of more data and wider validation of results due to the quantitative viewpoint of the mixed-method approach. Such an approach would also ensure a solid means to validate the functional architecture presented in this paper.

REFERENCES

[1] M. W. Blenko, M. C. Mankins, and P. Rogers, "The Decision-Driven Organization," *Harv. Bus. Rev.*, vol. 88, no. 6, pp. 54–62, Jun. 2010.

[2] P. Rogers and M. Blenko, "Who has the D?," *Harv. Bus. Rev.*, vol. 84, no. 1, pp. 52–61, 2006.

[3] J. Boyer and H. Mili, *Agile business rule development: Process, Architecture and JRules Examples*. Springer Berlin Heidelberg, 2011.

[4] M. L. Nelson, R. L. Rariden, and R. Sen, "A lifecycle approach towards business rules management," in *Proceedings of the 41st Annual Hawaii International Conference on System Sciences*, 2008, pp. 113–123.

[5] S. Schlosser, E. Baghi, B. Otto, and H. Oesterle, "Toward a Functional Reference Model for Business Rules Management," in *2014 47th Hawaii International Conference on System Sciences*, 2014, pp. 3837–3846.

[6] K. Smit and M. Zoet, "An Organizational Capability and Resource Based Perspective on Business Rules Management," in *Proceedings of the International Conference On Information Systems (ICIS)*, 2018, pp. 1–17.

[7] M. L. Nelson, J. Peterson, R. L. Rariden, and R. Sen, "Transitioning to a business rule management service model: Case studies from the property and casualty insurance industry," *Inf. Manag.*, vol. 47, no. 1, pp. 30–41, Jan. 2010.

[8] A. Kovacic, "Business renovation: business rules (still)

the missing link," *Bus. Process Manag. J.*, vol. 10, no. 2, pp. 158–170, 2004.

[9] D. Arnott and G. Pervan, "A critical analysis of decision support systems research," *J. Inf. Technol.*, vol. 20, no. 2, pp. 67–87, 2005.

[10] D. Arnott and G. Pervan, "A critical analysis of decision support systems research revisited: the rise of design science," *J. Inf. Technol.*, vol. 29, no. 4, pp. 269–293, Dec. 2014.

[11] M. Zoet, *Methods and Concepts for Business Rules Management*, 1st ed. Utrecht: Hogeschool Utrecht, 2014.

[12] K. Smit, M. Zoet, and M. Berkhout, "Functional Requirements for Business Rules Management Systems," in *Proceedings of the 23rd Americas Conference on Information Systems (AMCIS)*, 2017.

[13] T. Morgan, *Business rules and information systems: aligning IT with business goals*. Addison-Wesley Professional, 2002.

[14] Object Management Group, "Decision Model And Notation (DMN), Version 1.1," 2016.

[15] the Open Group, "ArchiMate® 3.0 Specification," 2016.

[16] B. Von Halle and L. Goldberg, *The Decision Model: A Business Logic Framework Linking Business and Technology*. CRC Press, 2009.

[17] K. Smit and M. Zoet, "Management Control System for Business Rules Management," *Int. J. Adv. Syst. Meas.*, vol. 9, no. 3–4, pp. 210–219, 2016.

[18] I. Graham, *Business rules management and service oriented architecture: a pattern language*. John wiley & sons, 2007.

[19] S. Liao, "Expert system methodologies and applications—a decade review from 1995 to 2004," *Expert Syst. Appl.*, vol. 28, no. 1, pp. 93–103, Jan. 2004.

[20] L. Bass, P. Clements, and R. Kazman, *Software Architecture in Practice*, no. 3. SEI Series in Soft. Eng., 2012.

[21] M. A. Babar and I. Gorton, *Proceedings of the 4th European Conference on Software Architecture (ECSA)*. Copenhagen, Denmark: Springer, 2010.

[22] N. Bateman, "Operating model: an exploration of the concept," Loughborough, UK, 2017.

[23] A. Murphy, J. Kirwin, and A. K. Razak, "Operating models - Delivering on strategy and optimizing processes," 2016.

[24] M. B. Kelly, "The telemanagement forum's enhanced telecom operations map (eTOM)," *J. Netw. Syst. Manag.*, vol. 11, no. 1, pp. 109–119, 2003.

[25] J. Huschens and M. Rumpold-Preining, "IBM Insurance Application Architecture (IAA) — An overview of the Insurance Business Architecture," in *Handbook on Architectures of Information Systems*, Berlin/Heidelberg: Springer-Verlag, 1998, pp. 669–692.

[26] M. Fischbach, T. Puschmann, and R. Alt, "Service-Lifecycle-Management," *Bus. Inf. Syst. Eng.*, vol. 5, no. 1, pp. 45–49, Feb. 2013.

[27] J. Schön, E. M. Thomaschewski and M. J. Escalona, "Agile Requirements Engineering: A systematic literature review," *Comput. Stand. Interfaces*, vol. 49, no. 1, pp. 79–91, 2017.

[28] M. Cohn, *User stories applied: For agile software development*. Addison-Wesley Professional, 2004.

[29] R. K. Yin, *Case study research: Design and methods*. Sage publications, 2013.

[30] P. Runeson and M. Höst, "Guidelines for conducting and reporting case study research in software engineering," *Empir. Softw. Eng.*, vol. 14, no. 2, pp. 131–164, 2009.

[31] A. Strauss and J. Corbin, *Basics of Qualitative Research: Techniques and Procedures for Developing Grounded Theory*, 3rd ed., vol. 3. Thousand Oaks, CA: SAGE Publications Ltd., 2015.

[32] H. E. Tinsley and D. J. Weiss, "Interrater Reliability and Agreement," in *Handbook of Applied Multivariate Statistics and Mathematical Modeling*, San Diego, CA: Academic Press, 2000, pp. 95–124.

[33] A. Böhm, B. Glaser, and A. Strauss, "Theoretical Coding: Text Analysis in Grounded Theory," *A Companion to Qual. Res.*, pp. 270–275, 2004.

[34] L. Bass, P. Clements, and R. Kazman, *Software Architecture in Practice Third Edition*, 3rd ed. Addison-Wesley, 2012.

[35] D. M. Buede and W. D. Miller, *The engineering design of systems: models and methods*. John Wiley & Sons, 2016.

[36] J. Vanthienen, "Ruling the business: about business rules and decision tables.," in *New Directions in Software Engineering*, 2001, pp. 103–120.

[37] Business Rule Solutions, "Rulespeak," 2017. [Online]. Available: http://www.rulespeak.com/nl/. [Accessed: 19-March-2020].

[38] K. Smit, J. Versendaal, and M. Zoet, "Identifying Challenges in BRM Implementations Regarding the Verification and Validation Capabilities at Governmental Institutions," in *PACIS 2017 Proceedings*, 2017.

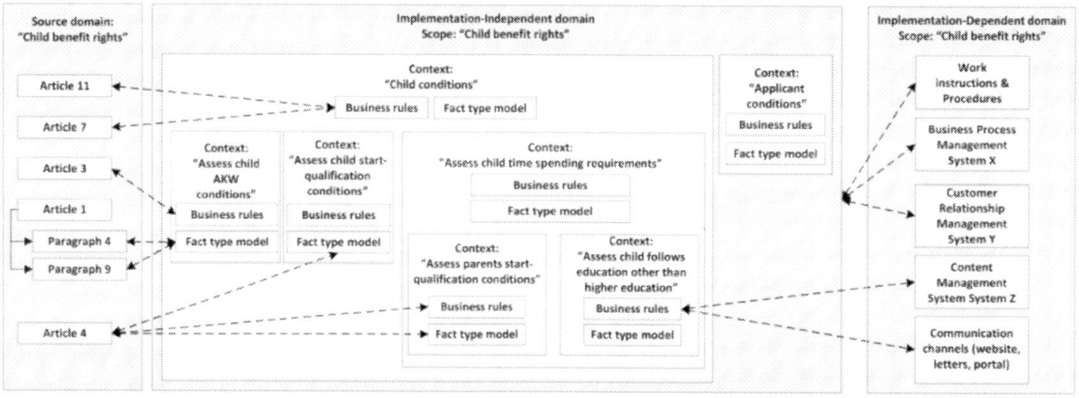

Figure 2. Example of a business decision with underlying business decisions and business logic

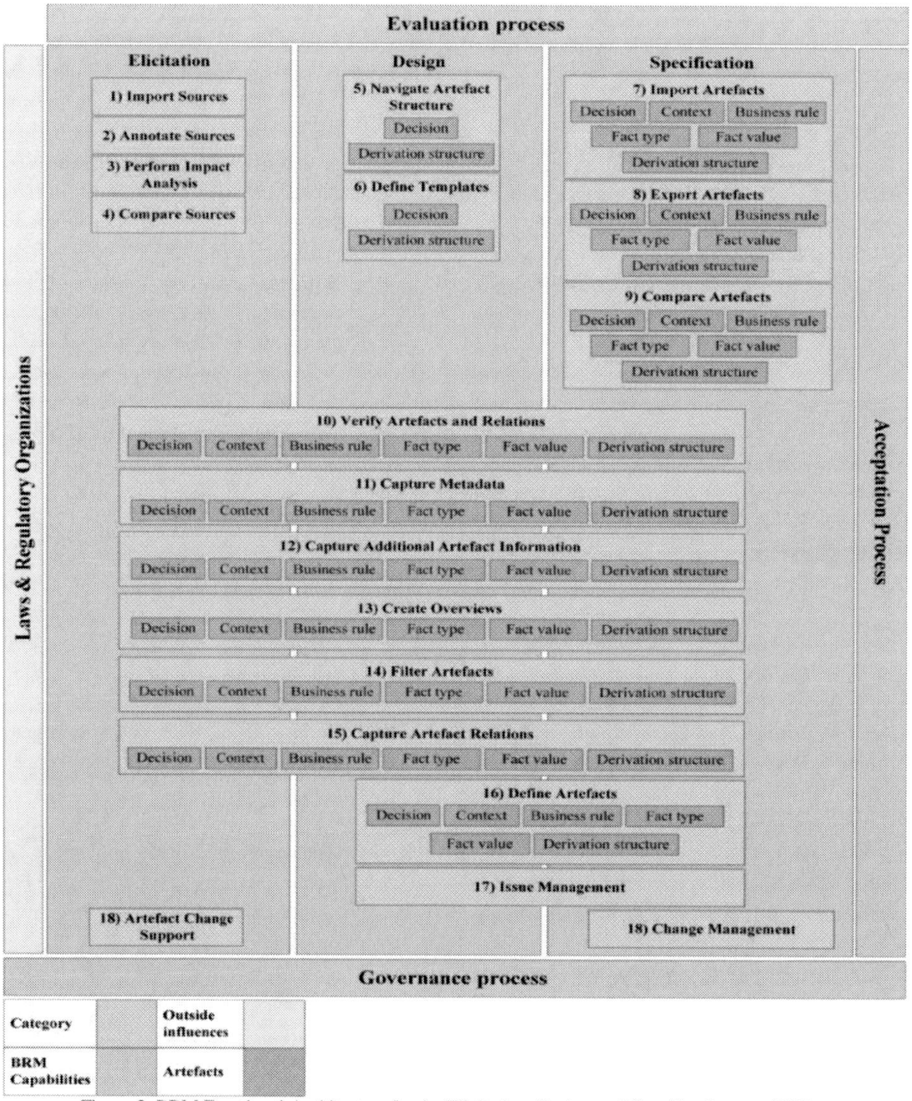

Figure 3. BRM Functional Architecture for the Elicitation, Design and Specification capabilities

Forecasting Electricity Usage in Industrial Applications with GPU Acceleration through RAPIDS AI Framework

Keh-Kok Yong
Accelerative Technology Lab
MIMOS Berhad
Kuala Lumpur, Malaysia
Email: kk.yong@mimos.my

Woan-Lin Beh
Faculty of Science
Universiti Tunku Abdul Rahman
Kampar, Malaysia
Email: behwl@utar.edu.my

Boon-Yaik Ooi
Faculty of Information and Communication Technology
Universiti Tunku Abdul Rahman
Kampar, Malaysia
Email: ooiby@utar.edu.my

Wai-Kong Lee
Department of Computer Engineering,
Gachon University
South Korea
Email: waikong.lee@gachon.ac.kr

Abstract— **Electricity usage prediction is important for planning and facility expansion in the industrial sector. Accurate prediction can save the operation and maintenance costs, increased the reliability of power supply and delivery system for future development. This paper is to compare various Exponential Smoothing models (Simple Exponential Smoothing, Holt Linear Trend, Holt Linear Damped Trend and Holt-Winters) and ARIMA (Autoregressive Integrated Moving Average) model in an attempt to predict the daily electricity usage in the industry in the production of Hammer and Pellet with high accuracy. The data used is from 30 September 2019 to 06 November 2019, which consist of only 39 observations after excluding the non-production day. These models are precise and modelled well when the time series data is in a short period and in short period forecasting. Accuracy level of each model is measured by comparing the Root Mean Square Error (RMSE) of forecasting value with the actual value. Based on the comparison result, the best model with the smallest RMSE value is given by Holt Linear Trend for the electricity usage for the production of Hammer (in Mill 1 and Mill 2) and the production of Pellet (in Mill 1). In the data of the electricity usage for the production of Pellet (in Mill 2), the smallest RMSE value is given by Holt Linear Damped Trend. To improve the training and forecasting speed, we adopt Graphics Processing Unit (GPU) acceleration through RAPIDS Artificial Intelligence framework.**

Keywords-component; Electricity Consumption Forecasting; Simple Exponential Smoothing; Holt Linear Trend; Holt Linear Damped Trend; Holt-Winters; Auto Regressive Integrated Moving Average.

I. INTRODUCTION

An increase in the consumption of domestic electrical current will cause higher utility costs. An accurate prediction of the future electricity usage in short-run and long-run may help the manufacturing industries and private investors to maximize their return and minimize the operation expenses [1][2]. Forecasting of electricity usage also helps the industry to plan and control on the future power system. Building an accurate and reliable forecasting model for electricity usage may provide valuable information for electricity system operators to formulate policies and plans for electricity [3]. Therefore, forecasting of electricity usage has become urgent and important for an industry [4]-[6].

There are many factors affecting the prediction accuracy of electricity consumption, such as economic condition [7], power facilities [8], population growth [9], weather conditions [10][11], festival season [12] and political influences [13]. Thus, forecasting on the electricity usage become challenges as the data often presents to be strongly nonlinear, random, more volatile and irregular [14]. It is due to the average yearly growth factor of electricity usage fluctuation. Also, the demand of it can change significantly in space and time related to different areas. Therefore, the long-run prediction of electricity usage may be impractical. The accuracy of the prediction in short-run can be improved by select a forecasting model that performs well with a relatively small sample size [14]. Apart from that, it has been found that making full use of more recent data which is closer to the forecast period is able to enhance the prediction performance [15].

Many researchers proposed different kinds of forecast models to predict the electricity usage in recent decades. The methods could be completely categorized into three groups: statistical analysis models, artificial intelligence models and grey forecasting models. Examples of the popular statistical analysis models include regression [16], logistic regression [6], simple Exponential Smoothing model [17][18], Holt-Winters model [19], univariate time series model [9][20], state space model [21], Kalman filter model [3] and Markov chain model [22]. However, statistical analysis models have some limitations, one of that is statistical models usually require that the sample data fulfil some statistical assumptions, such as normality assumption, thus limiting it practical application.

Artificial intelligence models such as artificial neural network [23][24], support vector machine regression [25][26] and deep neural networks [27] become popular in electricity consumption prediction. However, the prediction precision obtained from these models is totally rely on the number of the training sample data [4][28][29], which may not be applied in electricity usage data when the sample size is small.

There are different forecasting approaches including trend and seasonality and several comparative studies in the electricity consumption in the literature. Al-Ghandoor et al. [30] presented the electricity consumption of the Jordanian industrial sector based on multivariate linear regression. In the study, they found that industrial production outputs and capacity utilization are the two important reasons that affect demand on electrical power. Erdogdu [31] used

Autoregressive Integrated Moving Average (ARIMA) to estimate and predict the Turkish electricity demand. Taylor [32] found that Exponential Smoothing method is more reliable and appropriate for short period forecasting on electric consumption. Kavanagh [36] proposed double seasonal Exponential Smoothing variation of the Holt-Winters method to predict the short-term electricity loads for half hourly lead times for a day ahead.

The objective of this project is to compare various statistical approaches to forecast the electricity consumption of a factory. Such comparisons are crucial for the stake holder of the factory to factor in their operation cost in order to maximize production output and minimize production cost. The novelty of this work is to compare various statistical models to investigate the accuracy versus performance of these techniques especially with GPU acceleration. In order to achieve objectively compare the accuracy between the models, external factors such as weather and economic conditions will not be included in this study. This work is a subcomponent to our meta-predictor where accuracy and performance are important factors for the meta-predictor to autonomously select and combine predictions from multiple models.

In this paper, we proposed to use variety of linear models to find the best fitting to predict the future electricity consumption. The linear models that studied in this paper are Simple Exponential Smoothing model, Holt's Linear model, Holt's Linear Damped Trend model, Holt-Winters model, and ARIMA models. Electrical consumption forecasting classified into three categories: short period, medium period and long period. In this study, we focus on 5 working days; that is short term load forecasting. The data is collected from life current sensor transmitted to the cloud hosted for forecast processing. The training and forecasting are accelerated through GPU to achieve better speed performance with similar accuracy.

The paper is organized as follows. In Section II, it provides a review of methodology related works. In Section III, it briefly discusses experiments and performance results. Finally, Section IV concludes and discusses future work.

II. MEHTODOLOGY

A. Methods

We presented in here five approaches for forecasting the electricity consumption. Techniques chosen for this study are Simple Exponential Smoothing model, Holt's Linear model, Holt's Linear Damped Trend model, Holt-Winters Additive model, and ARIMA model. The details of the methods are discussed as following:

1) Simple Exponential Smoothing (ES) model

Exponential Smoothing (ES) is one of the generally used methods to discover the short-term dramatic changes in time series based on its past values. ES model is simple to estimate as it only requires a single parameter, which is the smoothing called as smoothing coefficient. Second, this model required less computational time and small data storage. The simple ES can be represented by the following equations:

$$R_t = \alpha y_t + (1-\alpha)R_{t-1}, \quad (1)$$

$$\hat{y}_t = R_{t-1}, \quad (2)$$

where R_t is the level at time t, α is the smoothing constant and $0 < \alpha \leq 1$.

2) Holt's Linear (HL) Model

Double ES is an extension to simple ES as the simple' ES approach does not fit well in the data when there is a trend. The double ES model is formed by two equations:

$$R_t = \alpha y_t + (1-\alpha)(R_{t-1} + c_{t-1}), 0 \leq \alpha \leq 1 \quad (3)$$

$$c_t = \gamma(R_t - R_{t-1}) + (1-\gamma)c_{t-1}, \ 0 \leq \gamma \leq 1 \quad (4)$$

where R_t is the level at time t, α is the weight for the level, c_t is the trend at time t, γ is the weight for the trend, y_t is the data value at time t. The one-step-ahead forecast at time t is given as

$$\hat{y}_t = R_{t-1} + c_{t-1} \quad (5)$$

Holt's Linear Trend (HLT) is a special case of double ES model with the forecast equation is given as

$$\hat{y}_t = R_{t-1} + hc_{t-1} \quad (6)$$

where h is the h-step-ahead forecast. However, when the data is with trend and seasonal, HLT may not be performed well, so HLT approach was extended to Holt-Winters method, which can help to measure strong trend patterns and seasonal pattern in the series.

3) Holt's Linear Damped Trend (HLDT) model

Holt's Linear Damped Trend (HLDT) includes a damping parameter, ϕ, where $0 < \phi < 1$. The equation is given as

$$\hat{y}_t = R_{t-1} + c_{t-1}(\phi + \phi^2 + \ldots + \phi^h) \quad (7)$$

$$R_t = \alpha y_t + (1-\alpha)(R_{t-1} + \phi c_{t-1}), \ 0 \leq \alpha \leq 1 \quad (8)$$

$$c_t = \gamma(R_t - R_{t-1}) + (1-\gamma)\phi c_{t-1}, \ 0 \leq \gamma \leq 1 \quad (9)$$

where R_t is the level at time t, α is the weight for the level, c_t is the trend at time t, γ is the weight for the trend, y_t is the data value at time t, and $\hat{y}_t$ is the one-step-ahead forecast at time t. If $\phi = 1$, the method is identical to HLT method. The short term forecasts for HLDT method are trended while the long-term forecasts are constant.

4) Holt-Winters (HW) method

The HW method, which is also called triple ES method, is a complex expansion of ES method and is used when there is trend and seasonality in the data set. HW additive method is chosen when the seasonal variations are roughly constant meanwhile HW multiplicative method is chosen when the seasonal variations are changing proportionally to the level of the data. This study will be applied only to the HW additive model:

$$\hat{y}_t = R_{t-1} + hc_{t-1} + s_{t-1} \tag{10}$$

$$R_t = \alpha(y_t - s_{t-p}) + (1-\alpha)(R_{t-1} + c_{t-1}) \tag{11}$$

$$c_t = \beta(R_t - R_{t-1}) + (1-\beta)c_{t-1} \tag{12}$$

$$s_t = \gamma(y_t - R_t) + (1-\gamma)s_{t-p} \tag{13}$$

where R_t is the smoothed estimate of the level at time t, c_t is the smoothed estimate of the change in the trend value at time t, s_t is the smoothed estimate of the appropriate seasonal component at t, α , β and γ are the smoothing parameters and p is the number of seasons per year as in eq. (13).

5) ARIMA Model

The ARIMA model consists of autoregressive (AR) part, a differencing (I) part and Moving Average (MA) part. The ARIMA (p,d,q) model can be expressed in a very general form:

$$(1-B)^d y_t = \vartheta_0 + \alpha_1(1-B)^d y_{t-1} + \ldots + \alpha_p(1-B)^d y_{t-p} + a_t - \theta_1 a_{t-1} - \ldots - \theta_q a_{t-q} \tag{13}$$

where B is the backward operator, ϑ_0 is the constant term, α_i is the AR coefficient, d is the order of the differencing, θ_j is the MA coefficient, where $j = 1,2,\ldots,q$, y_t is the data value at time t, and a_{t-q} is the random noise, which follows normal distribution. In this model, α_1 , $\alpha_2,\ldots,\alpha_p$, ϑ_0 and θ_1 , $\theta_2,\ldots,\theta_p$ are optimised by using maximum Likelihood Estimation (MLE) [37]. The best model is selected based on the Box-Jenkins methodology, which is composed of four main stages: model identification, parameter estimation, diagnostic checking and model application [37]. The stationary and invertibility conditions for the selected models should be fulfilled when fitting ARIMA model [38].

B. GPU Acceleration

The training and forecasting process can be time consuming when the data size is large; GPU can be used to accelerate these processes. In this paper, we adopt the RAPIDS AI framework that provides a series of libraries to accelerate machine learning techniques through GPU. These python based libraries use NVIDIA CUDA® primitives for low-level compute optimization. It scrutinizes the data parallelism with adopting high-bandwidth memory. Figure 1 shows the high-level architecture of RAPIDS.

In particular, we use cuDF, which is CUDA dataframe. This is a powerful data representation layer. It contains pandas-like functionalities for low level CPU and GPU components performing a heterogenous parallel computing. It eases up data scientists to manipulate data input/output, mimicking the CPU version of dataframe. On the other hand, we also use cuML, which is a GPU Machine Learning Algorithms library. It comes with Holt-Winter implementation in GPU.

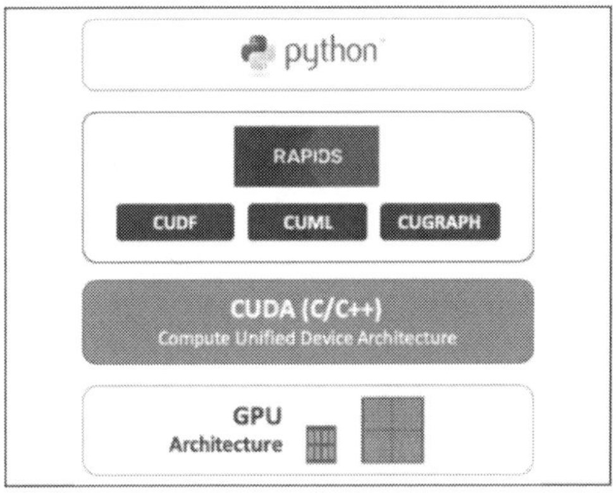

Figure 1. High level of RAPIDS AI architecture framework

C. Forecasting and Performance Accuracy

The static forecasting will be carried out for the next 5 working days. The performance of accuracy in forecasting will be investigated by root mean square error (RMSE) [37], which is shown as follows:

$$RMSE = \sqrt{\frac{1}{n}\sum_{i=1}^{n}(y_i - \hat{y}_i)^2} \tag{14}$$

where y_i and $\hat{y}_i$ are the observed and predicted values at time t respectively. The models with the lowest scoring from the four methods will be the best forecast models and can be used for control purpose in future.

III. Results and Discussion

The dataset used in this study is collected from a real plastic molding factory with 4 different milling machines. These are newly purchased machines, as a result, these 2 months historical records are not extensive enough. There are four sets of the data containing 39 observations (from 30-09-2019 till 06-11-2019) of the total electricity load for the production of Hammer and Pellet in Mill 1 and Mill 2. NVIDIA P100 GPU was used for the evaluation, which has 16GB GDDR5 RAM with CUDA version 10.2.

In this study, the data with same electricity consumption is removed. Then the last five observations of these four series are used for forecasting and the rest of the observations formed the training data for parameter estimation. This section mainly demonstrates the prediction process and parameter estimates of the five models, simple ES, HLT, HLDT, HW, and ARIMA and the fitting data. We implement a batch version of trustworthiness that provides reasonable low execution times for dataset up to 39 observations. In addition, after the fitting results are obtained, the accuracy of the five models is analysed and compared with the original data. Figure 2 shows plots of these four series in daily usage and the plots show that trend and seasonality exist.

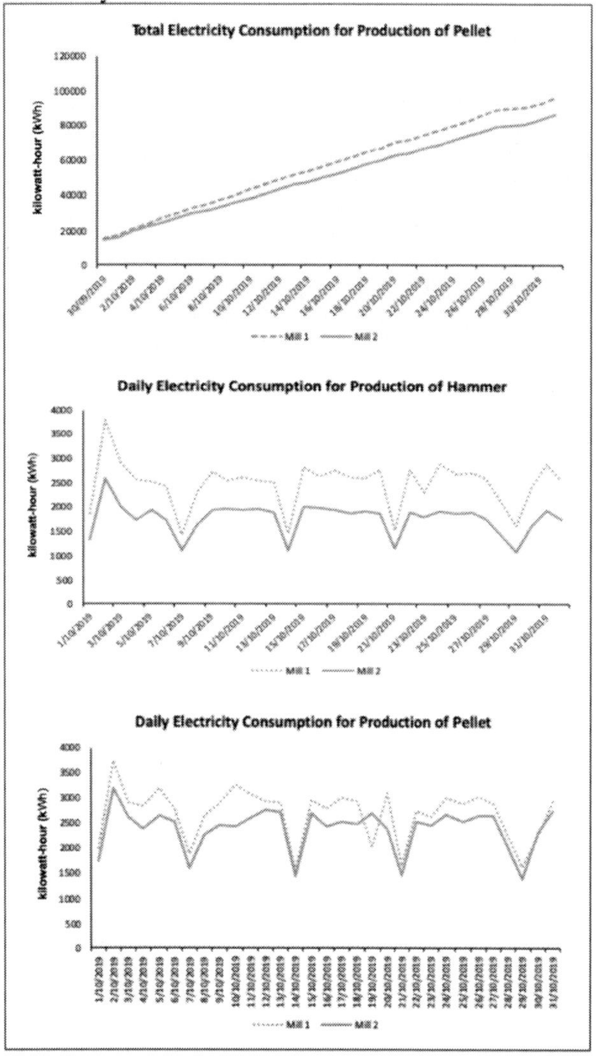

Figure 2. Daily data of the electricity load (in kWh) for the production of Hammer and Pellet in Mill 1 and Mill 2 in the period 01/10/2019 - 30/10/2019.

TABLE I. DAILY ELECTRICITY CONSUMPTION ESTIMATION OUTPUTS OF ES METHODS FOR PRODUCTION OF HAMMER.

	Mill 1				Mill 2			
ES models / Parameters	Single ES	HLT	HLDT	HW-Additive	Single ES	HLT	HLDT	HW-Additive
Alpha	0.9990	1.0	1.0	0.05264	1.0	1.0	1.0	0.05264
Beta	-	0.1	0.1	0.05264	-	0.1	0.1	0.05264
Gamma	-	-	-	0.9474	-	-	-	0.9474
Phi	-	-	0.9973	-	-	-	0.9955	-
Sum of Square Error	1.9364e+08	1.5050e+07	1.0969e+07	2.6639e+06	9.8410e+07	7.0899e+06	4.9372e+06	961291

TABLE II. DAILY ELECTRICITY CONSUMPTION ESTIMATION OUTPUTS OF ES METHODS FOR PRODUCTION OF PELLET.

	Mill 1				Mill 2			
ES models / Parameters	Single ES	HLT	HLDT	HW-Additive	Single ES	HLT	HLDT	HW-Additive
Alpha	1	1	1	0.05263	1	0.9	0.9	0.05263
Beta	-	0.1	0.1	0.05264	-	0.2	0.2	0.05263
Gamma	-	-	-	0.7895	-	-	-	0.8947
Phi	-	-	0.9959	-	-	-	10.9999	-
Sum of Square Error	2.2676e+08	1.7594e+07	8.5834e+06	3.9511e+06	1.7782e+08	1.3128e+07	1.0064e+07	1.6888e+06

For the various implemented models, we briefly illustrate the finding here. TABLES I-II present the estimation outputs of simple ES, HLT, HLDT and HW for the daily electricity consumption of the production of Hammer and Pellet in Mill 1 and Mill 2 respectively. The values of the sum of square errors shown in the TABLE I-II are used to identify the dispersion of the training data in the fitted model. TABLE III presents the ARIMA models that fitted to the four series, the models are selected based on minimum values of Akaike Information Criterion. The performance of accuracy in the forecasting is shown in TABLE IV. From the TABLE IV, it can be seen that the RMSE values of the HLT model are smaller than the ARIMA model and others ES models in the series of Hammer (Mill 1 and Mill 2) and Pellet (Mill 1), and HLDT is the smallest for Pellet (Mill 2). In other words, ES model, HL and HLDT models are more precise in predicting the electricity consumption total data in the production of Hammer and Pellet in Mill 1 and Mill 2.

TABLE III. ARIMA models with its' sum of square error (bracket) for the daily electricity consumption.

	Hammer	Pellet
Mill 1	ARIMA(6,1,0)	ARIMA(6,1,2)
Mill 2	ARIMA(6,1,1)	ARIMA(2,0,0)

	Hammer	Pellet
Mill 1	ARIMA(6,1,0) (1.09166e+05)	ARIMA(6,1,2) (4.2045e+04)
Mill 2	ARIMA(6,1,1) (1.70421e+05)	ARIMA(2,0,0) (1.84790e+05)

TABLE IV. THE RMSE OF THE ARIMA AND ES MODELS.

	Mill 1		Mill 2	
Models	Hammer	Pellet	Hammer	Pellet
Single ES	8126.87	9071.80	5853.39	7877.87
HLT	123.00	500.95	174.33	76.20
HLDT	132.30	745.45	279.14	51.02
HW-Additive	512.38	656.76	387.28	512.38
ARIMA	369.59	721.54	606.60	586.19

GPU computing is at a tipping point, as we compare the execution time and correctness of GPU many-core and CPU implementation against CPU multicore. TABLE V shows the timing performance of CPU and GPU implementation. CPU implementation is provided by statmodels library, while GPU implementation is adopted from cuML. The GPU performance is shown in brackets. We can observe that the GPU can provide around 3× performance improvement in training and forecasting, compared to the CPU implementation. The result turns out that it cannot take full advantages of all the available CUDA cores on the GPU device. The dataset size is too small.

TABLE V. THE TRAINING AND FORECASTING TIME COMPARISON (MS), CPU VS GPU (BRACKET).

	Mill 1		Mill 2	
Models	Hammer	Pellet	Hammer	Pellet
Single ES	69.5 (24.3)	71.5 (23.3)	59.6 (21.0)	69.2 (22.8)
HLT	69.1 (22.2)	72.7 (22.3)	60.5 (23.8)	71.5 (24.1)
HLDT	68.5 (23.1)	70.5 (22.9)	62.4 (21.9)	68.3 (28.2)
HW-Additive	68.7 (22.3)	71.5 (23.8)	69.1 (22.3)	70.2 (24.9)

IV. CONCLUSION

This study aims to compare various ES models and ARIMA model based on RMSE criteria in forecasting the daily electricity usage total data in the industry. From the results of data analysis that has been done, it was found that the model of Holt's Linear with lowest RMSE is the most appropriate model in forecasting the daily electricity usage total data in the production of Hammer (in Mill 1 and Mill 2) and the production of Pellet (in Mill 1). Holt's Linear Damped Trend model gave the lowest RMSE in the production of Pellet in Mill 2. These models are more appropriate when compared with Holt-Winters Additive model and ARIMA model. GPU acceleration is also useful to speed up the training and forecasting with approximately 3× performance gain. However, our experiment shows that there is approximately 40 milliseconds speed up. It is not a significant result, as the current dataset is small. Thus, it requires more new sensors to be used for collecting bigger historical dataset, then, it will be worthwhile from GPU acceleration. For future work, external factors that possibly affecting electricity consumption should also be included and more technique will be included.

REFERENCES

[1] K. Fisher-Vanden, E. Mansur, and Q. Wan, "Electricity shortages and firm productivity: Evidence from China's industrial firms," Journal of Development Economics, vol. 114, pp. 172-188, 2015.

[2] A. Hunt, A. Collard-Wexler, and D. O'Connell, "How do electricity shortages affect productivity? Evidence from India. American Economic Review," vol. 106, no. 3, pp. 587-624, 2016.

[3] H. M. Al-Hamadi and S.A. Soliman, "Long-term/mid-term electric load forecasting based on short-term correlation and annual growth." Electric Power System Research, vol. 74, pp. 353-61, 2005.

[4] Y. H. Chung, "Electricity consumption prediction using a neural-network-based grey forecasting approach," Journal of Operational Research Society, vol. 68, 1259-1264 (2017).

[5] M. E. Lebotsa, C. Sigauke, A. Bere, R. Fildes, and J. E. Boylan "Short term electricity demand forecasting using partially linear additive quantile regression with an application to the unit commitment problem," Applied Energy, vol. 222, pp. 104-118, 2018.

[6] F. Wang, Y. Yu, X. Wang, H. Ren, M. Shafie-Khah, and J.P.S. Catalao, "Residential electricity consumption level impact factor analysis based on wrapper feature selection and multinomial logistic regression," Energies, vol. 11, pp.1180, 2018.

[7] H.T. Pao, "Forecast of electricity consumption and economic growth in Taiwan by state space modelling," Energy, vol. 34, 1779-1791, 2009.

[8] A. Khosravi, S. Nahavandi, D. Creighton, and D. Srinivasa, "Interval type-2 fuzzy logic systems for load forecasting: A comparative study," IEEE Trans. Power System, no. 3, vol. 27, pp. 1274-1282, 2012.

[9] A. Hussain, M. Rahman, and J.A. Memon, "Forecasting electricity consumption in Pakistan: The way forward," Energy Policy, vol. 90, pp.73-80, 2016.

[10] M. G. Fikru and L. Gautier, "The impact of weather variation on energy consumption in residential houses," Applied Energy, vol. 144, pp.19-30, 2015.

[11] I. Staffer and S. Pfenninger, "The increasing impact of weather on electricity supply and demand," Energy, vol. 145, pp. 65-78, 2018.

[12] T. Sun, T. Zhang, Y. Teng, Z. Chen, and J. Fang, "Monthly electricity consumption forecasting method based on X12 and STL decomposition model in an integrated energy system," Mathematical Problems in Engineering, pp. 1-16, 2019.

[13] T. Dietz, C. Leshko, and A. M. McCright, "Politics shapes individual choices about energy efficiency," in Proceedings of the National Academy of Science, vol. 110, no. 23, pp. 9191-9192, 2013.

[14] K. Li and T. Zhang, "Forecasting electricity consumption using an improved grey prediction model," Information, vol. 9 no. 204, pp. 1-18, 2018.

[15] Y. F. Huang, C. N. Wang, H. S. Dang and S.T. Lai, "Evaluating performance of the DGM(2,1) model and its

modified models," Applied Science, vol. 6, no. 73, pp. 1-12, 2016.

[16] Z. Mohamed and P. Bodger, "Forecasting electricity consumption in New Zealand using economic and demographic variables," Energy, vol. 30, pp. 1833-1843, 2005.

[17] E. Osteragova and O. Ostertag, "The simple exponential smoothing model," in Proceedings of the Modelling of Mechanical and Mechatronic, Sep. 2011, pp. 380-384.

[18] N. A. Abd Jalil, M. H. Ahmad, and N. Mohamed, "Electricity load demand forecasting using exponential smoothing methods," World Applied Science Journal, vol. 22, no. 11, pp. 1540-1543, 2013.

[19] Y. W. Lee, K. G. Tay, and Y. Y. Choy, "Forecasting electricity consumption using time series model," International Journal of Engineering & Technology, vol. 7, no. 4.30, pp. 218-223, 2018.

[20] M. Bouzerdoum, A. Mellit, and A.M. Pavan, "A hybrid model (SARIMA-SVM) for short-term power forecasting of a small-scale grid-connected photovoltaic plant," Solar Energy, vol. 98, pp. 226-235, 2013.

[21] K. Nagbe, J. Cugliari, and J. Jacques, "Short-term electricity consumption forecasting using a functional state space model," Energies, vol. 11, pp. 1120, 2018.

[22] W. Zhao, J. Wang, and H. Lu, "Combining forecasts of electricity consumption in China with time-varying weights updated by a high-order Markov chain model," Omega, vol 45, pp. 80-91, 2014.

[23] F. Kaytez, M. C. Taplamacioglu, E. Cam, and F. Hardalac, "Forecasting electricity consumption: A comparison of regression analysis, neural networks and least square support vector machines," International Journal of Electric Power, vol 67, pp. 431-438, 2015.

[24] Y. C. Hu, and P. Jiang, "Forecasting energy demand using neural-network-based grey residual modification models," Journal of Operational Research Society, vol 68, pp. 556-565, 2017.

[25] A. Kavousi-Fard, H. Samet and F. Marzbani, "A new hybrid modified firefly algorithm and support vector regression model for accurate short term load forecasting," Expert System Application, vol. 41, pp. 6047-6056, 2014.

[26] G. Cao and L. Wu, "Support vector regression with fruit fly optimization algorithm for seasonal electricity consumption forecasting," Energy, vol. 115, pp. 734-745, 2016.

[27] D. L. Marino, K. Amarasinghe, and M. Manic, "Building energy load forecasting using Deep Neural Networks," in Proceedings of the IEEE Industrial Electronics Society (IECON 2016), Oct. 2016, pp. 7046-7051, doi: 10.1109/IECON.2016.7793413.

[28] C. Pozna, R. E. Precup, and J. K. Tar, "New results in modelling derived from Bayesian filtering," Knowledge Based System, vol. 23, pp. 182-194, 2010.

[29] S. Ding, K. W. Hipel, and Y. G. Dang, "Forecasting China's electricity consumption using a new grey prediction model," Energy, Elsevier, vol. 149, pp. 314-328, 2018.

[30] Y. Yan, C. Liu, B. Qu, Q. Zhao, and F. Ji, "Application of Grey Forecasting Model to Load Forecasting of Power System," in Proceedings of the Information Computing and Applications (ICICA), Oct. 2011, doi.org/10.1007/978-3-642-27452-7_27.

[31] A. Al-Ghandoor, I. Al-Hinti, A. Mukattash, and Y. Al-Abdallat, "Decomposition analysis of electricity use in the Jordanian industrial sector," International Journal of Sustainable Energy, vol. 29, no. 4, pp. 233-244, 2010.

[32] E. Erdogdu, "Electricity demand analysis using cointegration and ARIMA modelling: A case study of Turkey," Energy Policy, vol. 35, no. 2, pp. 1129-1146, 2007.

[33] J. W. Taylor, "Short-term electricity demand forecasting using double seasonal exponential smoothing," Journal of the Operational Research Society, vol. 54, no. 8, pp. 799-805, 2003.

[34] K. Kavanagh, "Short term demand forecasting for the integrated electricity market," Student Journal of Energy Research, vol. 2, no. 1, pp. 1-10, 2017.

[35] G. E. P. Box, G. M. Jenkins, and G. C. Reinsel, "Time series analysis: forecasting and control," 3rd ed., Prentice-Hall, Inc, 1994.

[36] S. B. Folarin and O. S. Iyiol, "Causality and invertibility of autoregressive integrated Moving Average (ARIMA) model," Asian Journal of Current Engineering and Maths, vol. 2, pp. 260-266, 2013.

Access Control Method for the Offline Home Automation System

Mikołaj Pabiszczak
Gido Labs
Poznań, Poland
Email: m.pabiszczak@gidolabs.eu

Monika Grajzer
Gido Labs
Poznań, Poland
Email: m.grajzer@gidolabs.eu

Łukasz Sawicki
LARS Andrzej Szymański
Niepruszewo, Poland
Email: lukasz.sawicki@lars.pl

Abstract—**The paper proposes a Decision Support System for controlling access to the core functionalities of speech-based, embedded home automation devices working fully offline. The system is based on the Keyword Spotting technology recognizing custom keywords from a non-English language. Even though the performance of this technology in the scientific set-ups is relatively high, the reported false positive rates are still not sufficient for commercial application. Therefore, in our solution, we incorporate a number of computationally lightweight modules that considerably reduce the rate of false alarms while retaining an acceptable access rate.**

Keywords–voice-controlled home automation; Access Control; Decision Support System; Keyword Spotting.

I. Introduction

Home automation systems supplied with speech-based interfaces are becoming increasingly popular and are currently used to command a variety of home appliances, such as, e.g., thermostats or lighting [1]. In such systems, Automatic Speech Recognition (ASR), being a part of the core Dialogue System, is a resource-consuming task, which may use a significant amount of device resources – especially if implemented on embedded devices. Therefore, voice-controlled systems and applications are usually not continuously performing ASR, but rely on the Access Control method that activates this technology only when needed. Such a methodology constitutes a Decision Support System (DSS), which contains intelligence for analysing acoustic-based knowledge [2] – coming primarily from Voice Activity Detection (VAD) and Keyword Spotting (KWS) technologies. VAD detects when speech occurs in a signal collected by the microphone and switches the device to the listening mode, while KWS aims at detecting, if the particular keyword phrase has been spoken (such as, e.g., "Hey, Siri" or "Alexa"). Other methods of Access Control for home automation devices may include also Speaker Recognition (SR) technology, which is based on voice biometrics and allows only authorized users to gain access to the system [2].

Due to the complexity of speech processing, many components of the Access Control and ASR procedures are often performed in the cloud. Cloud-based audio processing may, however, raise privacy issues – the audio recording is stored at external premises and may potentially be reviewed by the third parties [3]. This creates a need for solutions working locally, fully offline. Developing such systems for embedded devices is challenging due to the scarcity of computational power and other resources, especially battery power. In addition, an Access Control solution should be characterised by a very low False Positives Rate (FPR) in order not to raise false alarms and not to grant unauthorised access to the core home automation system. Especially in the case of the KWS module, even though the most recent research results are very promising, the reported FPR levels are still not sufficient for commercial application when applied without any supporting intelligence [4]–[6]. Moreover, the KWS systems are typically aimed at recognising English speech/speakers [4]–[6]. In order to produce a system working for a less common language (such as, e.g., Polish), it is necessary to gather a training database of examples, which is both time-consuming and financially expensive. Providing a well-performing system with only a small-size database available is very challenging.

To address the above challenges, we propose in this paper a DSS that would work on an embedded device and allow to efficiently make decisions on granting access to the voice-controlled home automation system. The decision-making engine of this solution exploits the knowledge extracted from the audio signals – collected by the device microphone with the support of KWS and SR modules. A core part of the proposed Access Control DSS system is the KWS module and the related inference engine. Hence, in this paper, we primarily present our research on these technologies, focusing on the design of 1) a KWS module for recognising a keyword from a non-English language (in our case Polish), and 2) computationally lightweight procedures that address the problem of high FPR and allow to significantly reduce the number of false alarms in the test environment. The presented results depict the comparison of false positive and True Positive Rates (TPR) of different DSS schemes investigated by us while addressing the research problems identified above. In this paper we will focus on the Access Control design, nevertheless it should be noted, that this is an initial stage of the entire voice-based interface, which is typically followed by an ASR-based dialog system responsible for recognizing speech and for command understanding. The design of the these latter modules is, however, out of the scope of this paper.

The rest of the paper is organised as follows: in Section II, we present a short overview of related work, followed by the description of the proposed DSS system and the methodology taken to implement its components for embedded devices in Section III. In Section IV, we discuss in detail our results and, finally, in Section V we present conclusion and suggestions for further improvements as well as future work.

II. Related Work

In the voice-controlled home automation systems, the devices offer user interfaces, which are designed to control an access to the core system functionality [7]–[9]. As the most straightforward solution, they are composed of VAD/KWS module [5]. The KWS system, which has been trained on examples including silence or background noise samples, can also play the role of a VAD solution. This makes the KWS module a core part of the Access Control technologies. Most recent research on KWS systems focuses on applying neural networks – with particular interest in the Convolutional Neural Networks (CNNs) [4]. In this context, an increasing attention was given to the so called Residual Neural Networks architectures (ResNet), which incorporate skip connections between blocks of selected layers. This kind of architecture was first used to train extremely deep networks aimed at image recognition and was then exploited for the audio processing tasks, such as KWS and SR technologies [5][10]. ResNets are characterised by a lower complexity and faster training phase and were proved to obtain very good performance even for relatively small-sized networks – reaching the accuracy of 95% [5]. While such results are impressive, they are far from being industrially applicable: assuming that FPR is 2% [5] and the system makes a prediction every second, there will be 72 false alarms in one hour — a number unacceptable from the point of view of an end-user.

In addition, the KWS-based Access Control technology may also be accompanied by the SR system to form a biometric-based DSS, which can identify speakers and grant them proper permissions [11]. Nonetheless, even combining the modules together does not improve the FPR of the Access Control DSS as a whole. Some approaches to address this problem introduce pushing a button [8], detecting the audio louder then a certain threshold [7] or rely on more advanced features – such, e.g. in [9], where KWS is followed by additional reasoning using Hidden Markov Models and re-checking in the cloud. The latter kind of solutions, used, i.a., by Apple, Google or Amazon, are often very complex and likely too resource-consuming for small embedded devices. On the other hand, many related works on voice interfaces do not consider the methods of Access Control explicitly [12][13], neglecting the aspect that has tremendous impact on the practical implementation of such solutions. This calls for new approaches that would offer required effectiveness on embedded devices.

III. System Architecture

We are considering a DSS system that is controlling access to embedded home automation devices. It is working locally on the device without any access to the Internet and cloud-based resources. The proposed system architecture is depicted in Figure 1.

In the envisioned design, if the user wants to activate the home automation device, he/she has to say the specified keyword and wait for a signal (buzz), which will confirm granting an access to the core ASR-based dialogue system of this device. The signal will be generated only if the user 1) has spoken the correct keyword and 2) was authorized as one of the known users.

The straightforward approach to the design of an Access Control DSS for the embedded devices would incorporate only the blocks of KWS and SR marked dark-grey in Figure 1. Combined together, they grant system access to the authorized users who have uttered particular keyword phrase. In the course of our research, we have investigated introduction of additional subsystems (light-gray boxes in Figure 1) that would allow to decrease the FPR of the entire Access Control DSS, without

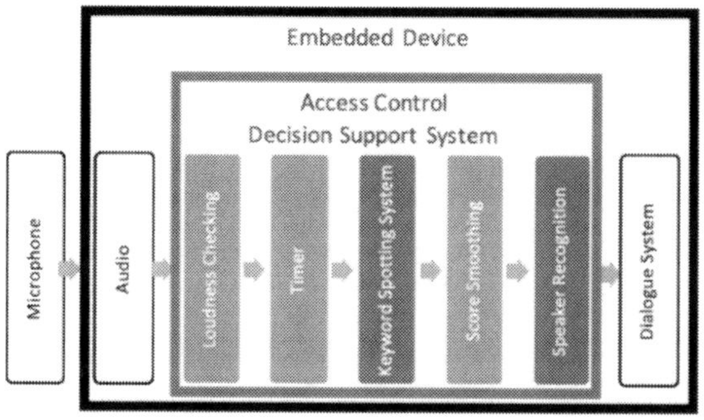

Figure 1. System design. Light-gray boxes represent new modules added in the course of research.

a significant loss in its TPR.

The first new element – "Loudness Checker" – requires the incoming audio to have a certain minimum level of loudness. The second one, called "Timer", limits the time duration of an audio buffer that is being processed – if the triggering word is not observed shortly after that, it may be assumed that the audio resulted from some background noise or other conversational sounds and does not need to be processed further. Such design also allows to lower the resource consumption, since the predictions performed by the KWS and SR modules are no longer executed continuously. The third system – "Score Smoothing" – performs the smoothing of the results obtained from KWS.

These decision-making subsystems together form an Access Control DSS, where at each step decisions are made based on the knowledge collected on the previous steps. The detailed description of each element is presented in the following subsections.

A. *Keyword Spotting module*

The KWS system is based on the neural network with ResNet architecture "res8" from [5], which is characterised by a small number of network parameters (approx. 110K). This architecture is comprised of 3 residual blocks, each containing: convolutional layer with ReLU activation, Batch Normalization, another convolutional layer similar to the first one and the second Batch Normalization. Between these blocks skip connections are present (the so called residual connections). Such a sequence of blocks is preceded by a convolutional layer with ReLU activation together with an average pooling layer. The output of last residual block is fed into an average pooling layer, flattened and fed into dense layer of size corresponding to the number of labels that can be recognised.

The system in [5] was trained for the English keywords. Since our system is targeting Polish language speakers and the keyword itself is atypical (a trade name of the product of a polish company), the challenge was to produce a well-performing classifier having available only limited database of related audio samples. Hence, a procedure called "transfer learning" was used. In this approach an already-trained neural network targeting a similar problem was used as a "feature extractor" and only its last layer (i.e. the classifier) was trained by using a smaller, problem-specific dataset. In our case, a "res8" network [5] was used as a feature extractor, which was trained on the Google Speech Commands Dataset (GSCD) for recognizing 10 keywords from this dataset and the labels of "silence" and "unknown". In order to train the classifier layer of our solution, with 2 outputs (keyword vs. non-keyword), we have gathered a dataset of 698 positive examples of the selected keyword from 36 people. For the negative examples, we have recorded a larger database of phonetically representative Polish speech. In addition, for the training phase 80% of examples were augmented with background noises of variable loudness, originating from the GSCD dataset. These background noises were also used to create negative examples of silence (i.e., the lack of speech).

The input of the neural network requires $1s$ of audio. Hence, for the system working in real-time, a sliding window of $1s$ that moves by $0.2s$ is used (i.e., the audio for the two adjacent predictions coincides in 80%). Those parameters were established experimentally, as a compromise between satisfactory spotting of utterances and computational burden. 40 Mel-Frequency Cepstral Coefficients acoustic features are then calculated for such a window, normalised, and fed into the ResNet, which acts as a binary classifier returning a numerical score. The score may be considered as the probability that the analysed audio snippet contains the desired keyword. Typically, if the score is higher than a certain threshold, it is assumed that the keyword was uttered. In our case, a threshold corresponding to the Equal Error Rate (EER) was taken, which was calculated with the use of a Receiver Operating Characteristic (ROC) curve and its Area Under Curve (AUC) obtained for the data in the test set. This way the operating point of our system (neural network) was specified.

B. Additional Modules

The Loudness Checking module is the first block of the proposed Access Control DSS, which constantly reads the audio input from the microphone and checks its mean amplitude. If it is above a certain threshold, the audio from the microphone is fed into neural network classifier. This threshold was set experimentally, as it depends on: 1) the particular microphone used, 2) the format of the audio encoding, and 3) a microphone driver.

The Timer module, directly following the Loudness Checking, processes only the signals which are considered strong enough. Since the duration of the desired keyword is typically not longer then $1s$, the timer module limits the audio input, being processed by the KWS model, to the first $1.2s$ of the signal (the lacking part of the $1s$ sliding window in the beginning of listening is filled with zeros). With the overlapping between consecutive frames of 80%, this gives the input to the KWS module of maximum 7 frames, which constitutes an attention window of size 7.

The third module, named Score Smoothing, contains the final evaluation engine and is introduced directly after the KWS block. It implements an additional logic introduced to extract the most meaningful knowledge from the KWS module output. Based on our observations (see Section IV), the FPR is too high if an access is granted after observing only a single frame containing the keyword. Therefore, the Score Smoothing module aims at smoothing the scores of the KWS classifier. Based on the observations from the initial field trials, our approach for this block is based on calculating the mean of the last n predictions – in the beginning of listening, when less number of predictions is available, the lacking results are assumed to have score 0 (we experimented with n equal to 3 and 4). This way, a single, strong trigger could still be considered as a positive activation. The Score Smoothing module makes a decision based on the observed mean value – once it exceeds the threshold set for KWS, the input audio signal is put for further processing by the SR module.

C. Speaker Recognition module

The SR module takes as input a single frame, which is fed from the Score Smoothing module as the one with the strongest trigger. The system is based on the ResNet neural network – following the architecture specified in [10] and the related model, which was further trained by us with low learning rate, on the database containing voices of 100 polish speakers. In the test on the database of 36 polish speakers (Section III-A), where a single speaker was identified, the EER of the new model was 1.7% (comparing to 2.27% of the original one by [10]). If one of the known speakers is found, the system grants the access to the ASR-based dialogue system.

IV. Evaluation

We performed the evaluation of the 3 main components, which were introduced to the proposed Access Control DSS (light grey in Figure 1) – with the aim to estimate their influence on both FPR and TPR measures. We report those measures, since they present the system performance in the operating point, which was specified by the selected system set-up (in case of the KWS module – by the threshold corresponding to the EER). The focus of the executed trials was on the new modules, which closely cooperate with the KWS module – further integration with the SR module is a part of the future work. We performed two tests in diversified conditions: the first one was used to determine the influence of the various components and their combination on the false positive activations caused by the background voices, which may occur in the household. The aim of the second test was to identify the influence of the selected designs on the TPR and false alarms in a challenging task, where speech samples included words that are phonetically similar to the keyword or are household-related.

The entire DSS system was implemented on a RaspberryPi 3B (CPU: 1,2 GHz quad-core ARM-8 Cortex-A53 (64-bit); 1 GB RAM). The device was equipped with a custom-made microphone matrix with 5 independent microphones. The experiments were conducted as field trials where real hardware was used. Unless stated explicitly, the parameters of the other modules were set as described in Section III.

A. FPR measures for different DSS designs

The aim of the first test was to estimate the FPR of the enhanced Access Control DSS, consisting of various combinations of proposed subsystems, in comparison to the standard Access Control method based only on the single KWS module. During the trials, 18min and $14s$-long audio of varying loudness was analysed. Radio conversations were chosen as the audio source, containing the voices of various people. The activation keyword was not present in the audio recordings. The DSS system was processing this audio and the number of false alarms was counted at the output – reflecting the number of positive access activations made after the system has wrongfully detected the keyword. FPR was calculated as the ratio of the number of these false alarms to the number of all analysed audio frames (equal to 5471).

TABLE I. FPR VALUES FOR VARIOUS ACCESS CONTROL DSS DESIGNS.

Design	FPR [%]
Reference system - only KWS	**2.23**
Loudness Checking	0.90
Loudness Checking + Timer	0.64
Score smoothing – avg. over 3 last frames	1.43
Score smoothing – avg. over 4 last frames	1.30
Loudness Checking + Timer + Score Smoothing [avg.3]	0
Loudness Checking + Timer + Score Smoothing [avg.4]	0

The results of this test can be found in Table I. For a reference system containing only the KWS module, FPR of 2.23% is obtained. Adding a Loudness Checking module allows to reduce FPR 2.5 times – to the value of 0.9%. This result is, however, still not satisfactory for commercial applications. The additional use of a Timer module enables to reduce the number of false alarms by a factor of 3.5 (in comparison to the reference system) and to obtain FPR of 0.64%. For the combination of KWS with a Score Smoothing module, using the average of the last 4 predictions gives the FPR of 1.3% and the average of the last 3 – 1.43%. In case of the system for which all three modules were incorporated into one processing pipeline (in two variants – with Score Smoothing using 3 and 4 predictions) the number of false alarms is reduced to zero. The results show that this set-up is the most promising one.

B. *Estimation of DSS system performance*

The aim of the second test was to obtain the values of TPR, FPR and accuracy for the key Access Control DSS designs. Among the 3 new modules, the Score Smoother is the one that can potentially have negative impact on the TPR measures. Therefore, we have been investigating which configuration – with averaging over 3 or 4 frames – will result in better overall performance. In this trial the audio signals were recorded live from 13 users (both female and male). For each person, the test consisted of uttering the keyword 30 times and uttering 10 other words 3 times each. Approximately 20% of them were phonetically similar to the keyword, which makes this trial particularly challenging. For each utterance, the binary result assigned by the Access Control DSS system at the Score Smoother output was recorded.

TABLE II. TPR, FPR AND ACCURACY FOR DIFFERENT ACCESS CONTROL DSS DESIGNS.

Design	TPR [%]	FPR [%]	Acc. [%]
Reference system - only KWS	90.77	5.90	92.44
Score smoothing [avg.3]	**86.41**	**4.87**	**90.77**
Score smoothing [avg.4]	84.10	4.87	89.62

The results are presented in Table II. The reference set-up with only KWS module present obtains TPR of 90.77% and FPR of 5.9% with overall accuracy of 92.44%. Such a result can be considered comparable with the results reported in the literature (e.g., approx. 95% in [5]) – this is a very good result bearing in mind that the neural network was trained on a smaller set of examples and that it was tested on the dateset containing also the words phonetically similar to the keyword. The DSS design with the Score Smoothing module using the last 3 predictions gives overall better results than the one with 4 predictions – obtaining TPR of 86.41% and FPR of 4.87% with accuracy of 90.77%. Hence, we have decided to include this variant in the final system design.

This final system set-up was also assessed towards the imposed delay – with regard to the KWS-related functionality (the detailed analysis of the SR module is part of the future work). Within the proposed Access Control DSS, the main component introducing delay is the Keyword Spotting System (please refer to Figure 1), since it consumes much more computational resources than the other DSS blocks. Hence, their delay can be assumed negligibly small. For the KWS module, the obtained delay is measured as the time between the moment of loading the audio from a microphone buffer and the moment of obtaining the result of prediction. In the investigated set-up, it varies between 0.4-0.5s, which is small enough to be considered practically applicable.

C. *Lessons learned*

Even though the second trial has shown the decrease in the TPR for the final DSS system variant of approx. 4% in comparison to the reference set-up, we consider it to be still applicable and acceptable, taking into consideration the very positive impact on the reduction of false alarms observed for this solution in the first trial. In addition, we have noticed in the course of conducted experiments that the observed False Negatives corresponded mostly to a lousy articulation/quiet speech, which could have been improved by the speakers and yield better results in the repeated trials. For an FPR reported in the second trial, which is still high, it is important to remember that a fifth of the testing words was phonetically very similar to the keyword and, as a result, the performed test was a challenging one. In general, the negative examples in this trial rarely occur in the beginning of the speech, and the chance of finding them in the attention window set out by Timer module is low. Thus, the FPR reported in the trial may be thought of as a "worst-case scenario". Considering the obtained results, we have decided to choose for the final DSS system the design for which the Score Smoothing module is using last 3 predictions and the system is equipped with Timer and Loudness Checking modules.

V. CONCLUSION AND FUTURE WORK

We have proposed a DSS system, which grants access to the voice-controlled home automation devices. It was introduced in order to decrease the FPR and diminish the number of wrongful activations while the home automation device is continuously processing the collected audio signals. For this purpose, 3 modules of the new DSS system were proposed to accompany KWS and SR technologies, which are typically used to activate an ASR-based dialog system only if the specified keyword is pronounced by the known system users. The performed evaluation enabled to assess these candidate solutions and select the best performing variant. The selected design allowed to considerably reduce the FPR of the entire DSS system while retaining acceptable TPR and keeping overall accuracy above 90%. Substantially, in the performed trails, the proposed solution allowed to entirely suppress false alarms caused by background radio voices, while the reference set-up generated approx. 122 unwanted activations per 5471 analysed frames. As a result, with the proposed computationally lightweight modifications, we have come up with an Access Control DSS that is commercially applicable.

As a part of the future work, we plan on further improving the system efficiency by experimenting with substituting the Loudness Checking subsystem with more sophisticated VAD. With a larger amount of available user data, we are also considering the possibility to substitute the output stage of Score Smoother with a trained classifier. Moreover, we envision to perform an evaluation of the entire Access Control DSS, including the SR module, in realistic set-ups with possibly high number of end-users.

ACKNOWLEDGEMENT

The research was supported by the National Centre for Research and Development in Poland under the grant no. POIR.01.01.01-00-0044/17

REFERENCES

[1] C. J. Baby, F. Khan, and J. N. Swathi, "Home automation using web application and speech recognition," in 2017 International conference on Microelectronic Devices, Circuits and Systems (ICMDCS), 2017, pp. 1–6.

[2] A. Kaklauskas, Intelligent Decision Support Systems. Springer International Publishing, Cham, 2015, ch. 2, pp. 31–85, in Biometric and Intelligent Decision Making Support, ISBN: 978-3-319-13659-2.

[3] A. Cuthbertson. Google defends listening to private conversations on google home: But what intimate moments are recorded? [Online]. Available: https://www.independent.co.uk/life-style/gadgets-and-tech/news/google-home-recordings-listen-privacy-amazon-alexa-hack-a9002096.html [retrieved: 11, 2020]

[4] T. N. Sainath and C. Parada, "Convolutional Neural Networks for Small-footprint Keyword Spotting," Proc. 16th Annu. Conf. Int. Speech Commun. Assoc. INTERSPEECH 2015, 2015, pp. 1478–1482.

[5] R. Tang and J. Lin, "Deep residual learning for small-footprint keyword spotting," in 2018 IEEE International Conference on Acoustics, Speech and Signal Processing (ICASSP). IEEE, 2018, pp. 5484–5488.

[6] C. Lengerich and A. Hannun, "An end-to-end architecture for keyword spotting and voice activity detection," arXiv preprint arXiv:1611.09405, 2016.

[7] C. Sidhartha, S. Siddharth, S. S. Narayanan, and J. H. Prasath, "Voice activated home automation system," in National Conference on Man Machine Interaction 2014, vol. 1. ASDF, India, 2014, pp. 69–72.

[8] K. A. Lee, A. Larcher, B. Thai, B. Ma, and H. Li, "Joint application of speech and speaker recognition for automation and security in smart home," in INTERSPEECH 2011, 12th Annual Conference of the International Speech Communication Association, Florence, Italy, 01 2011, pp. 3317–3318.

[9] Siri Team. Hey siri: An on-device dnn-powered voice trigger for apple's personal assistant. [Online]. Available: https://machinelearning.apple.com/research/hey-siri [retrieved: 11, 2020]

[10] W. Xie, A. Nagrani, J. S. Chung, and A. Zisserman, "Utterance-level aggregation for speaker recognition in the wild," in ICASSP 2019-2019 IEEE International Conference on Acoustics, Speech and Signal Processing (ICASSP). IEEE, 2019, pp. 5791–5795.

[11] M. Vacher et al., "Speech and speaker recognition for home automation: Preliminary results," in 2015 International Conference on Speech Technology and Human-Computer Dialogue (SpeD). IEEE, 2015, pp. 1–10.

[12] Y. Mittal, P. Toshniwal, S. Sharma, and D. Singhal, "A voice-controlled multi-functional smart home automation system," in 2015 Annual IEEE India Conference (INDICON), 10 2015, pp. 1–6.

[13] G. López, V. Peláez, R. González, and V. Lobato, "Voice control in smart homes using distant microphones: A voicexml-based approach," in Ambient Intelligence, D. V. Keyson et al., Eds. Berlin, Heidelberg: Springer Berlin Heidelberg, 2011, pp. 172–181.

Incorporating Diversity in Academic Expert Recommendation

Omar Salman, Susan Gauch, Mohammed Alqahatani, Mohammed Ibrahim, Reem Alsaffar
Computer Science and Computer Engineering Department
University of Arkansas
Fayetteville, AR, USA
e-mail: {oasalman, sgauch, ma063, msibrahi, rbalsaff}@uark.edu

Abstract—**Expert recommendation is the process of identifying individuals who have the appropriate knowledge and skills to achieve a specific task. It has been widely used in the educational environment mainly in the hiring process, paper-reviewer assignment, assembling conference program committees, etc. In this paper, we highlight the problem of diversity and fair representation of underrepresented groups in expertise recommendation, factors that current expertise recommendation systems rarely consider. We present a novel way to model experts in the academic setting by considering the demographic attributes in addition to skills. We use the *h*-index score to quantify skills for a researcher and we identify five demographic features with which to represent a researcher's demographic profile. We highlight the importance of these features and their role in bias within the academic environment. We present three different algorithms for scholar recommendation: expertise-based, diversity-based, and a hybrid approach. To evaluate the ranking produced by these algorithms, we propose a modified normalized Discounted Cumulative Gain (nDCG) version that supports multi-dimensional features and we report the diversity gain from each method. We used a tuning parameter to calibrate the balance between expertise loss and diversity gain. Our results show that we can achieve the best diversity gain increase when the tuning parameter value is set around 0.4, giving nearly equal weight to both expertise and diversity.**

Keywords-Expert Recommendation; Diversity; Fairness; nDCG.

I. INTRODUCTION

We are witnessing a significant change in the amount of the available information. The introduction of social media, blogs, the internet of things, and knowledge sharing communities have dramatically increased the amount of the available knowledge online [1]. This has led modern economies to shift to knowledge-based economies where the intellectual capabilities and expertise of the people determine their values in their enterprise and society [2]. However, determining the level of a person's expertise is a significant challenge because it is quite difficult to assess the amount of knowledge that individuals carry in their minds. Hence, enterprises and companies are beginning to rely on documenting people's expertise, and expert recommendation systems have been developed to identify the right individuals for a task. These systems are mainly dependent on the written artifacts of the experts to determine their expertise. For example, early systems consider the internal documents othe enterprise to extract the skills of individual employees [3].

Expert recommendation systems have been used in academia in the hiring process or finding reviewers or assembling a conference program committee. Although there have been promising developments, most expert recommender systems have not addressed the issue of demographic discrepancies and the need to have a diverse team [3]. Additionally, systems based on machine learning trained on biased training data perpetuate that bias in their recommendations, damaging underrepresented groups [4]. To address this issue, we propose three different approaches with the aim of providing accurate expertise, team diversity, and fair recommendation. Our contribution can be summarized as below:

- Propose a novel way to model an expert in the educational setting using a multivariate profile.
- Present new expert recommendation algorithms that consider different demographic attributes.
- Propose a modified metric that evaluates ranking based on different attributes.

II. LITERATURE REVIW

The process of expertise recommendation has been extensively surveyed by Balog et. al in [3]. The interest in expertise recommendation and expert modeling in academia has been discussed in [3][5]. Although there has been little attention to study an expert demographic profile in academia, Cochran-Smith and Zeichner [6] defined it to include the status of an individual with respect to gender, race, ethnicity, socioeconomic background, and age. Any attempt to model an individual's demographics is complicated due to the fact that people tend not to explicitly provide such information. Hence, there are several approaches to predicting their demographic information from publicly available information such as their name [7]-[13].

Bias in expertise recommendation within academia has received a fair amount of attention by many researchers. One study published by Nature magazine [14] shows that women are usually underrepresented in the peer review where only 20% of the reviewers are women. A similar study [15] shows that women and authors from emerging countries were underrepresented as editors and in peer reviewers. Because this problem is a focus area for the National Science Foundation (NSF), they developed an automated reviewer selection system that considers different demographic features when selecting reviewers [16]. The problem of bias in a peer review process is not limited to gender and race, but it can be seen from other angles, such as the geolocation of the reviewer. For example, a study in [17] shows that the US dominated the peer review process by 32.9% while its publications represent only 25.4% of publications between 2013 and 2017.

III. Problem Formulation

Given a set of conferences with n experts (i.e., authors) E such that $E = \{e_1, e_2, e_3, \ldots, e_n\}$, our goal is to build a fair ranking system R that can be used to recommend experts to join a conference program committee. To achieve that, we will try to solve the following two problems. First, we need to quantify the set of expertise that each expert possesses. Hence, we define the set S that contains the expertise score for each expert in E such that $S = \{s_1, s_2, s_3, \ldots, s_n\}$ where s_i is a scalar number represents the expertise score for expert e_i where $1 \leq i \leq n$. Second, we will define a demographic profile for each member of the set E with respect to a set of categorial features F with cardinality m such that $F = \{f_1, f_2, f_3, \ldots, f_m\}$. Hence, for expert e_i, we have the set $D = \{D_1, D_2, D_3, \ldots, D_n\}$ where $D_i = < d_{i1}, d_{i2}, d_{i3}, \ldots, d_{im} >$ that represents the demographic profile based on features in the set F. Finally, recommendation algorithms (FUNC) will be proposed based on S, D, or both that provide different ranking for the set E such that FUNC(S,D) $\rightarrow$ R where $R = \{R_1, R_2, R_3, \ldots, R_p\}$ where p is the number of ranking produced by FUNC.

IV. Expert Modeling

A. Expertise Profiling

Expertise profiling can be defined as a record that shows the proficiency of specific knowledge areas that an expert possesses [18]. It can be viewed as a vector of scores that shows the competency of each skill for that expert. In academia, there has been considerable interest in developing expert profiles due to the demand of having experts to review papers, participate in conference program committees or grant review panels, or finding talented individuals to join research teams. There have been different attempts to measure the amount of expertise that an expert has in academia as in [4][16][19]-[22]. One method that we propose here is to use the *h*-index as a metric to assess the scientific performance of a researcher. *h*-index was proposed by Hirsch in 2005 to measure the researcher's quality and productivity [22]. It is a robust single-number metric that uses the number of publications to indicate the quality of the researcher's output and the citation count to represent the quality of the expert's work. *h*-index scores are also employed by funding bodies and employers to determine funding, career decisions, promote and award committees [23][24]. Using a single score number to assess researcher expertise helps to rank those candidates and finally makes these decisions much easier [25]. It has been incorporated in many scholarly databases such as Google Scholar, Web of Science, Scopus, and Publish or Perish. In this research, we will use *h*-index as provided by Google Scholar as our metric to represent the expertise score for each researcher, as it tends to offer more excellent coverage and accuracy for computer scientists compared to other bibliometric databases [26].

B. Demographic Profiling

Many academic institutions and scholars realized the significance of including the demographic features in an expert profile for the reason that such data can be used in discrimination countermeasures, achieving fairness goals, complying with state and local regulation with respect to fair and diverse employment opportunity. In this research, we will represent the demographic profile using five important features that have been considered major sources of bias in the academic environments that are: gender [27][28], race [28][29], career stage [30], institution geolocation [17], institution ranking [17]. To build that profile, we will incorporate different techniques of feature predictions and web crawling to collect the attributes of the demographic profile as some features are explicitly included in researcher personal home pages while others might not be included due to privacy concerns, and hence prediction tools will be employed to predict such a feature.

To predict the gender and race, we will use NameSor software described in [13].The software uses a database of name information of more than 4 billion names [31] with the help of a novel machine-learning algorithm to provide a matching probability for the gender and race. One challenge is identified by [13] with respect to predicting gender with Chinese names. We manually validated any name that had a gender confidence probability of 0.6 or less, and we found that a gender matching accuracy of 80% with respect to Chinese names and 92% percent with respect to others, and we manually rectified any discrepancies. However, the accuracy was not as high when predicting race, specifically predicting African American as the system provides an accuracy of 15% by labeling many White scholars as African American. Hence, we manually verified every scholar labeled as African American by NamSor to correct any errors. Nevertheless, the software predicts other races with an acceptable accuracy of 75-80%. Once scholar gender and race have been predicted, we map it from categorical to binary values by using the concept of protected parameters where minorities are assigned a value of 1 and the majority will be penalized by having a value of 0. For example, gender will have these values (0 for male and 1 for female) while the race of White and Asian has 0, and other races will have a value of 1.

Career stage extracted from the Google Scholar (GS) page and mapped to binary values by having two classes (junior = 1, senior = 0). We define senior researchers as any researcher who has the academic rank of an associate professor, a senior lecturer, or above. Any academic rank lower than associate professor is considered a junior researcher. Geolocation is collected using the same method of the career stage. We map this to a developed country (Binary value: 0) and developing country (Binary value: 1) as per the last United Nations countries classification [32]. The last attribute is the affiliation rank, for which we used the TIMES computer science university ranking system [33] and mapped it to 0 if the university rank is less than the mean of TIMES computer science university ranking and 1 otherwise.

V. SCHOLAR RECOMMENDATION

In the previous section, we demonstrated the expertise and demographic profiles that are considered the main inputs to our recommendation algorithms. Now, we are ready to describe our proposed scholar recommendation algorithms that address the issue of recommending an expert. We consider the case of recommending a researcher to join a team of conference program committee. We will address this problem from three different aspects: expertise, demographic diversity, and a balanced approach between expertise and diversity.

A. Expertise Recommendation Approach

As discussed above, we quantified the skills of scholars using *h*-index, where the higher the score is, the higher the expertise that such scholar has. To add a researcher to a team (e.g., conference program committee), we get the *h*-index of every author who published an article in that conference, extract GS *h*-index, and recommend the scholar that has the highest *h*-index. One advantage of this approach is that it maximizes the expertise in the process of the recommendation. However, it might lead to a systematic bias by favoring one demographic group over the other by failing to address the issue of demographic diversity. For example, the expertise-only approach does not consider the issue of the gender gap and the race gap. Hence we might end up with a team of the same race or gender. Another concern is by favoring highly cited researchers; it minimizes the opportunities for junior researchers to attend such research teams, which negatively impacts their chances to advance their careers. Additionally, most highly cited researchers are employed by the top rank universities, and this approach would less favor those researchers from lower-tier universities.

B. Diverse Recommendation Approach

The second algorithm utilizes the demographic profile for a scholar as the basis by which to recommend a researcher. In this approach, we calculate the diversity score for a researcher. The diversity score is simply the sum of the binary score for demographic features, where d_i is the diversity score for each feature and n is the number of demographic features in the profile (see (1)). For example, if the demographic profile for a researcher is (gender = woman, race= African American, Career Stage = professor, University rank = 2, Country = United States) then the corresponding diversity score is (1+1+0+0+0 = 2). We refer to this algorithm as **(DIV)** where the scholars will be ranked according to their diversity score and in descending order. In case two or more researchers have the same score, the algorithm will randomly pick one to be recommended.

$$\text{Score(DIV)} = \sum_{i=1}^{n} d_i \qquad (1)$$

C. Hybrid Recommendation Approach

The previous two approaches each have advantages and disadvantage. The first approach enhances the expertise of the team but fails to address the problem of forming a diverse team. The diversity approach solved that problem, but again it might cause an unacceptable drop in the expertise level of the team. Hence, a hybrid approach is introduced. That introduces a tuning parameter (α) to balance these approaches, as shown in (2):

$$\text{Score(H)} = [\alpha * \text{Score(DIV)}] - [(1-\alpha) * \text{Score (EXP)}] \qquad (2)$$

Our goal, in this case is minimizing the utility loss, which results from favoring the diversity over the expertise to the minimum, hence we will test different values for α. To make both scores comparable, we will measure the performance using score scaling such that Score (EXP) and Score (DIV) will be normalized so that both scores will get a value between (0 and 1). Equation 3 will be used in our normalization process

$$\text{Score(H)norm} = \frac{Score_i - \min(Score)}{\max(Score) - \min(Score)} \qquad (3)$$

VI. EXPERIMENT

A. Dataset

We will test our recommendation algorithms by recommending scholars to join an existing conference program for three of The Association for Computing Machinery (ACM) conferences that have high impact factors [34]. These conferences' Program Committees (PCs) were previously found to be less diverse than the set of accepted authors [35][36]. For the year 2017, we collected information about all the authors and PC members for SIG-CHI (The ACM Conference on Human Factors in Computing Systems), SIG-MOD (International Conference on Management of Data), and SIGCOMM (The ACM Conference on Data Communication). Using information on their Google Scholar page and home page, we collected the demographic information, discarding researchers in industry and that missing demographic information. The total profiles in our dataset are 1217 and can be seen in Table I.

TABLE I. DATASET DESCRPTION

Conference	PC members	Authors
SIGCHI17	213	436
SIGMOD17	130	290
SIGCOMM17	23	125

B. Baseline and Metric

For each dataset, we generate different K ranking, where K is the ranking cutoff, using our proposed algorithms and the following baseline:

Baseline: We used the Expertise Approach that selects candidates based on qualifications (*h-index*) only as our baseline (see Section V-A) for comparison.

Metric 1: Diversity gain based on mnDCG: We will compare the baseline with other approaches using normalized discounted cumulative gain (nDCG) by calculating the diversity gain at each rank. However, nDCG works with one feature at a time, hence, we had to modify the nDCG metric to support multi-feature ranking gain. Thus, we propose multidimensional normalized Discount Cumulative Gain (mnDCG) that can be calculated in three steps. First we calculate the DCG per feature as in (4) where n is the maximum rank and score (*f, i*) is the score for feature *f* for the candidate *i* in the expert demographic profile. Once DCG is calculated, then Ideal Discounted Cumulative Gain (IDCG), is calculated for each feature by ranking candidates in a descending order based on that feature. Now, nDCG for that feature can be calculated using (5). The process repeats itself for all features and the mnDCG is the average nDCG gain over all features as shown in (6).

$$DCG = \left(\sum_{i=1}^{n} \frac{2^{score(f,i)}}{\lg(1+i)}\right) \quad (4)$$

$$nDCG_f = DCG_f / IDCG_F \quad (5)$$

$$mnDCG = \frac{1}{k}\sum_{j=1}^{k} nDCG_f \quad (6)$$

Metric 2: F-Measure: We will use the F-measure as harmonic mean between the diversity and expertise gain.

VII. RESULTS AND DISCUSSIONS

Table II displays the result of evaluating our diversity approach against baseline and RAND recommendation algorithm which randomly picks candidates. We tested our proposed algorithms on each conference separately and measure the diversity gain by recommending top K experts for different values for K. We reported the diversity gain using mnDCG for each ranked set of candidates produced by our ranking algorithms. As Table II presents, the DIV algorithm always outperforms the other algorithms with respect to diversity. We also notice that the expertise algorithm produces the poorest diversity performance as compared to other algorithms, including random, indicating that it produces program committees that do not reflect the demographics of the community as a whole.

TABLE II. MNDCG DIVERSITY GAIN RANKING PRODUCED BY RAND, EXPERTISE, AND DIVERSITY ALGORITHMS

Conference	Rank@K	RAND	DIV	Expertise
SIGCHI17	50	0.222	0.617	0.113
	100	0.23	0.66	0.122
	Total (436)	0.639	0.847	0.602
SIGCOMM17	50	0.374	0.679	0.29
	100	0.494	0.804	0.523
	Total (125)	0.639	0.804	0.602
SIGMOD17	50	0.207	0.563	0.164
	100	0.312	0.66	0.227
	Total (290)	0.648	0.821	0.608

Nevertheless, promoting diversity comes at the cost of expertise. Hence, we tested our balanced approach presented in Section V-C that incorporates the results from the diversity algorithm (DIV) and the expertise algorithm using a linear tuning parameter (α). Table III shows these results averaged over the three conferences. We report the expertise saving to represent the amount of expertise retained after incorporating diversity, and the diversity gain relative to the baseline expertise algorithm. We use F-measure to combine the two diversity and expertise gains into a single metric. We report the result using α using steps of 0.1 to find the best value. α of 0 indicates the expertise only algorithm and α 1.0 indicates the diversity only algorithm. The highest F-measure is achieved when alpha is 0.4 indicating a 60% contribution from the expertise ranking and 40% from the diversity algorithm.

TABLE III. HYBRID ALGORITHM EVALUATION

α	Diversity Gain	Expertise Gain	F-Measure	Diversity Gain%	Expertise Saving %
0	0.603	1	0.752	0%	100%
0.1	0.642	0.998	0.781	6.60%	99.80%
0.2	0.659	0.993	0.792	9.40%	99.30%
0.3	0.69	0.975	0.808	14.50%	97.50%
0.4	0.731	0.922	**0.816**	**21.30%**	**92.20%**
0.5	0.784	0.829	0.806	30%	82.90%
0.6	0.813	0.771	0.792	35%	77.10%
0.7	0.829	0.671	0.742	37.70%	67.10%
0.8	0.832	0.609	0.703	38.10%	60.90%
0.9	0.832	0.608	0.703	38.10%	60.80%
1	0.824	0.554	0.662	36.70%	55.40%

To illustrate the effect of our approach, we provide the participation of members of underrepresented groups using the baseline recommendation algorithm versus our hybrid approach (with α = 0.4, rank@K = 50) in Figure 1. For example, the results show that our balanced, hybrid algorithm, has increased the females in SIGCOMM from 22% to 44%, the developing countries in SIGMOD from 16% to 56%, and racial minorities from 4% to 14% in SIGCHI with 92% expertise saving.

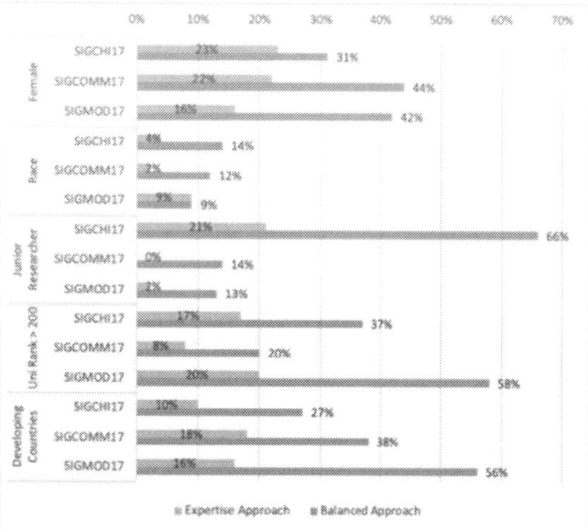

Figure 1. Demographic gain with average expertise loss of 7.8% @ K = 50 using α = 0.4.

We also test our hybrid approach by recommending the same PC size from a pool of the real PC and conference authors and compare it to the demographic distributions of the real PC, as shown in Figure 2. Our algorithm increased the representation of all demographic groups on average across the three conferences. The average expertise loss, as measured by the nDCG on the *h*-index, was 1.3%, a small penalty to pay for increased diversity.

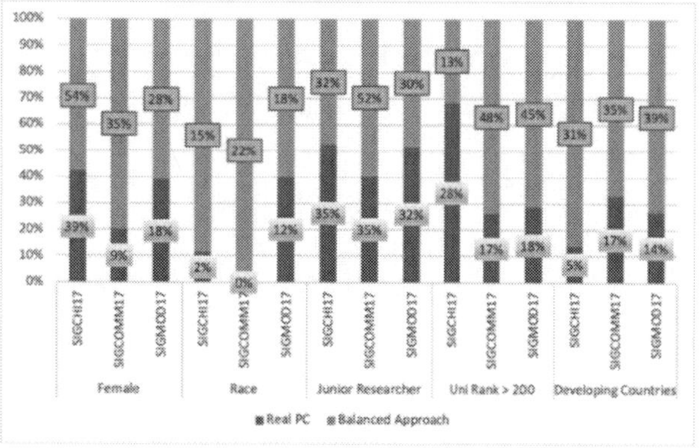

Figure 2. Demographic difference between real PC and balanced approach [α = 0.4].

VIII. Conclusion

The paper presents an approach to incorporate demographic fairness in expert recommendations in academia. It also introduces a more comprehensive way to represent demographics in researcher profiles in order to achieve fairness, increase demographic diversity, and ensure that members of underrepresented demographic groups have access to career opportunities. Our profiles include five attributes that have been shown to be sources of explicit or implicit bias in academia, i.e., gender, race, career stage, academic rank, and affiliation geolocation. We use these demographic features within an expert recommender system in academia. The paper presents and evaluates three scholar recommendation approaches: 1) the expertise model; 2) a new diversity model; and 3) a balanced approach between that balances diversity gains against loss of expertise. We consider a specific example of expert recommendation in academia that is recommending researchers to join a conference program committee. We created a dataset of 1217 researcher profiles from the three top ACM conferences for 2017. We evaluate our algorithms using a modified nDCG metric, mnDCG, that measures gain across multiple dimensions. Our evaluation shows our diversity approach provides a better diversity gain; however, this comes with the cost of expertise. Hence, we developed a hybrid recommender system that incorporates linear optimization through a tuning parameter. Our results show that the best parameter value for the three conferences studies is approximately 0.4, i.e., 40% weight to the diversity recommendation and 60% weight to the expertise recommendation.

In the future, we will extend the demographic profile design to contain continuous values to provide a wide range of demographic groups for the same attribute. We will apply these new profiles to fair group formation algorithms [36]. We intend to assign different weights to each demographic feature based on different mechanisms and study whether this leads to a better demographic representation. Also, we plan to study the demographic composition of different academic conferences in other domains.

References

[1] M. Winans. *10 Key Marketing Trends for 2017 Customer Expectations and Ideas for Exceeding Customer Expectations.* [Online]. Available from: URL:ftp://ftp.www.ibm.com/software/in/pdf/10_Key_Marketing_Trends_for_2017.pdf [retrieved: October, 2020]

[2] W. Reinhardt, B. Schmidt, P. Sloep, and H. Drachsler, "Knowledge worker roles and actions—results of two empirical studies," Knowledge and Process Management, vol. 18, pp.150-174, Jul. 2011.

[3] K. Balog, Y. Fang, M. de Rijke, P. Serdyukov, and L. Si, "Expertise retrieval," Foundations and Trends® in Information Retrieval, vol. 6, pp.2–3, Feb 2012.

[4] D. Pedreshi, S. Ruggieri, and F. Turini, "Discriminationaware data mining," Proc. of KDD, ACM Press, Aug. 2008, pp. 560–568.

[5] J. Tang et al., "Arnetminer: Extraction and mining of academic social networks," Proc. of KDD, ACM Press, Aug. 2008, pp. 990-998.

[6] M. Cochran-Smith and K. Zeichner, Studying teacher education: The report of the AERA panel on research and teacher education, Routledge, 2009.

[7] J. Michael, "40000 namen, anredebestimmung anhand des vornamens," C'T, 2007, pp. 182-183.

[8] I. Perez. *Gender-guesser*. [Online]. Available from: https://pypi.python.org/pypi/genderguesser [retrieved: October, 2020]

[9] M. Vanetta. *Gender Detector* [Online]. Available from: https://github.com/malev/genderdetector [retrieved: October, 2020]

[10] R. Knowles, J. Carroll, and M. Dredze, "Demographer: Extremely simple name demographics," Proceedings of the First Workshop on NLP and Computational Social Science, Nov. 2016, pp. 108-113.

[11] J. Ye et al., "Nationality classification using name embeddings," Proc. of the 2017 ACM on Conference on Information and Knowledge Management, Nov. 2017, pp. 1897-1906.

[12] C. Strømgren. *Genderize.io*. [Online]. Available from: https://genderize.io/ [retrieved: October, 2020]

[13] S. Mattauch, K. Lohmann, F. Hannig, D. Lohmann, and J. Teich," A bibliometric approach fo detecting the gender gap in computer science," Communications of the ACM, vol. 63, pp. 74-80. Apr. 2020.

[14] J. Lerback and B. Hanson, "Journals invite too few women to referee," Nature, vol. 541, pp. 455-457, Jan. 2017, doi:10.1038/541455a

[15] H. Yin, B. Cui, and Y. Huang, " Finding a wise group of experts in social networks," Proc. of International Conference on Advanced Data Mining and Applications, Dec. 2011, pp.381-394. Springer, Berlin, Heidelberg.

[16] S. Hettich and M. Pazzani, "Mining for proposal reviewers: Lessons learned at the national science foundation," Proceedings of the 12th ACM SIGKDD International Conference on Knowledge Discovery and Data Mining, Aug. 2006, pp. 862-871.

[17] Publons. *Global State Of Peer Review*. [Online]. Available from https://publons.com/static//Publons-Global-State-Of-Peer-Review-2018.pdf [retrieved: October, 2020]

[18] K. Balog and M. De Rijke, "Determining expert profiles (with an application to expert finding)," Ijcai, vol. 7, pp. 2657-2662, Jan. 2007.

[19] K. Chandrasekaran, S. Gauch, P. Lakkaraju, and H. Luong, "Concept-based document recommendations for citeseer authors," The International Conference on Adaptive Hypermedia and Adaptive Web-Based Systems, Jul. 2008, pp. 83-92.

[20] A. Pudhiyaveetil, S. Gauch, H. Luong, and J. Eno, "Conceptual recommender system for CiteSeerX," Proceedings of the third ACM conference on Recommender systems, ACM, Oct. 2009, pp. 241-244.

[21] B. Sateli, F. Löffler, B. König-Ries, and R. Witte, "ScholarLens: Extracting competences from research publications for the automatic generation of semantic user profiles,"PeerJ Computer Science, vol. 3, e121, Jul. 2017.

[22] J. Hirsch, "An index to quantify an individual's scientific research output," Proceedings of the National academy of Sciences, vol. 102, pp.16569-16572, Nov. 2005.

[23] *Measuring Research Success:H-index Scores in Science*. [Online]. Available from: fromhttps://conductscience.com/measuring-research-success-h-index-scores-in-science/ [retrieved: October, 2020]

[24] L. Tang and G. Hu, "Evaluation woes: Metrics can help beat bias," Nature, vol. 559, p. 331, Jul. 2018.

[25] W. Schreiber and D. Giustini, "Measuring scientific impact with the h-Index: a primer for pathologists," American journal of clinical pathology, vol. 151, pp. 286-291, Feb. 2019.

[26] J. Bar-Ilan, "Which h-index?A comparison of WoS, Scopus and Google Scholar," Scientometrics, vol. 74, pp. 257-271, Feb. 2008.

[27] L. Bornmann and H. Daniel, "Reliability, fairness and predictive validity of committee peer review," BIF Futura, vol. 19, pp. 7-19, 2004.

[28] M. McConner, "Black women in leadership: An assessment of the gender inequality and racism that exists among black women leaders in higher education," The Journal Higher Education Management, vol. 29, pp. 78-87, 2014.

[29] L. Perna, D. Gerald, E. Baum, and J. Milem, "The status of equity for black faculty and administrators in public higher education in the south," Research in Higher Education, vol. 48, pp. 193-228.

[30] S. Gallo, L. Thompson, K. Schmaling, and S. Glisson, "Participation and motivations of grant peer reviewers: a comprehensive survey of the biomedical research community," Science and engineering ethics, vol. 26, pp. 761-782, Apr. 2020.

[31] D. Menéndez, "Damegender: writing and comparing gender detection tools," EasyChair, Apr. 2020.

[32] United Nations. *UN World Economic Situation and Prospects (WESP) Report*. [Online]. Available from: https://www.un.org/development/desa/dpad/publication/world-economic-situation-and-prospects-2019 [retrieved: October, 2020]

[33] Times Higher Education. *World University Rankings 2019 by subject: computer science* [Online]. Available from: https://www.timeshighereducation.com/world-university-rankings/2019/subject-ranking/computer-science#!/page/0/length/25/sort_by/rank/sort_order/asc/cols/stats [retrieved: October, 2020]

[34] *Conference Rank* [Online]. Available from: https://cn.aminer.org/ranks/conf [retrieved: October, 2020]

[35] O. Salman, S. Gauch, M. Alqahatni, and M. Ibrahim, "The Demographic Gap in Conference Program Committees," Proc. of the 17th International Conference on Applied Computing (AC 2020), Nov. 18-20, 2020 (in press).

[36] M. Alqahatni, S. Gauch, O. Salman, M. Ibrahim, and R. Alsaffar, "Diverse Group Formation Based on Multiple Demographic Features," Proc. of the 12th International Conference on Knowledge and Discovering in Information Retrieval (KDIR 2020), Nov. 2-4, 2020.